THE ATOM SPIES

THE ATOM SPIES

BY OLIVER PILAT

G. P. PUTNAM'S SONS   NEW YORK

Preface

SINCE the events described are still controversial, some question may be raised about the narrative method used in portions of this book. Where a charge has been made under oath, as before a Congressional committee, and the defense has been a refusal to talk for fear of self-incrimination, it has been supposed that the charge may be credible, subject to a notation of any formal denial elsewhere. Where contradictory versions have been produced in court, the jury's verdict has been followed. If a Soviet courier is depicted as too bored to read a stolen description of the trigger heart of the atom bomb, or a repentent dupe is portrayed in an attempt to wash escape funds down a toilet as "dirty money," these are not romantic fictions, but fact. Though some weaving of testimony has been required, the details and the quotations, save for a rare connecting phrase, come from the record.

Authorities on various phases of the subject have been consulted, but no hesitancy has been shown in discarding their views where they conflicted with the considered opinion of the author. In a word, the author alone is responsible for the presentation. The experts consulted included Irving H. Saypol, the prosecutor at two atomic trials, and now a New York Supreme Court Justice; Dr. Eugene Rabinowitch, editor of the *Bulletin of the Atomic Scientists;* Ladislas Farago, formerly of the Psychological Warfare Section of Naval Intelligence; Elliot E. Cohen, editor of *Commentary* magaine; Joy Davidman, poet and novelist; Gardner (Pat) Jackson of the CIO; John W. Carrington, and a semi-anonymous man named McGuire. My wife Avice was patient and helpful, and the *New York Post* deserves a bow for assigning me originally to study the background and history of several of the atom spies, and for granting a leave of absence during the writing of the book.

For Jeffrey and Betsy

Contents

Preface   v

1. The Lost Secret   3

2. The Several Lives of Harry Gold   26

3. The Cover-up   57

4. Klaus Emil Julius Fuchs   79

5. A Net Is Torn   105

6. Chicago and Berkeley   132

7. Escape and Confession   165

8. Ruth and David Greenglass   199

9. The Conspirators   230

10. Trial and Punishment   263

Index   303

THE ATOM SPIES

1. The Lost Secret

ON Sunday morning, June 3, 1945, about six weeks before a super-solar flash in the sky over Alamogordo ushered in the Atomic Era, a fat little man with discouraged shoulders and a pouting face walked up a steep flight of stairs at 209 North High Street, Albuquerque, New Mexico, and knocked at the first apartment. A young fellow wearing bathrobe and slippers opened the door. "Mr. Greenglass?" inquired the stranger, and as the other nodded, he slipped inside, saying, "Julius sent me," rather breathlessly, with all the emphasis on the first word. Greenglass said, "Oh." After closing the door, he walked to a table containing his wife's purse, opened it, and removed a piece of cardboard two or three inches long, a jagged piece from the instruction side (not the side showing the picture of the little girl) of a box of Jello, raspberry flavor. From a pocket, the visitor produced a similar fragment. The two pieces, held in air, so obviously belonged together that a careful matching was unnecessary. David Greenglass smiled triumphantly; though he was a burly 190-pounder, with unruly black eyebrows and black hair, he gave an impression of good nature. "My wife Ruth," he said with a wave of his hand. The visitor nodded his head toward the red-cheeked, blue-eyed girl, scarcely out of her teens, who was also wearing a bathrobe and slippers. "I'm Dave from Pittsburgh," he said, in an unexpectedly round tone.

"What a coincidence," said Ruth Greenglass, tritely, while her

3

roving glance picked out each week-end disorder in the combination living room and bedroom. "Your name is David and so is David's."

"We weren't exactly expecting anybody today," David Greenglass told Dave from Pittsburgh, who was really Harry Gold from Philadelphia. "This is a surprise. Will you have something to eat?" Gold said he had eaten breakfast. He kept his head slanted and his eyelids down as though he were listening for something. "Do you have any information for me?" he demanded. Greenglass replied, "I have some, but it will have to be written out." Ruth Greenglass went into the cubbyhole of a kitchen to make some fresh coffee, but by the time she returned the two men were shaking hands, having agreed that Gold would come back at 3 P.M. for the information which he required about Los Alamos.

Harry Gold read a mystery story for a couple of hours in his room at the Hotel Hilton, and ate his lunch there. He had registered under his right name, without baggage, the previous evening, after a visit to the North High Street address around eight o'clock, had aroused only a tall, stoop-shouldered man with white hair who said the Greenglasses were out somewhere but would surely be back in the morning. Precisely at three o'clock, Gold returned to the Greenglass apartment. David was wearing his Army uniform, with T/5 insignia showing he was a corporal. Ruth had made tea, and laid out some little cookies. David had a report ready, consisting of several sheets of 8-by-10-inch ruled white paper showing various schematic, or unscaled, drawings of flat-lens mold experiments for detonating an atom bomb on which he had been working in the smallest of the three ultra-secret technical shops at Los Alamos.

A couple of pages of descriptive matter about the various letters and symbols on the sketches, as well as a sheet containing a list of possible recruits at Los Alamos were included. "On this list," said Greenglass, "I want to explain about one man, why I put his name down. I talked to people about him a little bit. He might not seem to be good material, but there is a story—"

4

Harry Gold cut him short. "Such procedure is extremely hazardous, it's foolhardy!" he said, with intense irritation. "Why do you do things like that? Under no circumstances, ever, should you try to proposition anybody to help in the work. You ought to be more circumspect in your conduct. Never give anybody the slightest hint that you are furnishing information on the outside."

David Greenglass shifted his heavy shoulders, and frowned, but his words were mild. "Julius wanted a list of people who were sympathetic with Communism and who might help furnish information," he said. "You come from Julius, don't you?"

The inference was: Julius is your boss, isn't he? Harry Gold saw no reason to explain that he did not even know Julius Rosenberg. "I'll take the list," he said.

Rosenberg had originally cut the Jello box in two halves as a recognition device during a January meeting in New York with the Greenglasses. He had given one part to Ruth, explaining that her courier would bring the other part. He had implied that the courier would be a woman they had met earlier that evening, but arrangements had been changed by Anatoli A. Yakovlev, Rosenberg's Soviet superior in New York.

Gold had objected as loudly as he dared when Yakovlev handed him the Jello box fragment. It was vital, it had to be done, insisted Yakovlev. Gold said he thought it inadvisable to endanger his very important trip to see Dr. Klaus Fuchs at Santa Fe by adding this extra task. Yakovlev said Gold did not apparently understand this was also an extremely important business; in short, he must go to Albuquerque as well as to Santa Fe. "This is an order," Yakovlev had hissed, when Gold remained unconvinced. As usual, the Soviet agent had planned everything. Gold must take a circuitous route, he said, going first to Phoenix, then to El Paso, and finally to Santa Fe. From Santa Fe he could travel by bus to Albuquerque in a couple of hours.

Because he was able to secure only a limited vacation from his job in Philadelphia, Gold omitted the indirect approach to New Mexico by way of Arizona and Texas. He went directly to Santa

Fe, arriving around 2:30 P.M., on Saturday, June 2, an hour and a half before his rendezvous. Walking around town, he stepped into a museum and picked up a Chamber of Commerce map of Santa Fe, as a way to avoid asking directions from some stranger. He marked the Castillo Street Bridge on the map. Promptly at four o'clock, Klaus Fuchs came driving down Alameda Street to the bridge in his battered Chevrolet coupe. The British scientist picked up Gold, addressing him as Raymond. The two went for a short drive in the country, during which Fuchs spoke in some detail of the scheduled test at Alamogordo. He did not expect a successful explosion before 1946, he said, though recent progress had been impressive. Just before their parting in Santa Fe, Fuchs had turned over to Gold a sizable packet of typewritten notes. From there he went to visit the Greenglasses in Albuquerque.

Gold had been trained to leave as soon as he took documents, or to put it the other way around, to take no documents until he was ready to leave. An informant might claim innocence if seized with information still in his possession; after the transfer, both were vulnerable. Therefore, on that Sunday afternoon in June, though safely indoors with the Greenglasses in Albuquerque, Gold got jumpy as soon as he accepted the corporal's report. "I've got to go," he said, getting up from the table. David Greenglass smiled. "Wait a second and we'll go with you," he said. Ruth Greenglass mentioned seeing Julius just before leaving New York in February, and followed that up with a reference to Julius' wife Ethel, without drawing any comment from Gold, who handed a sealed white envelope to David. Greenglass fingered the fatness of the envelope, but did not tear it open to see how much money it contained.

"Will it be enough?" said Gold, as though urging examination of the money.

"Well, it will be enough for the present," said Greenglass, dropping the unopened envelope into his pocket.

"You need it badly," said Gold, more as a statement than as a question.

6

"We've had expenses," conceded Greenglass. "You know. Ruth's miscarriage in April, there were doctor's bills, and she couldn't work, and there were other expenses."

Ruth bit her lip. "I'm ready to go," she announced.

Gold glanced hurriedly from husband to wife and back again in an uncertain fashion. "I'll see what I can do about getting some more money for you," he promised.

"That will be nice," David said, as they left.

Gold hinted he would prefer no escort beyond a certain point by remarking that he would know where he was when he reached the USO building. They walked along a slanting back street to the USO. Greenglass said he expected a real furlough, not a week-end pass like the present one, but twenty days or more, around Christmas time, and that he might return then to New York.

"If you want to get in touch with me there," he said, "phone my brother-in-law, Julius." He gave Julius' phone number at Knickerbocker Village in New York. Gold said it was just possible he might see the Greenglasses before Christmas, since he was planning another visit to the Southwest in the early fall. The Greenglasses went tactfully into the USO after saying good-by to Gold, who kept on walking. When they came out of the building again, Gold was gone. They returned in silence to the apartment, opened the envelope, and found $500 in bills.

David Greenglass turned over the money to his wife. "We can live on it," he said. "You can get along on it, can't you? What's the trouble then?"

Ruth spoke rapidly, "Julius said we were sharing information for scientific purposes. Now I see how it is: you turn over the information and you get paid. Why, it's just—it's just C.O.D.!" Her voice broke as she burst into tears. David shook his head slowly and took her in his arms, giving her what comfort he could. Before he caught his bus back to Los Alamos, she was cheerful again, having planned precisely how to divide the money: $400 as a deposit in the morning at the Albuquerque

Trust and Savings Bank, $37.50 for a war bond, and the rest for household expenses.

Somewhere in Kansas, on the train riding to Chicago, Harry Gold examined his historic haul. Though he possessed some scientific qualifications as a chemist, Gold found Fuchs's theoretical discussions of the application of fission to the manufacture of a new weapon rather heavy reading. After glancing at a sentence here and a sentence there, he put away the pages in a manila envelope with a brass clasp, printing DOCTOR on the outside. The Greenglass material was simpler, and illustrated, but the corporal's spidery handwriting proved difficult to decipher. After a few minutes, Gold abandoned that also and put it in a second manila envelope marked OTHER.

Gazing through the imperfectly cleaned window at merging images of flat, fertile land, Gold congratulated himself on the economy and efficiency of his operations. Including twenty minutes with Fuchs, and two short encounters with the Greenglasses, the total time spent with informants on the trip scarcely exceeded an hour. No money had been spent besides the $500 to the Greenglasses, since Dr. Fuchs had waved aside $1,500 brought to him by Gold at a previous rendezvous and had not been tempted again. Characteristically, Gold excluded his own expenses, which were slight; as usual, he was traveling in an upper, and eating odds and ends from vendors rather than meals in the expensive diner. A pair of restless youngsters in a seat across the aisle attracted his attention. Gold gave them some of his candy, explaining to their parents, "I have a couple of my own at home." Then he returned to an unseeing stare at the Kansan countryside.

Gold reached New York on the evening of June 5, in time for his prearranged rendezvous with Yakovlev, a thin, nervous man in his thirties who was registered as a clerk at the Soviet Consulate for espionage purposes. The meeting place was way out in Brooklyn where Metropolitan Avenue runs into the borough of Queens. Gold took his customary circuitous route, trying familiar tricks to throw off possible surveillance, such as waiting on a subway platform or in a train, apparently engrossed in a newspaper, until the doors began to close, and then squeezing through at the last second. The appointment was for 10 P.M. and the neighborhood seemed lonely and frightening to Gold, as he slid into a deserted side street nearby as a final test. His greatest asset in these matters, a feeling as to when he was under observation, told him he was all right, but he had to make sure.

Almost on the stroke of ten, Gold and Yakovlev saw each other in the distance. They approached leisurely to afford each other an opportunity to decline the encounter, if necessary. After a quiet greeting, they walked together about a block, stopped to chat, exchanged newspapers, then separated hurriedly. The paper delivered by Yakovlev with his inevitable hand tremor was just a newspaper, but the one from Gold held in its folds two manila envelopes—marked DOCTOR and OTHER—containing sufficient data, for any modern, industrial country with substantial funds, man power, and scientific know-how to go far along the road toward producing an atom bomb of its own.

Keeping a schedule worked out by them in May, the pair met again two weeks later. This rendezvous was set for early evening, at the end of the Flushing elevated line, on Main Street, Flushing. Sitting in a convenient bar, Yakovlev had Gold elaborate on the details of his New Mexican trip. Toward the end of the two-and-a-half-hour meeting, Yakovlev revealed that the two envelopes had gone immediately to Moscow, causing a sensation. The information from Greenglass was "particularly excellent and very valuable," said Yakovlev, words which from him meant highest praise. Even so, he was guilty of understatement. Six years later, the eyes of John A. Derry, a production chief of the Atomic Energy Commission, widened with astonishment at sketches by David Greenglass duplicating those handed to Harry Gold in 1945. "Why they show the atom bomb," said Derry, "substantially as perfected!" By this he meant, explained the AEC expert, not the test bomb of Alamogordo, not the maiden attempt at

Hiroshima, but the implosion-type, the third and most important of the wartime series, the Nagasaki bomb.

2

Espionage to acquire the secret of a new weapon had plenty of historical precedents, but this was a somewhat different kind of weapon, and a somewhat different kind of espionage. The atom bomb rang down the curtain on a second world war in a quarter of a century; Jovian thunderbolts themselves could have been no more dramatic than the explosive mushrooms which obliterated two Japanese cities. The international quality, costliness, and secrecy of the project to free the energy hidden in matter and make military use of it created an overwhelming impression. Americans began to think of the bomb as a sort of domestic talisman which would ward off another world war for an indefinite period. Because atomic attack had given the Japanese a face-saving alternative to national hara-kiri, and had resulted in surrender, it was assumed the bomb would stop any possible aggressor in the future. National optimism enlarged the probable zone of immunity. Cautious citizens could be excused for joining the others, however, when even Maj. Gen. Leslie R. Groves, the military head of the Manhattan Engineering District Project, under whose wing the bomb was hatched, expected no reasonable foreign facsimile before 1960. Less sanguine estimates from individual scientists received little attention. The announcement in 1949 that an atomic explosion had occurred in Russia came, therefore, as a great shock to most Americans. The subsequent hazily outlined spy revelations produced an almost traumatic numbness in some quarters. There was a spreading sense of helplessness and defeat, easy to understand but quite unjustifiable, on the basis of the facts.

The very scale of the wartime precautions taken by the 250-man security force directly under General Groves had seemed to guarantee secrecy. There were the ordinary measures: screening of employees, censorship of mail at installations, and compartmentalization of information. There were extraordinary arrangements, ranging from the aliases assigned to foreign physicists, such as Baker for Bohr and Farmer for Fermi, to the private asylum used for an officer or two who cracked up under strain. Several hidden cities were created, with an aggregate population exceeding 150,000. Stories were told when their telling became permissible, how firemen from the outside could not reach a wartime blaze at Oak Ridge because they lacked credentials, how Harry S. Truman, then a Senator from Missouri on the trail of war waste, was refused admittance to the plutonium plant at Hanford by a guard who spoke jovially about the manufacture of bubble gum there, and how Dr. J. Robert Oppenheimer, head of the scientists at Los Alamos, was required to put this curious place listing on the birth certificate of his daughter Toni in 1944: "Rural Area, Sandoval County, New Mexico."

John Campbell, patron saint of the science fiction writers, had been dealing in a literary sense with atom bombs for a decade when the FBI called on him one day, in the interests of national security, to stop it. Campbell had quite an argument on his hands before he succeeded in persuading the government that to abandon his favorite subject, abruptly and without good reason, might be extremely suspicious. Operating on a similar theory, General Groves allowed small quantities of uranium compounds to be shipped as usual to Russia during the early part of the war rather than arouse questions by an embargo.

Conscious of an ace in the hole which would top any other military hand, the United States moved serenely into the postwar period. Disarming may have been more hurried and sweeping as a result. Foreign policy itself may have been affected. The Potsdam conference occurred about a week after the Alamogordo blast. On July 24, 1945, President Truman mentioned to Marshal Stalin at Potsdam that the United States had developed an unprecedentedly destructive weapon which might be used, if necessary, against Japan. Former Secretary of State Byrnes reported on this in his book, *Speaking Frankly*.

> Stalin's only reply was to say that he was glad to hear of the bomb and he hoped we would use it.
>
> I was surprised at Stalin's lack of interest. I concluded that he had not grasped the importance of the discovery. I thought that the following day he would ask for more information. He did not. Later I concluded that, because the Russians had kept secret their developments in military weapons, they thought it improper to ask about ours.

The complementary side of intense Soviet secrecy at home was intense Soviet espionage abroad, but quite obviously this possibility did not occur to the American Secretary of State.

The Canadian spy-ring revelations in the winter of 1945-46 offered the United States a chance to shake itself loose from its illusion about a magic secret weapon. The chance was lost largely because American leaders did not want to jeopardize efforts to work out a reasonably postwar basis for living in the world with the Soviet Union.

During UN debates on atomic energy in 1947, the deafish but keen ear of Bernard Baruch caught references in Soviet speeches which could only come from the heart of United States classified knowledge on the subject. He passed along his suspicions to the State Department. Hints from other sources, including the revelations by Whittaker Chambers and Elizabeth T. Bentley, forced counterespionage authorities gradually to enlarge their estimates of possible Soviet penetration of United States military secrets. Scientists were trying meanwhile to put over the idea that the general principles underlying all processes were widely known, that there might be thousands of little technical secrets about an atom bomb, rather than one central secret. They said further that the disparity between the level of United States technical competence in nuclear weapons and that of perhaps half a dozen other industrialized countries, including Russia, could not last more than a few years. Somehow these warnings failed to puncture the American illusion about the exclusive bomb. In this and other fields, the conclusion was inescapable that the Atomic Energy Commission and the Joint Congressional Committee on Atomic Energy had failed miserably to live up to their educational responsibilities to the American people.

When disillusion came, it carried a double dose of bitterness because of a widespread notion that the atom bomb, by itself, could win a major war. This was nonsense. The atom bomb was never a decisive weapon; it had to be integrated with more traditional forms of military strength to be decisive.

In the wake of disillusion, some people wanted to blame everything on the Soviet atomic espionage coup. Thus it was said the theft of the bomb had caused the war in Korea, though the fighting there grew out of a pretty complex international situation. High United States taxes were traced to loss of "the secret," because of budgetary increases to provide general rearmament, though on that rearmament rested American hopes of reaching an eventual, stabilizing deal with Russia to keep the world peace.

Conceding that espionage might have advanced production of a Soviet atom bomb by a year or two, the comparative situation in the United States early in 1952 did not justify alarmism. So far as the original uranium-plutonium bombs were concerned, the American stockpile still ran into the hundreds compared to a Soviet stockpile running into the tens, according to the best available estimates. During 1951, small tactical bombs had been developed and tested in Nevada to meet specific battlefield requirements. Strategic-type atomic weapons, tested at Eniwetok, had been simplified and improved for handling by small jet-propelled bombers. Work on nuclear reactor engines for submarines and airplanes was proceeding rapidly in various plants from Schenectady to San Diego. An improved gaseous diffusion plant was getting under way at Paducah, Kentucky, and one to process uranium ore with greater efficiency at Fernald, Ohio. Finally, more than a billion dollars had been allotted to the new

13

The Atom Spies

United States effort on the Savannah River near Aiken, South Carolina, to build a hydrogen bomb, a thermo-nuclear weapon one thousand times more destructive than an atom bomb, if it were feasible to build one, which seemed likely.

The question posed by all these new installations and developments was whether, so far as it was possible to judge on the basis of the American wartime experience, they were being penetrated quickly and thoroughly by Soviet espionage.

The importance of finding a close answer to this question was multiplied by a possibility that this weapon might really be decisive, where the atom bomb was not. Conceivably, the future of the planet was at stake. Albert Einstein, one of the purest intelligences ever to adopt the United States as a home, dismissed the early notion that the explosion of a flock of atom bombs would cause a chain reaction destroying the globe. If this were possible, he said, it would have happened long ago through the impact of cosmic rays. As to the hydrogen bomb, he was not so sure. Explosion of enough of them might produce such deadly radioactivity, drifting with the prevailing wind over land, as to eliminate most life in its wake, he declared.

Subtle Communist propaganda in this field had to be recognized, and rejected, as a preliminary to judging any question about atomic energy. At the end of the war, for example, West Coast Stalinists operating through the Hollywood Writers Mobilization were instructed to work with friendly physicists belonging to the Federation of Atomic Scientists on a campaign for sharing atomic secrets with the rest of the world. The unconscious corollary was that spy-proof United States secrets did exist. The next phase of the campaign was to demand that the United States pledge never to use such a destructive weapon again, which focused world attention on the American bomb, rather than on the fundamental issue of aggressive war, wherever instituted, and by whatever weapons. The FAS as an organization never urged a unilateral pledge by the United States not to use the bomb.

Richard J. Collins, a screen writer who broke with the Party

14

after taking part in this campaign, testified in 1951 before a Congressional investigating committee that he was asked to work up a series of radio programs on the "terror aspect of the bomb" to influence scientists as well as ordinary citizens. One of these programs, he said, "was called 'Happy Birthday, Dear Earth Star,' which was about some people on another planet who have gone through this before and who watch the earth join—you know—the other stars, as a result of an atomic explosion."

An even more startling example of Soviet success in reaching behind United States mental defenses was provided by the penetration of an organization known as the National Committee on Atomic Information. This was set up in Washington after the war to explain the official United States attitude on atomic energy to the public. Each of the national organizations which maintain lobbies in the capital, church groups, women's organizations, farm groups, labor unions, and the like were invited to send one representative as a member of the commission. After some months, discerning United States physicists began to question the angling of committee releases. Quiet investigation revealed that one of the employees of the committee, a harmless-looking individual selected on the recommendation of a CIO representative since exposed as a Communist, had been using this unequalled American forum to distribute diluted Soviet propaganda. When the functionary realized his activities were under scrutiny, he resigned without formality and dropped completely out of sight.

The theoretical possibility of making a hydrogen bomb was perfectly well understood in 1945. President Truman decided at that time not to press forward toward developing one, according to an informative and uncontradicted Washington column by the Alsop brothers, because his advisors, two eminent and patriotic scientists, Dr. Vannevar Bush and President Conant of Harvard, believed it would take the U.S.S.R. from ten to fifteen years to produce an ordinary atom bomb. This advice proved inaccurate. On February 1, 1950, President Truman therefore authorized a hydrogen-bomb program, along with continued examination of "those factors that affect our program for peace and this country's security."

The Federation of American Scientists, which was the Federation of Atomic Scientists under a new name, criticized the Presidential directive obliquely by issuing a statement built around the contention that "if we build H-bombs, the Russians will build them also," without any evidence whatever that the Russians were not already trying to build them.

Suppose the assumption were made, for the sake of safety, that the Russians had jumped into the hydrogen-bomb race ahead of the United States? Would this be a basis for panic? Not necessarily. United States industrial capacity was several times greater than that of Russia. United States scientists, though fretting to some extent over secrecy rules, were freer and superior in quality on the average than the Soviet scientists. The national technological level in the United States was definitely higher. One false and unnecessary prop to national self-esteem—the illusion of an unmatchable secret weapon—had vanished, but there was no need to discard with it a reasoned belief in the country's ability to equip itself for almost any contingency.

Fairly persistent reports, from not particularly reliable sources, suggested that Stalin had set June, 1952, as the deadline for the production of new weapons, including a hydrogen bomb. United States scientific leaders were chary of public comment, but they did not seem alarmed over these reports. Their attitude suggested that they believed the United States to be still ahead in research. If the Soviet Union had any advantage, they implied, it was in propaganda, and in espionage.

3

The 1950-52 atomic trials and revelations destroyed whatever was left of two persistent and dangerous American illusions. One, of course, was the postwar legend that a magic gadget drawn

16

from the hidden core of matter could assure the United States of indefinite peace and security. The other was the prewar liberal myth that Communists presented no particular practical problem. Neither of these notions could withstand the impact of that single story of Harry Gold's 1945 vacation in New Mexico.

The liberal illusion about Communists dated back to the early days of the New Deal, when the late President Roosevelt was getting the capitalistic machine to run again, on a reform fuel, after a serious depression breakdown. In the enthusiasm engendered by FDR's social program, certain blind spots developed. Few liberals cared to recognize, for example, that there had been a radical infection among the young urban intellectuals who gave the New Deal so much of its driving power.

No doubt the propaganda of popular front organizations in the late thirties helped to create a feeling that Communists were something dreamed up by Red baiters. If Communists existed at all, this propaganda suggested, it was as individual harmless humanitarians on the good or left-of-center side—"our side"— as opposed to the selfish exploiters on the other side, the bad side. Sometimes the illusion took another form: there are Communists, but we can work with them, and use them. Sometimes it went only so far as thinking that if Hitler were wrong, Stalin must be right, to some degree. In all its forms, the mass illusion touched an amazingly large number of decent people.

President Roosevelt was a great man, but history will think the less of him for believing he could treat Stalin like just another big-city politician, to be pushed around with charm. His encouragement of the liberal illusion about Communists came close at times to intellectual and emotional irresponsibility. It affected his followers. Early in the war, it was said, Dean Acheson, then a subordinate official at the State Department, called on Donald Hiss to ask if any credence should be given to a whisper from A. A. Berle (who had just talked to a man named Whittaker Chambers), that Donald and his brother Alger Hiss were Reds. Ridiculous, said Donald Hiss, and Dean Acheson thanked

17

him for the reassurance. Somewhere around 1940, Mrs. Franklin D. Roosevelt invited leaders of the American Student Union into her parlor on one occasion to ask politely if there were any truth in reports that they were Communists. Of course not, the ASU boys and girls declared in a chorus of insulted virtue, and were duly thanked for their frankness by the First Lady.

Those who told such stories did not realize, perhaps, that Acheson's sense of honor among men, and his wide social sympathies were qualifications as important as his intellectual brilliance in handling foreign affairs, after he added up the score on Communists. They might not have known that Mrs. Roosevelt, a woman who did not mind being wrong at times if she could end up right, secured private reports on the ASU, on the American Youth Congress, and on other similar outfits, which she used publicly to disown and discredit them among fellow travelers, and that she fought the Communists openly, and usefully, in the American Newspaper Guild, of which she was a member. The fact remained that she and Acheson, by assuming honesty of response from a possible Communist, to a question put under such circumstances, were acting less than realistically at the time. In this they typified an attitude which affected the general public, Congress, the courts, the Department of Justice, and to some extent even a police agency such as the FBI.

The liberal illusion about Communists underwent an eclipse during the Hitler-Stalin pact, chiefly because the Party-line unions tried to sabotage national defense. Then the fortune of war brought the United States and the Soviet Union into standoffish alliance. The public took Russia to its heart. Midwest cities of unquestioned patriotism celebrated Red Army Day. General MacArthur wired warm military tributes to the Kremlin. Community leaders worked furiously for Russian relief. Domestic Communists tried to encourage the idea that they were more American than ordinary Americans by sabotaging their own unions in the drive to bring military help to Russia.

With a few exceptions, Americans lacked any appreciation of

the failure of the Soviet Union to reciprocate. They did not suspect the implacable distrust toward foreigners of all kinds, which was concealed at the heart of Leninist doctrine. As many as fifteen hundred NKVD members swarmed through the United States during the war, ostensibly as helpers in the dispatch of lend-lease material to the Soviet Union. As late as 1946, one thousand of these Russian secret policemen, who were picking up blueprints galore and everything else that was not nailed down, tarried in the United States as invited guests.

The United States did pretty well against its primary, known espionage opponents during the war. The *Kriegstagebuch,* or Nazi war-record book, kept by Admiral Wagner, revealed no acquisition of United States atomic secrets, according to a postwar survey of the Office of Naval Intelligence. FBI Director Hoover boasted in 1946 about foiling "the enemy's masterpiece of espionage." In a *Reader's Digest* article, he described how the United States received a tip in 1940 to watch for "lots and lots of little dots" as a new Nazi communication trick, and how this led in 1942 to interception of an order (under a dot on a suspicious piece of paper and visible only when magnified two hundred times) assigning Hitler's best spies to report on United States uranium experiments for the utilization of "atomic-kernel energy." Eventually the spies were intercepted before they could carry out the order.

On the other hand, Technical Corporal Greenglass, working in a shop at Los Alamos, could violate an elementary rule of espionage by making a conspicuous approach to a scientist, "That is an interestingly machined piece of material, sir," and receive a frank reply, "Yes, that is neutron source," plus an explanation which he could carry out in his head, past the unsuspecting guards at the gate. And Klaus Fuchs, casually dropping off colleagues from Los Alamos at the La Fonda Hotel in Santa Fe, where the bartender was an FBI agent, could drive openly to the Castillo Street Bridge for a rendezvous with Gold. Top-ranking scientists had counterintelligence agents assigned to them, for their protection as much as anything else, but Dr. Fuchs rated just enough below the top level not to get one.

Since winning the war was the primary national goal, detection of a native Communist with his ear to a keyhole, or his finger on a classified document, did not generally result in an arrest, which might have led to confession and exposure of an espionage net. Like everybody else, counterintelligence wanted to preserve the façade of allied unity. Suspected or known traitors in a laboratory were shifted to less secret work, or were eased into uniform, for assignment to some remote, but safe command. Communists recognized their comparative immunity and took full advantage of it. When General Strong, head of Army Intelligence, demanded in 1943 that Nathan Gregory Silvermaster, who was actually chief of a Soviet ring among government employees in Washington, be discharged from the Board of Economic Warfare as a Communist, the apparatus inspired a vigorous protest. With the help of a deceived Cabinet member, the Party slid Silvermaster back into a berth at the Agriculture Department, though Naval Intelligence as well as the FBI, had him tagged by this time as an NKVD operative.

Prewar Soviet espionage in the United States had been largely industrial. The Politburo envied American factory techniques. Since the Russian leaders operated on an organized system of suspicion, they did not trust industrial information which they could get in a co-operative way. To be genuine, the information had to be stolen, they thought. The Soviet industrial managers were unsure (though never for publication) about their capacity to evaluate modern industrial processes, since their experience in some fields was limited. They decided they wanted complete plans in actual use by leading United States corporations. As a result, many of the things secured surreptitiously by Soviet spies before the war were not secret; most of them, indeed, involved no criminal charge of espionage. The process trained recruits, however, and the border line between industrial and military espionage became increasingly blurred.

A new-type truck, an experimental tire from artificial rubber, or an improved insecticide for tropical use could be considered industrial or military, depending on the use to which it was put. Spies who developed routines for funneling American business and scientific know-how to the Soviet Union could do as well, it was assumed, with military secrets. This theory was not put into practice during the early war period to any extent, since the Soviet underground machines in North America got quite rusty and inefficient for want of regular use, proper care, and funds. Soviet energies and anxieties were focused elsewhere.

Into this espionage vacuum, according to the testimony of important operatives who later renounced their allegiance to Stalinism, various ambitious individuals from the Communist parties in the United States and Canada began to thrust themselves. They called attention to golden opportunities for a little discreet spying, particularly in ultra-secret atomic research. At first the Center in Moscow was uncertain; it had no exact measure for the situation. Yielding gradually to excitement over what were called postwar weapons—new weapons being developed in allied countries which could conceivably affect the postwar balance of power—the Center used the volunteers for all they were worth.

Once the Center realized the military importance of fission, it focused tremendous effort. "Take measures to organize acquisition of documentary materials on the atom bomb!" ran one order, including the rare exclamation mark, from the Center to net directors in North America. The Comintern roster of friendly scientists was utilized to the utmost. Local Communist groups, which had been cold shouldered, were squeezed suddenly for recruits. Marxist study groups at Berkeley, California; Chicago; Montreal, and elsewhere accustomed scientists to an ethic and manner of conspiracy in a short time. In one such case, a few weeks of intensive cultivation served to transform professional men on the fringes of the Communist movement into full-fledged informants.

It had always been recognized that the Communist parties in

each country provided an unequaled ready-made pool of espionage raw material. This time the pool was really drained of available man power; hundreds, perhaps thousands, of members were thrown into the work, in various capacities, without adequate training.

The Manhattan District Project employed 225,000 persons directly, 600,000 indirectly. To police 825,000 persons (most of whom actually had no access to secrets), the United States had 750 agents, including 500 from the FBI as well as the 250 with military intelligence or less than one agent to every one thousand workers. Since half the time, the precise things being guarded were not clear, leaks were inevitable. Perhaps the most undefended aspect of the atomic program were the large industrial concerns handling phases of the manufacturing processes. Some of these plants dealt with Communist-controlled unions. Though most of the union members were demonstrably loyal, Party control facilitated steady and successful espionage. With this experience in mind, the United States should have refused war contracts to plants where Communist unions were in control. Largely because of selfishness on the part of big business, such a rule was not invoked when the Korean hostilities began. It has still not been invoked.

The chief value to be derived from the factual reconstruction of atomic espionage during the last world war was that it could provide perspective as to the relative importance, and danger, of the various parts of the Communist machine in the United States and Canada.

There were three main levels, it appeared: the open Party, consisting of members, many of them scarcely more sophisticated politically than fellow travelers, who lacked direct contact with or knowledge of the Russians operating behind the scenes; the inner Party members, whose stomachs were strong enough to stand contact with the Russians; and the actual underground workers. There seemed to be a steady downward drift, from

22

open Party to inner Party to espionage apparatus, at times so strong a downward drift as to draw persons on the fringes of Party life into actual spying within a few weeks.

Having been pulled into industrial espionage in a more leisurely way back in 1935, Harry Gold had acquired a thorough schooling in protective techniques. Since decentralization was one cardinal rule, he felt quite unhappy over the extra rendezvous at Albuquerque in June, 1945. Danger to a spy increased by geometric rather than arithmetic progression, according to the number of persons touching the secret; doubling the number of contacts, he had been told, might easily quadruple the threat of exposure. In accordance with that principle, Gold had been instructed originally to drop all other contacts so as to concentrate on Klaus Fuchs. Yet a second important meeting had been squeezed at the last minute into a long jaunt involving split-second timing.

Gold's alarm over Greenglass' attempts to line up recruits was also reasonable. An informant for an espionage ring in wartime who wants to avoid a firing squad had better stay away from talent spotting, recruiting, or agitation.

Doubling in brass, as Greenglass was doing under orders from Julius Rosenberg, did not constitute smart or professional operation. There is some evidence that Harry Gold was not even in the same net as Julius Rosenberg. To bring him in, on an emergency basis, because the regular courier used by Rosenberg was indisposed, or was otherwise unable to make the trip, was a reckless act, in an espionage sense. It enabled Gold, six years later, in the first atom-spy trial in United States history, to serve as a government witness against Julius Rosenberg, of whom he might otherwise never have heard.

The mishandling of Rosenberg (who became the first American sentenced to death for atomic espionage) seemed particularly glaring. As early as 1942, he had gathered around himself a group of Communist engineers, for the purpose of collecting and passing on industrial and in rare cases military information of value to a stocky, middle-aged Soviet agent who used the name Golos (the Russian word for voice) in his public role as a travel agency manager, and simply John as a cover name for espionage. While carrying on this furtive activity, Rosenberg served as a civilian inspector for the United States Signal Corps, visiting in turn various East-coast factories which were making military equipment. He operated also as a radical ward heeler within the Communist-controlled Federation of Architects, Engineers, Chemists and Technicians. Before the war ended, Rosenberg was dropped from the Signal Corps as a card-carrying Communist. He called attention to his own exposure by a series of attempts to reverse his discharge. Despite all this, he continued as (a) an employment-and-grievance commissar for the FAECT; and (b) an amateurish Benedict Arnold, supervising still more clumsy contacts.

Retaining Rosenberg for espionage, under the circumstances, without even a cover name to hide his illegal activities, suggested recklessness or ineptness on the part of his Soviet superiors. In fact, most of the atom spies were laughable, by long-term, professional standards. They worked in largely improvised nets along highly unorthodox lines. They were boys, sent on errands earmarked for supermen. Their brashness may have contributed to their incredible success, as it certainly contributed to their eventual exposure. The method of their handling led to a conclusion which made a mockery out of the old liberal illusion about Communists. Quite obviously, the Soviet Union rated the conspiratorial phase of Communism above any other phase. It was willing to use untrained members as emergency spies because it considered the open-Party rank and file, then and now, to be expendable. The situation in 1952 differed from that of 1945 largely in an intellectual climate which had shorn the Communist party of sympathizers. Some forty thousand members remained, indoctrinated and more or less tractable. The extent of their participation in espionage during a possible war with Russia depended partly on the speed and thoroughness with which they were rounded up by counterespionage authorities, and partly on the degree to which those not rounded up were willing to be wasted as outriders for the Soviet conspiratorial apparatus.

2. The Several Lives
of Harry Gold

HARRY GOLD provides an almost classical example of the way the Soviet Union manages to turn dupes to fifth-column use in any free country. It wasn't clear when he was first arrested, but it has gradually become clear since then that Gold came out of the same stream of Communism which furnished the other agents used by the Russians in North America. If a partial account of Gold's activities has power to shock some Americans in 1952, and seems preposterous to others, it is because standard operating procedures in this field have not yet become public knowledge. As a spy, Gold didn't quite class as a professional. He was a gifted, part-time amateur, working with a somewhat haphazard net. His excellence in espionage was due largely to his slavish obedience to instructions. Though superlatively useful at times to his Soviet superiors, Harry Gold was not indispensable. The apparatus served by him never lacked available alternative recruits, ready and willing to run great risks for insignificant rewards. His designation as the courier to carry atomic secrets showed a high Soviet regard for his capacities. Nevertheless, other couriers could have been used for this espionage job of all jobs, with almost equal chance of success. Soviet gratitude for his service proved less than eternal; within a short time after his capture and confession, Gold was brushed off with the phrase "antileftist adventurer," and so he has remained, in Communist circles.

26

Exaggerated appraisals of Gold as "the most despicable traitor since Judas" and "the greatest spy in history" contribute little to the solution of the problem in internal security which he poses. At the present time, he has considerable importance because of his willingness to describe in considerable detail, the precise operation of the conspiratorial apparatus in which he was an odd-shaped but functioning cog.

Charged in 1950 with wartime espionage, punishable by death, Gold was so explicit about his crime as to amaze investigators. In asking Federal Judge McGranery to assign him a lawyer, Gold requested somebody of wide reputation who would allow him to co-operate with the FBI. John D. M. Hamilton accepted the assignment; in 1951, shortly before Gold was sentenced to thirty years in prison (later reduced somewhat to take into account time already spent in jail), Hamilton told the court that he had found the atom spy "the most selfless person" in his experience. Even discounting exaggeration in behalf of a client, a residue of that early American innocence which was a favorite theme of Henry James seemed perceptible. Though he headed the Republican machine in the United States during one presidential campaign, Hamilton was probably too much of an ordinary, out-in-the-open American to understand an opaque, circuitous character like Harry Gold.

Psychologically, Gold was a sport, or a freak. His variations from normal behavior increased his temporary value as an underground worker, but eventually marked him as an unreliable agent.

Always fiercely selfish in his own queer way, this withdrawn, mousy individual had a great capacity, almost compulsion, to live deviously. He learned to divide his thinking into compartments. In a sense this is what any husband does who manages to maintain a mistress without arousing his wife's suspicion, or any confidence man who pretends to be an honest salesman during week-end visits to his home. What set Gold apart, according to his own statements, was a gradually developed, eerie technique

27

for preventing thoughts of one phase from penetrating another. Unless he did this, he explained, life would have been too horrible to endure. When the partitions began to crumble, Gold would proliferate a new existence, like a crab growing a fresh claw after a fight. Before he landed in jail, Gold gave himself the luxury of at least three major existences. In one of these, a sort of dream of what he might have become, and might have done, if things had been different, Gold, though a bachelor, invented details of courtship, marriage, and children; he described marital pleasures and quarrels, separation, and pending divorce. He went so far as to transfer circumstances from the life of his mother to his imaginary marriage. He reshuffled family relationships, verbally killing off his flesh-and-blood brother and adopting in his place a young cousin who had admired him as a boy. Privately, he was ashamed of himself for this domestic betrayal—unknown at home because he remained a model, if secretive, son and brother on the surface—and to his shame was added the burden of betraying his religion, his community, and his country.

If Harry Gold eventually emerged in a fourth, and finally constructive role, that of repentant American, it was largely as a way of erasing his earlier confusions and relieving his crushing sense of guilt. He found in confession a relative peace of mind.

2

As the first-born of *émigrés* from Russia, Harry Gold grew up under conditions of poverty and anxiety. These did not make him a spy, obviously; many children of immigrants turn out well. If most of them find existence rather grim and unrewarding, that is perhaps the general lot. Wasn't it Thoreau who, without any reference to the special problems of immigrants, pointed out that most men lead lives of quiet desperation? It is perhaps less surprising, in view of their unstable sociological base, that so few second-generation youngsters land in jail than that so many rise to comparative peaks of business and professional competence.

All you can conclude with any certainty from Harry Gold's early life is that it fostered certain traits which fitted in with his monstrous later development.

Samuel and Celia Golodnitsky, his parents, came from Kiev. They commenced their flight from Russia toward a Western land of promise in 1907. They paused in Berne, Switzerland, where their son Heinrich was born on December 12, 1910. Reaching Ellis Island in July, 1914, the Golodnitskys were almost turned back because of two different spellings of their names on official papers. A hint from the New York immigration officer led them to shorten the name to Gold. Heinrich became Harry in 1922 when his parents were naturalized.

From 1914 to 1916, which for Harry represented the childhood period during which psychologists say basic approaches to people and situations are worked out, the Gold family was constantly on the move, struggling with a strange language and strange customs. They went briefly to Little Rock, Arkansas, and to Duluth, Minnesota; for six miserable months, they endured a Chicago slum. Finally they landed in a decayed section on the south side of the old Quaker town of Philadelphia. There Joseph, their second son, was born February 10, 1917. They had no other children.

Samuel and Celia Gold played minor but reasonably constructive roles in America. With the memory of what they had left behind them still fresh in their minds, they were grateful for small freedoms, and for small comforts. Yet they had the habit of apprehension; it would have been strange if their persistent fearfulness had not seeped down into the consciousness of Harry. Joseph arrived in a more settled atmosphere. He grew up sturdier and more cheerful than Harry. Being more than six years younger, he could not solve Harry's problems for Harry. His comparative social ease only served to highlight the older boy's nervousness.

The two Gold boys felt a deep affection for their parents and for each other. Their expression of it varied. Harry would do anything in the world for Joseph, if he considered it necessary,

29

but he was the sole judge of the necessity, and from day to day he was likely to be sharply critical or uninterested. Joseph had trouble grappling with his older brother's whims—after they grew up, he would say, "Harry is Harry, you know," with a forgiving shrug of his shoulders—but his prevailing attitude was admiration.

Neither of the parents could quite cope with Harry. Samuel never learned to speak English clearly, which whittled away his authority to some extent with the boys as they mastered the language automatically. Mr. Gold worried a good deal over his jobs, since cabinetmaking as a trade was losing ground to factory forms of manufacture. At times he had to take less skilled work for the sake of the family. When he finally secured what seemed like a steady job making victrola cabinets across the Delaware in Camden, New Jersey, he began to feel really at home in his adopted country, but even then he left the guidance of the kids pretty much to his wife. Celia Gold, a short, gentle woman, was a vigorous, canny housewife, a patriotic citizen, a community-minded mother who practiced charity and who in wartime refused to accept extra ration stamps from a neighbor. She tutored children of the neighbors in Hebrew, and taught her own boys to share their toys and milk with less fortunate youngsters.

Harry learned to avoid other children, who were likely to turn cruel after being treated kindly, but he was forever lugging in stray cats and dogs to be fed. A steady pet might have done Harry good, but there were no facilities for keeping one in a small cold-water flat. Celia fussed continually over Harry, and probably understood him as well as anybody, but all her affection and concern could not reach the core of his trouble.

Whether dietary deficiencies during childhood played a role is not certain, but whatever the reason, Harry grew at a lesser rate than the size of his parents suggested as reasonable. He was a butterball of a youngster, with little strength and virtually no comic sense or capacity for pleasing other kids, though he usually impressed adults to some extent.

30

Nobody could have called Harry Gold handsome as a boy, with his dark, almost swarthy skin, receding forehead, and anxious eyes. Nature gave him long lashes and Hollywood eyebrows, those romantic high arches pencilled in for actresses along with their pancake make-up, but these were not calculated to appeal to the polylingual roughnecks on the block. All children are savages in some respects; Harry's playmates would have been impressed by skill at games, but he classed as a dub even at marbles. A country kid might have found consolation wandering in the woods, but in Harry Gold's neighborhood, near Fifth and Shunk in South Philadelphia, any expedition out of sight of the stoop could be hazardous. Harry learned to walk warily, and to dread the street. Lacking the advice or comfort of an older brother, or a stronger or more wily friend, he stuck indoors as much as he could, clinging instinctively to his mother for protection and companionship.

His mother did what she could; she cheered him up and fed him sweets. Since Harry discovered reading early, she decided he was destined to become a scholar. She encouraged his bookishness on the theory that if he got good marks in school, if he proved smart in an academic sense, if he learned the lore of the word, he would laugh at the hoodlums in the end. She told him so constantly. In making friends, and influencing bullies during school recess, Mamma's advice had a certain pie-in-the-sky flavor; nevertheless Harry accepted it. As to the implied religious twist to some of his mother's suggestions, Harry never rebelled; he simply failed to see the point, in a gentle but eventually clear manner.

Though he started late, and was held back by several sequences of illness, Harry Gold did well enough in the classroom work at George Sharswood Public School, Second and Wolf streets. One teacher allowed him to correct examination papers. Harry worked feverishly, hour after hour, improving the efforts of his classmates in as near as he could come to their own handwriting. His theory was "everybody should pass"; they had a right to do so, he declared. Moving on to the South Philadelphia High School for Boys, and picking up scholastic pace, he completed the four years course in three and a half years, with an average which shoved him up into the top quarter of his class on graduation day. Except for membership in the Science Club, Harry Gold took no part in extracurricular activities. He did not watch games, or go to dances. He was never troublesome in class. So far as relations with classmates went, except for one or two who needed his scholastic help, he was a misfit, though he won the respect of his teachers. In English and science, where he showed special interest, his instructors wondered at times if something resembling insolence did not hover behind his smooth recitations. Matthias Richards, the principal, summed up the odd boy in a sentence: "He was very mild and quite introverted, but he got top marks."

Harry Gold received his high-school diploma in June, 1928. It was not until twelve years later that he won his college degree in his chosen subject of chemistry, and then only by virtue of the financial assistance of the Soviet spy apparatus.

In approaching his goal, however slowly, Harry kept turning the screws down, tighter and tighter, on his own free time. For seven out of twelve years, he maintained a backbreaking schedule of work and study, study and work. During the final five years, like a businessman driven by some inner compulsion to overwork when his business does not require it, Gold added a hidden schedule of espionage in behalf of a foreign power. Long before then, Harry Gold had squeezed most of the juice of his life. Dr. C. G. Jung has pointed out that some men and women become spies because of "the senseless emptiness of their lives." Espionage did provide Harry Gold with a badly needed sense of being useful. He got a thrill out of service for a cause which colored his most humdrum activities. He had been bothered to some degree by the realization that he rated as a bore with most of those he met. After he entered on a double life, being a bore classed as a duty, since the best spy was obviously the one who attracted least attention.

That Harry Gold exerted some control over his development was indicated by the way he eluded programs which displeased him. Shortly after graduation from high school, he took an apprenticelike job with the Giftcrafters, a respected woodworking outfit in Philadelphia. This was his father's idea; Samuel Gold pulled strings to arrange it. If cabinetmaking could carry him and his family halfway around the world, Samuel reasoned, something resembling it might give his son security. When the idea failed, paternal control over Harry Gold just about ended. Harry proved fairly handy, though unmuscular, at the work. He didn't enjoy the job, and he didn't get along with his fellow employees or supervisors.

From August to December, Harry Gold stuck to his job, making no open complaint, but showing by a deepening melancholy that things were not going well. Finally, around Christmas, an apparently inevitable quit-or-be-fired situation provided honorable escape.

Mrs. Gold tried next. Through a community contact, she helped Harry get a small job, requiring some knowledge of chemistry, in the distillery division of the Pennsylvania Sugar Co. in Philadelphia. The personal isolation, dignity, and detail of laboratory work reassured Harry Gold. His effort and politeness, and later his capacity, attracted the attention of Dr. Gustav Rich, the company's chief research chemist. Asked tactfully for advice, Dr. Rich agreed with Mrs. Gold that Harry was a promising boy who could stand more education.

Harry was always grateful to be noticed, no less advised, and his own inclinations followed the line of the doctor's advice. From that moment he began to put aside every penny he could out of his small salary; in two years he had saved the amazing sum of $2,500. In the fall of 1930, when he was approaching his twentieth birthday, Harry Gold took leave of absence from the company and became a day student in chemistry of the Towne Scientific School at the University of Pennsylvania. More than age separated him from his somewhat younger classmates. Since he did not live on campus, commuting ate up free time. He didn't dance or drink; he didn't dress properly; in undergraduate slang he was a wet smack. Many a smack dries out under the breeziness of collegiate banter, but not Harry Gold. His increasing seclusiveness involved self-defense as well as the necessity of picking up cash on the side in odd jobs.

The depression which began with the stock-market slide in 1929 took a new downward lurch in the winter of 1931-32, and Harry's father, like so many others, was laid off. Since Joseph was only a boy of thirteen in school, that left the family without income. Harry Gold did not dodge his duty. During his working period, his mother had refused board money, so he could build up his savings; now it was his turn. As a matter of course, Harry handed over more than $1,000 to his family, which went for food and clothes and rent. "We ate up Harry's money that winter," Samuel Gold recalled later.

When all his money was gone, on March 12, 1932, Harry dropped out of classes and retrieved his old job with Dr. Rich. Nine months later, the sugar company laid him off. Unemployment did not necessarily involve any disgrace at that time. The depression had gone so far that in some Eastern cities one out of every four or five families was on relief, and it was frightening, if you were close to the line. Within Harry Gold, fright took a queer turn and emerged as pride. He would never allow the family to go on relief, he announced. He would steal or starve first, he said.

Perhaps because he had so little grace in approaching strangers in his own behalf, Gold took the rebuffs of job hunting with great bitterness. After two heartbreaking months of paylessness, Harry landed a job with the Hollister Co., a soap-manufacturing concern in Jersey City. He worked there only from February to September, 1933, but it was during this period that he took his first faltering steps toward espionage.

The man who got Gold his job, according to FBI Director Hoover, was somebody in Jersey City "whom we shall call Troy

Niles." Under oath, at one of the trials, Gold named him as Tom Black. There may have been still another name involved. According to Hoover, Niles was an eccentric who liked to coil a pet black snake around his neck, and who would pitch marbles to a crow trained to catch them in flight. Gold testified that Black was a chemist, and a trusted friend, perhaps the only enduring friend in his life. There is some indication that the two had known each other in Philadelphia before Black moved up to the New York area. In any event Gold was tremendously grateful to Tom Black-Troy Niles. Toward Black's union, the Federation of Architects, Engineers, Chemists and Technicians, Gold felt naturally sympathetic. When Black talked Communism, which seemed to be in the air at the time, Gold listened. When Black went to Communist meetings, Gold tagged along, somewhat reluctantly.

This was the peak of the Communist "Third Period," so labeled by Lenin to describe the age of cataclysmic wars and revolutions which were to drown imperialism in a sea of blood, and usher in a golden way of life for all true believers. The young comrades in their blue work shirts or flat-heeled shoes saw no merit whatever in the expiring world of the bourgeois. They lived in a fine Marxian fury, rushing into city streets to announce their determination to fight for the workers' fatherland with their fists if necessary. They demanded an autonomous Negro republic in the South to end racial prejudice. They issued leaflets to R.O.T.C. students in Midwest universities urging the "peasants" to turn their rifles on their oppressors.

In seeking to convert Gold, Black found two soft spots: anti-Semitism and Russia. Gold had the idea that his boyhood troubles with rowdies in the street stemmed from religious prejudice. He might have been right. On the other hand, there might have been little or no anti-Semitism involved. An Irish Catholic boy of the extreme scholarly type, or a German Lutheran lad of the same quality, without strength or wit or charm, might conceivably have received the same rough treatment. In any event, the calculated Communist exaggeration of anti-Semitism, under the pretext of wiping it out (always with an implied promise of revenge) did have considerable attraction for Gold. Many Jewish families that had fled from persecution by the Czar after the unsuccessful Socialist revolution of 1905, even though they were not involved in that revolution, felt vaguely sympathetic toward the Bolshevik revolution when they heard about it later in the countries where they had taken refuge. They might be totally nonpolitical in their adopted country. Even so, they were inclined to take the new regime in Russia on faith because it had evened scores with their old enemy, the Czar. Frequently this sensitivity to anti-Semitism, coupled with a latent feeling for Russia, fell with particular impact on the children of the second generation. During long evening talks, Black made the most of his advantages, stressing Soviet efforts to bring about a higher standard of living for everybody in a country where millions were still dying, he said, for lack of enough to eat.

In addition to attending occasional Communist meetings in Jersey City with Black, Gold visited New York to check chemistry courses at a Communist school near Union Square. The courses failed to meet his needs, so he did not enroll. Party life appalled him, so he did not sign up or acquire a card. Most of the Party members seemed to be "wacked-up Bohemians," he told Tom Black. Fuzzy-minded at best in social and political understanding, Gold did not object to the black-and-white crudities of Party doctrine. He swallowed these whole. He was still parroting Stalinist propaganda, unconsciously, after he had confessed to espionage. Commentators who expressed horror that Gold could do what he did without having any connection with the Communists revealed merely their own naïveté. If Harry Gold shied away from the open-Party phase of Communism, it was because he avoided all social contacts except those of an inevitable or formal nature. The raucous young men and the sexy girls who gave him the jitters were not confined to the Communist party, though they had a little extra scope there through the cutting of family ties. Officially, promiscuity was discouraged in the Party

36

as a handicap to efficiency. However, Communist ethics were based on what was good for the working class. If the individual Party member, male or female, had some latitude in defining what was good for the working class, sleeping with a recruit might come under the head of ethics. Beyond this, there was a great deal of talk about sex among Communists who thought rebellion in one field should extend to others. There were also many successful marriages which grew out of the unconscious courting apparatus maintained by the Party. Harry Gold's reaction to the Communist line on sex revealed as much about him as it did about the Party members.

Shortening of the work week under N.R.A. in the fall of 1933 forced the Pennsylvania Sugar Co. to hire a few extra employees, so Gold was able to return to the security of the Philadelphia distillery and life at home with his family. He maintained regular contact with Tom Black on the basis of a mutual doctrinal interest in Communism, and it was during this period, apparently, that Gold hurdled the tests set ordinarily by the Party to establish a recruit's willingness to endure humiliation or dare illegal activity.

Reliable anti-Communist sources provide an account of how a Harry Gold became something of a Party hero in New Jersey during the early thirties by trying to convince a soldier on a bus to set up a core of disaffection and Communist propaganda within the armed forces. When the bus arrived at the next town, the soldier called a cop. Thrown into jail over the week end, this Gold put on a brave face before a judge who declared mere advocacy of revolution no crime; an overt act was required, he said. The judge's opinion, accompanying release of the prisoner, received extensive circulation in the Party press. Members of the Gold family showed reluctance after the 1951 trial to grant interviews, lest they interfere in some way with the FBI, which was still running down espionage leads, and Gold himself was in prison, unavailable for consultation, so there was no confirmation that he was the Harry Gold involved in this old case. Existence of two persons with the same name, acting on a similar impulse

The Atom Spies

in the identical geographical area would seem unlikely. Furthermore, when Gold was placed on a college campus in Ohio by his Stalinist mentors in 1938, his first move was to wander over to the Army Air Force research center at Dayton and try to subvert some of the young soldiers.

In April, 1935, Gold agreed to keep his eyes peeled for ordinary chemical methods which could be "passed on to the Russian people." This was a tactful approach to industrial espionage. Tom Black was already doing it, and it was partly to "get him off my neck about joining the Communist party," Gold said later, that he agreed to do likewise. An emotionally unstable person, Gold may have been attracted partly to the idea because it suggested a controlled, dignified form of activity, like laboratory work itself.

The Russians had a tremendous admiration for American efficiency, declared Black. They wanted U. S. industrial processes, but American businessmen refused to furnish data out of prejudice, the Soviet talent-spotter asserted. Those who did turn over data frequently "sabotaged" the figures, said Black. The way Black put it, Gold had an obligation to bring the light of technological progress to the land of his parents. Gold accepted this idealistic pitch without question, perhaps recalling that Black and the Party had provided a job in time of need on one occasion, and might do so again, if necessary.

Gold "floundered around very amateurishly for several months," without suspecting that part of the Stalinist technique was to let espionage recruits place themselves firmly on the hook. In November, 1935, he and Black went to New York for a rendezvous. Outside Penn Station, a square-chinned young man approached and passed by, twitching his right shoulder as a signal to them to follow him.

When they overtook the stranger, Black said, "This is Paul Smith," and disappeared. Paul Smith was a Russian employed at the Amtorg Trading Corporation, where NKVD men masqueraded as industrialists. Walking with Gold down a side street,

Smith immediately brought up the subject of a new process for the manufacture of absolute ethyl alcohol. "Your chief chemist in Philadelphia is working on it," said Smith. "What do you know about it?" Gold admitted he did not know much. "Well, that will be your first job," said Smith. "And you are not to see Tom Black again, ever. Understand?" Gold nodded, too overcome by Smith's sharply domineering personality to do any talking.

The Russian called Smith gave Gold a thorough schooling in industrial espionage: what to look for, how to get it, how to prepare it, how to transmit it. He led Gold through the normal routine for an espionage recruit, starting with a biographical sketch of himself, then biographical sketches of his relatives, business associates and friends, analyzing their weaknesses and interests. Gold must have nothing to do with the open Party, Smith directed. He must avoid Communist meetings and Communist friends. He must stop reading the *Daily Worker* and other Party publications. If he expressed political opinions at all, they should be of a reactionary character. . . . Most of this advice proved palatable to Gold. He modified it somewhat, to continue contact with Black, to register as a Democrat in politics, and to express occasional liberal opinions in the proper company, being careful never to appear more Leftist than his associates. He discovered this method worked better than an outright reactionary pose.

Gold was never able to get the ethyl-alcohol process desired by Smith, but he got other valuable material from his company and its chief subsidiary, the Franco-American Chemical Co. He turned over to Smith data on lanolin, the Clayton process for making soap continuously, a carbon-dioxide recovery method, and a number of processes relating to commercial solvents employed in formulating varnishes and lacquer.

In some respects, the Smith interview closed a circuit in Gold's life. It protected him from disillusionment. One obvious reason for the tremendous turnover among Communists in the outer or open Party was ideological dissatisfaction. The chance of this happening to Gold was minimized because he was forced to be ignorant of the shades of Party doctrine. The Communists were entering, in 1935, into a phase of pseudo-respectability and rapprochement, in which they all wore Sunday suits and decided to raise children and put money in the bank. Gold's ostensible turn of direction was paralleled to a certain extent by thousands of persons more or less under open-Party influence.

The Smith interview tended to deepen and rationalize a seclusiveness in Gold which was already odd and disturbing. Gold had been taking evening courses at the Drexel Institute as early as 1933. He seemed to be always taking courses, in everything from psychology to glass blowing. By 1935 he was well launched in pursuit of a night degree in chemical engineering. Such a heavy schedule of study after a long day at the distillery left no leeway for relaxation or fun. Adding a secret career in industrial espionage slammed the door on the normal diversions of a young man, ranging from sport to sex, though not necessarily in that order.

Even before he became a spy, Gold rarely found the cash or the occasion for dating. Now he had an additional pretext for avoiding girls, since the romantic exchange of personal tidbits involved in the normal process of courtship would carry dreadful risks of self-betrayal.

Gold's secret affected his relationships with his fellow workers. He had joined the Federation of Architects, Engineers, Chemists and Technicians, but he resigned from the FAECT in accordance with a strict interpretation of Smith's wishes. When another union called a strike at the Pennsylvania Sugar Co., Gold stayed home rather than crash a picket line. After the strike ended, he came to his bench as though nothing had happened. Dr. Rich exploded at the sight of him. "What do you think you're doing?" he said. Gold said he was reporting for work. "You're on the night shift now," said the research director, mischievously. Tears swamped Harry Gold's protruding brown eyes as he explained he was taking a night course in organic chemistry at Columbia University in New York. Roaring with sudden laughter, Rich agreed to let the boy continue working.

Gold got a tremendous lift over the way he was fooling everybody in the distillery. If Dr. Rich suspected anything, "I'd be out on Shackamaxon Street in a minute," he told his friend Black. In chemistry, "Dr. Rich raised me from a pup," Gold used to say. Nevertheless, he saw nothing improper in deceiving his patron in the interests of a higher loyalty. His sense of values had already softened to this extent.

The restriction of Gold's snooping to industrial matters was beginning to fade. Once he stumbled on some information about tracer bullets. He offered it to Paul Smith, only to be told curtly, not that this was outside his field, but that the Soviet Union needed no further data on the subject.

In 1937, a man known to him as Steve replaced Paul Smith as contact, and early in 1938 a man called Fred replaced Steve. Fred came to the conclusion that the Pennsylvania Sugar Co. was about mined out, and that Gold had better switch to the Philadelphia Navy Yard. Gold was shocked at the idea of leaving his safe haven with Dr. Rich. He could not get decent pay anywhere else without a college degree in chemistry, he said. If he left the Pennsylvania Sugar Co., it would be to complete his college training somewhere, he announced. Gold stuck to this stand, even when Fred became abusive. In midsummer, 1938, Fred changed his tune. Going back to college might be a good idea, he agreed. M.I.T. was the best place, he said; all Gold's expenses would be paid there. Gold had already made tentative arrangements to go to Xavier University, a Jesuit institution out in Cincinnati. He stalled on the alternative suggestion until it was too late to go anywhere except Xavier. He had saved some money, not much, but with $10 or so a week from Fred, he got along for the next two years. Gold paid for his tuition, in a sense, by infiltrating Army Air Force research at Dayton. Without exaggeration, it could be said that Gold, in a switch on a great Amer-

41

ican tradition, had worked his way through college by betraying his country.

In the summer of 1940, when he was almost thirty, Harry Gold returned to Philadelphia with his prized college degree in chemistry, won with highest honors. He moved into an improved job, working directly under Dr. Rich in the Pennsylvania Sugar Co. research laboratory. Almost simultaneously, he was promoted by the apparatus from the role of informant to that of courier.

Gold's psychological partitioning was proceeding rapidly. He made a practice of working abnormal hours—fifty, sixty, seventy, a week—in the laboratory. He did this partly because when he got going on a problem, food or sleep meant little until the problem was solved. He wanted also to create tolerance for periodic unexplained absences. He did chores for other laboratory workers so they would cover up for him, if necessary. Analytical chemistry fascinated Gold; at times he would say he found his only happiness in the laboratory. He was particularly fond of working at night. But there were only so many hours in the day. Sixty hours a week, plus time for the graduate courses he persisted in taking, filled his life to overflowing. To prevent a crack-up under strain and lack of rest, after adding spy work to everything else, Harry Gold treated himself as if he were more than one person. He tried, in each phase of his life, "to stay on a single track." When he had to shift, the analogy which came to his mind was "turning a switch." By means of this invisible switch, he kept the tension of the dark hours of risk taking from invading his comfortable laboratory, and prevented normal evaluation of what he was doing to his country from penetrating his semiautomatism as a spy.

Mrs. Celia Gold became upset over Harry soon after his return from Cincinnati. For years she had been trying to divert him from what she considered moodiness. With less and less success, she sought to interest him in a synagogue service, a civic meeting, or a neighborhood dance. He had no time for such things, he said. After a while she was unable to induce him even to take her to the opera, a musicale, a ballet performance, or a movie. Harry still lived at home, but he seemed almost invariably preoccupied, tense, and secretive. He was becoming a stranger in his own home. Mrs. Gold realized that something horrible was happening inside Harry's mind, far beyond her own affectionate reach.

3

Late in the afternoon of December 26, 1946, the phone rang at the New York laboratory where Harry Gold was working alone. "This is John," announced the metallic voice of Anatoli Antonovich Yakovlev, thirty-five-year-old graduate of Moscow's Engineering Economic Institute, who was listed as a clerk at the Soviet Consulate in New York.

Yakovlev's inquiry, "Have you been all right?" was code for "Are there any suspicious strangers hanging around?" or more precisely, "Have you been free from surveillance?" Gold's "I am fine" gave assurance that the coast was clear. "I'll meet you at eight o'clock tonight," said Yakovlev, and hung up, without consulting Gold's convenience or naming the place.

Gold knew that the Earl Theatre, up near the Yankee Stadium in the Bronx, was indicated. Promptly at eight, Gold strolled to the proper corner of the upstairs lobby. There was no sign of Yakovlev. Instead, a formidable man, standing two or three inches above six feet, with blond hair and very sharp features, came up to him abruptly and said, "Do you know how to get to Paul Street?"

Restraining a facial twitch, Gold replied, "Yes, I'm going there myself a little later," and produced a torn piece of paper from his pocket. The stranger had his piece ready to complete the paper marriage. Gold's half read: "Directions to P . . ." and the other: ". . . aul Street."

The outsized Soviet agent walked "with a catlike stride almost on the balls of his feet" to a nearby fountain in the lounge, took a gulp of water and dried his mouth with a huge hand. To Gold, who had followed, the man said, "John is getting ready for a trip. He'll be on the southeast corner of Forty-second Street and Third Avenue at ten tonight." Then he left.

Both the new rendezvous and the old Paul Street recognition device recalled Harry Gold's most successful trip as a courier, his atomic journey to Santa Fe and Albuquerque in June, 1945. That crucial New Mexican trip had been planned in May, 1945, at a table in the rear of Volk's café, at the southeast corner of Forty-second Street and Third Avenue. Then in July, 1945, at the second, more leisurely encounter with Yakovlev after Gold returned from the Southwest, an emergency plan for the future had been worked out.

The time might come soon, Yakovlev had said, when he would have to leave and be replaced by a new contact. Under his direction, Gold had taken the top sheet from a memo pad of the perfectly respectable Philadelphia laboratory supply house of Arthur H. Thomas Co., had scribbled the sentence about Paul Street diagonally across it, had torn the paper, and the sentence, in half, keeping part himself and giving the other part to Yakovlev. It had been understood that the person bringing Yakovlev's half of the paper, and using the agreed recognition phrase, would be Yakovlev's successor, Gold's new Soviet superior, sixth in a series beginning with Paul Smith. After Smith, Steve, and Fred had come Sam (Semen M. Semenov, an Amtorg official), and after Sam had come John (Yakovlev). Though a year and a half had elapsed, Yakovlev's predicted departure was apparently at hand.

Punctual as ever, Gold met Yakovlev at ten for what he suspected would be a formal farewell. Yakovlev was a native of Borisoglevsk, Voronezh, U.S.S.R., a man about five feet nine with a long nose, a light complexion, and gaunt cheeks. He always looked half starved. He had a habit of brushing a dark brown lock of hair off his forehead with a hand which would start trembling at times, for no apparent reason. His disqualifications for United

44

States espionage included extremely poor English and a complete incapacity to sense surveillance. Instead of going into the familiar Volk's bar this time, Yakovlev suggested a walk, as a result of which they wound up in another bar on Second Avenue near Forty-second Street.

After the waiter wiped their table and took an order for two beers, Yakovlev apologized for having failed to show up as scheduled at their meeting place in the Earl Theatre lounge ten months previously. He had been forced to lie low, he said. If it came to a choice, he emphasized, it was always better to pass up a chance of getting information than to do anything which might endanger the apparatus. He recalled a period toward the close of 1945, already known to Gold, when a very important person with information on his person about the atom bomb came to New York. Discovering that the man with the information was accompanied everywhere by a counterintelligence man, Yakovlev had decided to avoid contact. Now the time had come, he said, to go to another country, and to pass Gold on to his successor.

"The man in the theater?" said Gold.

Yakovlev nodded, and was silent. Gold also found nothing to say. The waiter brought the beer.

"You didn't come to the theater last month," said Yakovlev. "What happened to you?"

"What happened to me?" Gold asked. Receipt in the mail of free tickets to a New York sporting or theatrical event, without any covering letter, had been arranged by Yakovlev as a warning to Gold of a meeting. Early in December, an envelope containing two tickets to some fights in Madison Square Garden had reached Gold's Philadelphia home. Unfortunately, the warning had come too late. Gold was supposed to go to the theater on the date and hour given by the tickets, but by the time he received them, the fights had already been held. With a subtle sense of triumph under his blandness, Gold explained that the envelope had been mailed to 6328 Kindred Street, instead of 6823 Kindred Street, Philadelphia 24.

The delay in delivery, for which neither he nor the post office could really be blamed, Gold said with increasing insolence, had made it impossible for him to reach New York in December in time to keep a November meeting.

Yakovlev tightened his lips. "Have you heard anything from Dr. Fuchs since I saw you last?" he demanded. Gold said he had heard nothing recently from Dr. Fuchs.

"You should begin now to plan for a mission abroad," said Yakovlev, in a businesslike tone. Gold was to go first to London, the Soviet agent explained, then by plane to Paris, in March, 1947, and there meet a physicist, presumably Fuchs. Yakovlev passed over a sheet of onionskin paper bearing typed directions as to making contact, and Gold studied them as well as he could in the dim light of the bar.

The immense importance of this contact, said Yakovlev, required that Gold should make certain of getting time off from his job well in advance. Any loss in salary would be made up, and money would be available for expenses, he said. Would there be any trouble over the leave of absence, Yakovlev inquired. Gold said he expected none; there was some pressure at Abe Brothman Associates at the moment, but laboratory work was due to slacken soon.

"Brothman?" said Yakovlev, in horrified tones.

Gold tried to bluster. "You reached me there by phone," he said.

"Yes, but I didn't understand—" Yakovlev shook his head with frustration, letting the lock of hair flop across his forehead. He brushed it away with a trembling hand. "You work for Abe Brothman?"

The Russian fumbled in a pocket and tossed a bill on the table, got up and almost ran out of the bar. Gold trotted in his wake. He couldn't quite catch Yakovlev, but he kept close enough, like Alice following the White Rabbit, to hear mumbled phrases about damage, terrible damage, damage that could never be repaired.

Coming to an abrupt stop on the sidewalk, Yakovlev glared at

Gold. "I will not see you again," he said, enunciating each word distinctly. He skipped across the street between passing cars. This time Gold made no effort to follow. Yakovlev left the United States by ship the next evening. Gold never did see him again, or the other Russian, the tall one with the razor face who walked catlike on the balls of his feet.

4

Of all Harry Gold's spy contacts, Abe Brothman was the only one who balked at discipline. He rarely showed up for a rendezvous on time. Frequently he didn't appear at all. He forgot promises, ignored precautions, talked recklessly, and tried to use his secret Soviet connections to chisel business contracts for himself and jobs for his friends. Because of his unreliability, he was dumped by one branch of Soviet espionage, only to establish indirect relations later on with another branch that was less finicky. Despite his disqualifications, Abe Brothman had been turning over valuable information to the Russians ever since his Young Communist League days at Columbia University in the early thirties.

Yakovlev washed his hands of Brothman in 1944. He told Gold to avoid the man as of no further use. Later he became more emphatic; Gold should completely forget Brothman, he said, because Brothman was hot, that is, in imminent danger of exposure. Despite these warnings, Gold continued to see Brothman, as he had continued to see Tom Black despite Paul Smith's order. Obeying orders was Gold's great strength, yet in these cases he disobeyed. "I just forgot the warnings about Brothman," he said, on one occasion. "I had so much on my mind I just forgot."

There was more to it than that. As a spy, Brothman was reckless, impractical, and ornery, but as a person he held great appeal for Gold because of his scientific capacity, his generosity, and his affection. He had managed to penetrate Gold's routine deceptions and had forced Gold to construct an entirely new, imaginary

47

existence. Repudiation of Brothman would have meant, in a sense, repudiation of Gold's own dream for himself.

Gold and Brothman first met in New York on September 21, 1941, at a rendezvous arranged by Sam (Semen Semenov). An unimpressive man of medium size wearing undistinguished clothes, Gold had traveled up from Philadelphia by train in the early evening, reading one of his favorite mystery stories on the way. Arriving precisely at ten o'clock at a prearranged spot on the sidewalk of a cross street not far from Penn Station, Gold waited for fifteen minutes, raising his drooping lids from time to time sufficiently to note the license plates of cars drawing up to the curb.

Gold avoided looking directly at the cars or at anybody in the vicinity. The blank look of his sallow face suggested sleepiness more than anything else. He might have been a bookkeeper or a bookmaker or just an idle fellow, so little was there in his appearance to stir speculation. A sedan parked nearby. Calmly checking the license plate against a card drawn from his wallet, Gold took a couple of steps, turned the door handle, and slid into the front seat, alongside the driver, saying "How are you, Abe? It is Abe, isn't it? I bring you regards from Helen."

The driver started nervously when Gold got in, but settled back after the recognition sentence. "I'm Abe all right," he said, freeing a hand from the wheel for a gesture or the beginning of a handshake. He wore no hat, and his wedge-shaped face looked top-heavy because of a receding hairline and a flat pompadour. Ignoring the hand, Gold said he was Frank Kessler. He worked out of town as a chemist, he said. Brothman expressed delight at being able to deal with a scientist, because Helen (Elizabeth T. Bentley, the Vassar graduate turned Soviet courier) had been terrible on technical stuff. "That girl thinks flange is a kitchen stove," said Brothman. "She can't decipher her own notes. I told John [not Yakovlev, but Jacob Golos], I said, 'John, you've got to get me somebody who knows what I'm talking about.' "

Gold said he did not know John or Helen. Following instructions from Semenov, he asked Brothman about the health of his wife Naomi and their little girl.

Brothman boomed that they were both fine. Was Kessler married? Gold, who had run into difficulties with one previous contact who thought all bachelors were irresponsible, got the inspiration to announce that Kessler was married. Did he have any kids? Yes, he had two, lied Kessler-Gold; they were nonidentical twins named Essie and David. How old were they? They were six, said Gold; they were born in 1935 when he was visiting Cincinnati on business. He stopped the avalanche of questions for a while by reciting an anecdote about Cincinnati, recalled from his college days.

Brothman leaned forward to turn on the car radio, and caught the closing rounds of the Louis-Nova heavyweight championship fight at the Polo Grounds, culminating in a terrific single right hand punch by Joe Louis which rendered Lou Nova helpless. After the fight, Brothman switched the talk to baseball. With all his previous contacts, Gold had remained at arm's length, but he seemed unable to keep any distance between himself and Brothman. Gold played no sports, not even handball, Brothman's favorite, as it developed, but he did study baseball statistics, and he could dredge up from memory details of games, scores, and the quirks of famous players, going back years. It was his chief and almost only conversational gambit of importance, good for an evening, but not enough for continual contact with a man like Brothman, whose curiosity was insatiable.

When the pair adjourned to a cafeteria to continue their talk, Gold canvassed his cash to see what he could afford to eat. Brothman promptly wrested from him the fact that he was spending approximately $7 of his own money on train fare and food to keep the rendezvous, since he received no expenses from the apparatus at this time.

With great contrition, Brothman recalled that he had failed to show up at two previous meetings which had been scheduled between them. So Gold had been spending his own money for nothing, he exclaimed. Brothman ended up by forcing a $10 bill on the amazed Gold.

With a man like Brothman, those nonidentical twins could not remain in arrested motion. Obviously they grew older, and did well or poorly at school. Their mother had to be described and embellished. At subsequent meetings, Harry Gold invented little yarns about his imaginary children to satisfy Brothman's insistent curiosity: Essie broke a leg, and David got polio, but they both recovered, as most real children seem to do.

To keep his standing with Brothman, Harry Gold found himself reminiscing about romances which might actually, he thought, have flowered in his life, if he had not been too busy. He started with Gloria, a very beautiful girl "with one blue eye and one brown eye," whom he met on a trolley car in Philadelphia and saw on a few occasions later.

He would have married Gloria, said Gold, except for the opposition of a rich young man, named Frank, whose uncle ran a peanut-chew business. While he was courting the girl with the one blue eye and the one brown eye, he met a friend of hers, a young, gawky, long-legged model named Arabella, who worked at Gimbel's in Philadelphia, he told Brothman.

Arabella gradually put flesh on her bones and developed into a comely young lady. Her mother was a miserable housekeeper, and her father a gambler, but Gold courted her anyway, he said. Another suitor was an uncouth person known as Nigger Nate, who "conscripted girls for brothels." Gold described how he routed this underworld character by a combination of bluff and brawn, and thereby won the hand of the fair Arabella. After several postponements for financial and other reasons, said Gold, with all the corniness of invention characteristic of those old-time radio serials, he and Arabella were joined in the holy bonds of matrimony. Neighbors contributed to the wedding by sending in good things to eat after the ceremony. Such an incident, involving not Harry's wife, for he never married, but his mother, had often been narrated in the Gold family circle. As a grown man in his thirties, Gold was indulging in a sort of adolescent dream about replacing his father in the affections of his mother.

Harry's imaginary honeymoon in Atlantic City was full of comic misadventures as well as of a great deal of solid sexual satisfaction of a sort which he had missed entirely in his life. After the honeymoon, he told Brothman, he and Arabella rented a room-and-a-half apartment in Philadelphia. This was his first mention of Philadelphia to Brothman. Previously he had been simply an out-of-town chemist. Now he was spotted geographically. From an espionage point of view, the change was enormous.

Gold hardly noticed. Having lived in moderate circumstances with his parents up to this time, he was busy drawing on his memory of a richly furnished apartment owned by Morrell Quentin Montgomery, an acquaintance of twenty years and a laboratory associate, to picture how luxuriously he and Arabella lived at home.

All this intimate if largely imaginary chitchat, developing in the course of regular espionage meetings with Brothman, was contrary to a basic principle of personal concealment in spy work. Nobody realized that better than Harry Gold. His other contacts had known him only as a disembodied personality with a cover like Martin or Raymond which could be a first or a last name, or nothing at all. Gold had gotten off on the wrong foot with Brothman by mentioning those lively nonidentical twins, and he had been unable to call a halt.

At one meeting, Brothman asked Gold to do some work for him on a tough problem in analytical chemistry at his Philadelphia laboratory, which by then had been described though not named. Gold agreed to do so. Soon he had to provide an address in Philadelphia to which Brothman could send wires, and letters, about the work. Gold was still known to Brothman as Frank Kessler. He solved this problem by announcing that he could always be reached care of an old friend, Harry Gold, thereby bringing Gold into the picture for the first time. Trying desperately to repair that blunder, Gold gave a misleading vague new address for himself. He and Arabella had just purchased a new home in Abington, a wealthy northeast suburb of Philadelphia, he told Brothman.

Grateful for the free part-time chemical assistance, and genuinely impressed by Gold's competence, Brothman offered Gold a full-time paying job in 1945. Gold refused on the ground that Arabella was so pleased with life in Abington that "she would not consent to be transplanted to New York." The twins, Essie and David, were enchanted with their school, and the neighbors were so considerate, and democratic.

The excuse about Abington was "partly false but it was based on truth," Harry Gold explained later. "My mother and I had purchased a home and I didn't want to be transplanted to New York." What he was doing, again and again, was attributing the views of his actual mother to his imaginary wife. "My mother and I . . ." What about Samuel Gold, Harry's father, in his sixties by then but sturdy and reliable as ever, holding down a good woodworking job with the Zeyher Manufacturing Co. in Philadelphia, and contributing more than anybody else to the purchase of the new $5,000 row house on Eldred Street, in the comfortable but scarcely fashionable Oxford Circle area in Philadelphia? What about Joseph, Harry's younger brother, also a bachelor, a veteran with a job at the Naval Aviation Supply Depot in Philadelphia, who had contributed heavily to the purchase of the house, and in whose name it was actually carried? Why were Samuel and Joseph elbowed aside in Harry's stories?

Joseph, the huskier, more adaptable of the two brothers, had served in the Army during the war, whereas Harry Gold had been rejected and placed in 4F, because of extreme hypertension. In his periodic additions to his imaginary biography, Gold began to take care of Joseph.

His younger brother, he told Brothman, had been killed during a parachute jump in Hollandia. Joseph had served there, though he had returned with three combat ribbons and a tough case of malaria, so the story was not precisely false. It just wasn't true. Carrying the push of brotherly jealousy a step further, Harry Gold told Brothman how his younger cousin Joe, who had regarded him as a hero during boyhood days, and who was perhaps the only person who ever did regard him as a hero, had been adopted by his parents as a substitute for the lost Joseph. No such adoption ever took place.

Toward the end of 1945, the Pennsylvania Sugar Co. sold out to the National Sugar Refinery Co. Dr. Rich was replaced and a sweeping reorganization left no room for Harry Gold. Visiting New York in February, 1946, Gold mentioned to Brothman that he was afraid of losing his job in Philadelphia (not that it had been gone for several months). He was promptly and warmly invited to accept $100 a week, almost twice what he had been receiving in Philadelphia, as chief chemist for Brothman's engineering firm, which was showing some signs of growth. Gold accepted. In doing so, he mentioned for the first time that his real name was not Kessler, but Gold. This seemed safe to him, since by this time he had created in front of Gold an entirely new and fake personality with twins, an adopted brother, and a spurious suburban environment. He reveled in his domestic fairy tale, and found traveling easier than it had been, because he could always produce one of his well-grooved anecdotes about his wife or children, without worry of exposure. Better even than baseball, children could be counted on to fill the empty holes in conversation which sometimes developed.

Celia Gold was inconsolable when Harry told of his impending move to New York. Promises that he would come home to Philadelphia every single week end failed to dry her tears. She didn't know what it was, but she divined that something was wrong with him. Her expressed concern about his health reached toward the unvoiced troubles which must be churning in his mind. Why didn't he tell her what was bothering him, she demanded. Gold said he was all right, she was just kicking up a fuss because he wanted to take the only job open to him. Harry's father and brother tried to stay neutral. They preferred to have him stay at home, they said, but he was a man, and if his work led him to New York, maybe he had to leave. They were careful, naturally, not to go quite that far in the presence of Mrs. Gold.

Harry Gold got so upset over his mother's plaints that he postponed going to work in New York until June, 1946, four whole months after he accepted Brothman's offer. When he did go, he explained to Brothman that Arabella and the twins would stay in Abington temporarily. They were already upset over their inability to see him except week ends, he declared; if anything prevented him from returning on week ends, they would be heartbroken.

Espionage activity for Gold slackened during this period, as a sequel to upheaval and reorganization of the apparatus following the Gouzenko revelations in Canada. The spies were keeping their heads down for a while. The change should have permitted Harry to develop a more normal pattern of living, but somehow it did not work out that way. He rarely started a conversation, even with friends, or looked directly at anybody who came up to him. Sometimes he would walk away from people in the middle of a phrase. He had no minor vices, no real diversions. Suggestions of a social nature bounced off his shell; he was too busy, he said.

He really was busy. When he did not return to Philadelphia for the week end, his work week at the Brothman laboratory ran to one hundred hours or more. Frequently he worked all night, catching daytime catnaps, like Edison, on a cot in the laboratory. He rented a furnished room somewhere which he rarely visited. Occasionally he stayed overnight with the Brothmans. If and when he got home to Philadelphia, Harry Gold relaxed by listening to baseball games by radio or reading mystery stories. He had stacks of these mysteries in his bedroom, and he would read them late at night, when he was too tired to sleep.

Anybody who worked that hard, argued Mrs. Gold, was doing it deliberately. Harry insisted that Brothman kept pushing him to finish this or that experiment, on the ground that success or failure of the entire organization rested on his shoulders, which was no doubt true. However, when Mrs. Gold threatened to go up to New York and say a few words to Brothman, Harry got really upset. If she did that, he would leave home entirely, he said. She didn't test out his threat.

In New York, Gold began to complain from time to time to Brothman, and to others in the Brothman social and business circle who had gradually acquired a sense of his imaginary family, that Arabella was not acting like a proper wife. She was taking his unavoidable absences too hard, he said. She refused point blank to live in New York. As time went on, Gold told how Arabella had slipped into an affair with an elderly but rich realtor whom she had met in Abington. She really loved Harry Gold, but she was trying to punish him for working away from home, the chemist said.

Finally, he and Arabella separated. She refused to let him visit the twins, Essie and David. If he persisted in trying to approach the children, she threatened to start divorce proceedings. Unwilling to abandon hope of an eventual reconciliation, Gold told how he went back to Philadelphia for the melancholy pleasure of standing in a park at a safe distance, watching his children at play. Actually he spent the week end in bathrobe and slippers at the Eldred Street family home, listening to the radio and reading mysteries. He frequently seemed on the verge of exhaustion in New York, so much so that even Brothman urged him to take it easy. Harry Gold complained to Brothman about being "horribly entangled" in a web of lies. He longed for something to "brush aside the whole loathsome structure" so he could "be himself" again, he said. His words did not make too much sense, and he seemed to be talking more to himself than to anybody else.

There came a day when two courteous FBI men arrived at the Gold home in Philadelphia to ask some questions. Harry Gold said it was nothing important, after they left, but he was obviously upset, and the others in the family were more upset. Several weeks later, Mrs. Celia Gold ran up and down stairs in the process of airing out some winter clothes, and crumbled suddenly to the ground in the back yard with a fatal heart attack. All of Gold's suppressed feeling of guilt toward his family focused at the news. He realized that his mother had immediately sensed that the illegal activity, whatever it was, which interested the FBI, provided a clue to his strange behavior over the years, and that this realization had been too much for her.

"I killed my mother," Gold told one of the minor Brothman employees. "Did you hear me? I killed my mother!"

The employee had become hardened by then to the strange and probably quite imaginary family yarns spun by Gold. "Is that so?" he said politely.

3. The Cover-up

HARRY GOLD fell into the hands of the FBI in 1947, but unfortunately, the Bureau could not hold him. Carelessness in counterespionage and Gold's verbal slipperiness contributed to the escape. The effects of this mischance were enormous. The United States lost an immediate opportunity to shut off arteries all over the country which Gold was bleeding for military information. Not only was the net served by Gold able to remain in existence another three years, but Gold himself was left free to resume contact with it, after a period of hibernation known among spies as going private. Many American scientists believed in 1947 that the supposed monopoly of the uranium-plutonium bomb was a fake and an illusion. If Gold had confessed at that time, his confession might have convinced United States political authorities that these scientists were right. The logical assumption would then have been that the Russians were already projecting plans beyond the ordinary atom bomb into the realm of thermonuclear weapons. In other words, a chain reaction of public disillusionment might have been set off which would have led President Truman to advance, by a year or two, his 1950 decision to start intensive work on the development of a hydrogen bomb.

The FBI is a generally efficient outfit, properly respectful of the civil rights of those whom it interrogates, for which every citizen who has ever heard of the ruthlessness of certain branches of foreign secret police remains devoutly thankful. In its 1947

57

encounter with Gold, however, it seems to have been excessively courteous. It put an already recognized spy, Abe Brothman, on his word of honor not to talk to Gold until the FBI reached Gold. Brothman's reaction may be gauged by the fact that he invariably referred to the FBI as the Rover Boys. After Gold claimed he had a stack of blueprints at home in Philadelphia which he had failed to turn over to Jacob Golos, Soviet spy chief, two FBI agents paid him a visit and accepted at face value his assurance that he must have been mistaken, he didn't have any documents there at all. If the agents had gone down into the cellar, they would have found a closet jammed from floor to ceiling with incriminating data.

Golos, a kindly, middle-aged man with a weak heart, whose real name was Raisin, and whose cover name was John, used a travel agency called World Tourists, Inc., as a screen for his underground work. Before the war, the FBI had noticed him exchanging packages in a suspicious manner with Gaik Badalovich Ovakimian, one of the great Soviet spies. In January, 1940, according to the *Washington Post*, Attorney General Murphy filed charges of military espionage against eight persons and three business houses, including Jacob Golos and World Tourists, Inc. Golos subsequently pleaded guilty to violation of the foreign agents registration act and received a suspended sentence. For several years thereafter, up to the time of his death in 1943, the FBI kept him under intermittent surveillance.

The FBI was led directly to Brothman by the Communist defection of Elizabeth T. Bentley. She was an idealistic and quite emotional girl, a Vassar graduate and a former schoolteacher, who became attracted to Communism in her late twenties as an antidote to the excesses of Fascism which she witnessed during a depression-year visit to Italy. Introduced to Golos in New York by an Italian Communist, Miss Bentley served first as a letter drop, to whom incriminating communications from Stalinist spies in Mexico and Canada could be mailed. She became Golos' secretary and assistant, and eventually his mistress. For the ailing, introspective man she called Timmy and Yasha, she developed a great affection. When he died in her arms on Thanksgiving Day of 1943, espionage lost most of its flavor for her. Things she had been able to endure with Golos at hand suddenly seemed unendurable. Contact with garden-variety Soviet agents, who were alternately spineless, shallow, and brutal, deepened her disillusionment. In 1945 she went to the FBI with her story, which was treated with reserve pending investigation. Meanwhile the apparatus had been getting concerned over her displays of temperament. During a lonely walk along the New York water front, her Soviet superior, Al, who was really Anatol Gromov, first secretary of the Soviet Embassy, tried her loyalty by the traditional money test for spies. Deciding that this was a "showdown," as she wrote in her book about her experiences, called *Out of Bondage*, published in 1951, she said, "Don't be silly, Al. Of course I'm not a traitor. Come to think of it, I could use a little extra money." Whereupon Gromov handed her $2,000, got a signed receipt, and left her with every indication of pleasure. Miss Bentley later turned over the money to the FBI.

After testing enough of her story to find it genuine, the FBI tried to use Miss Bentley as a stalking horse to lure Soviet agents out into the open. This did not work too well, perhaps because the earlier suspicions about her began to be revived. By late 1945, the apparatus was warning members to stay away from Helen, which was her Party name. One of those warned was Brothman, who had been in direct contact, first with Golos and Miss Bentley together, then with Miss Bentley alone, before she was replaced as a courier by Harry Gold. Miss Bentley was inclined to be contemptuous of Brothman, to whom Golos had given the revelatory nickname, "The Penguin," but she knew very well what he had been doing, in an espionage sense.

When the FBI finally pounced on the Penguin in 1947, they were deflected to some extent by another woman, Miriam Moskowitz, a tall, willowy girl with light hair and a passion for white blouses, print skirts, and sunglasses in the wintertime. A college graduate, thirty-one years old in 1947, Miss Moskowitz had gone to work originally for Brothman as a secretary. When he set up his own small engineering consultant firm, she became his accountant and entire office staff. Eventually she ranked as a full partner, in charge of business details, not only of the engineering company but also of a later concern organized to manufacture cosmetics. Like Brothman, Miss Moskowitz was a veteran Communist. She was also a shrewd woman fighting for business survival. Keeping Brothman and Gold from flying at each other's throats under the stress of imminent exposure and the weight of their accumulated misunderstandings required great poise and tact, but she managed it. Curiously enough, her triumph over Miss Bentley in the 1947 situation received no mention whatever in the latter's book.

Normally, in matters of espionage, little was known and much had to be presumed. In this case, the gradual weaving of a rope of deception, which enabled Harry Gold, the most successful courier of the atomic era, to reach safety after the ground had been cut from under his feet, could be watched from beginning to end.

2

The first thing Harry Gold did upon reaching the Brothman laboratory in Elmhurst, Queens, around four o'clock on the afternoon of May 29, 1947, was to destroy the onionskin instructions from Yakovlev about an April rendezvous in Paris with a physicist, presumably Klaus Fuchs. The meeting had already taken place, or not taken place, in Gold's absence, but the paper itself might have aroused suspicion. It was the only suspicious-looking thing revealed by Gold's hasty glance around the laboratory. In accordance with a hoary tradition which must cause alimentary allergies in the profession, Gold therefore ate the evidence. He was still chewing when the two FBI agents, one very large and one quite small, put in an appearance. Miriam Mos-

60

kowitz, entering breathlessly in the wake of the agents, and peering around the larger one, thought Gold looked "superbly nonchalant." She told him so later, with a hug, though ordinarily this mushroom of a man made her squirm, because he treated her more like a piece of furniture than a woman. The agents glowered at Miss Moskowitz until she retreated with a mumble about Abe having gone home with a splitting headache and wanting to discuss some contract or other with Harry that evening, if possible.

Gold swallowed his espionage orders, and nodded. "Good night, Miriam," he said.

The agents may have congratulated themselves on reaching Gold before anybody could tip him off as to what was in the wind. If so, they were overoptimistic. They had first encountered Miss Moskowitz around eleven o'clock that morning, when they dropped into Brothman's Long Island City office. She had been co-operative, and had phoned Brothman at home. As soon as he arrived at the office, to confer with his visitors, Miss Moskowitz discreetly departed. After making sure she had shaken off surveillance, she went over to New York for Soviet guidance. The advice she received, not metaphorically but literally, was: "Tell the FBI to go to hell." This did not seem too practical, since by the time she reached the office again, Brothman had already given two fluent but contradictory stories to the FBI.

His first story when shown a portrait of Golos by the FBI men, was that he did not know anybody who looked like that, nor did the name Golos mean anything to him. (This last claim was true, since he knew Golos only by his cover name, John.) When the agents produced a photo of Miss Bentley, Brothman sang a new song, still off key. He knew her all right, he said. She was Helen, the secretary of the man whose picture they showed first. Brothman made quite a production out of telling the truth. "When you showed me that man's picture," he said, "and said you were investigating a violation of the United States involving espionage, I thought this might have some connection with a Russian spy ring, and for that reason I didn't want to be involved.

"I've spent three or four years building up a business, and I thought I couldn't stand the publicity which would result if I identified him. Then you showed me Helen's photograph and I realized you knew the story. If you will try to protect me from unfavorable publicity, I will be glad to tell you about it."

The agents glanced at each other without comment. "Now this man with the Russian name," continued Brothman, "he came to my office sometime in 1938 or 1939 and told me he had some connections with the Russian government. He said he might be able to get me some business with the Russian government. I guess he heard of me through advertisements for one of my inventions in the chemical engineering field which I had placed in the trade journals. I got lots of inquiries through those ads. I first loaned him blueprints for a vat or some machinery for a chemical process. We became quite friendly. I used to have dinner with Helen and him at restaurants. Once he gave me an album of Brahms's Violin Concerto, worth about $4. I had a very good phonograph at the time, and it seemed to me to be an unusual courtesy. Another time he gave me a book, Perry's *Chemical Engineers' Handbook,* worth about $6. We paid for our own dinners as a rule. Sometimes Helen came to my office for blueprints and plans. Then another party came instead of Helen, Harry Gold. I got to like Harry Gold. I got to feel he was a good man in chemistry. He did some chemistry experiments for me on his own, and finally I asked him to come to work for me. He is out at the laboratory now."

The agents gave Brothman plenty of rope. When he finished, they took him back and forth over his story, without developing any glaring inconsistencies.

Most of the blueprints turned over to Helen and Harry Gold were returned, Brothman said, but not all of them. The originals were around somewhere, he said; they were quite harmless. As to the invention which attracted Golos in the beginning, it was a piece of equipment designed to develop very intimate mixing between liquids and liquids, and gases and liquids, at a point of extreme turbulence, so as to accomplish an immediate uniform distribution of the added fluid to the circulated fluid at that point. It was applicable to the blowing of oils to make linoleum bases, the sulphination of oils to make hard-water soaps, the introduction of reactive gases or gases which were to be scrubbed in liquids. It covered the whole range of the process industries and could even be used to put air into hydrogenated oils.

When Brothman ran down gradually, like an unwound victrola, the smaller agent asked, mildly, "Are you a Communist?"

Brothman said he belonged to the Young Communist League for a while during the early thirties when he was a student at Columbia University, but that was more social than anything else. A man working eighteen hours a day to build up his own business had no time for politics, he pointed out. How did he get in touch with Golos when he wanted to? Brothman replied he didn't —well, on one occasion, he did reach him by a phone listed in the book under Mr. Chester, a Watkins exchange. Did he get any contracts from the Russian government? "We did get inquiries from the Amtorg Trading Corporation," said Brothman, "and I seem to think they were traceable to this man's intervention. We quoted jobs, but we never did get one. We quoted a job as late as last September."

Finally he signed a formal statement: "In 1938 or 1939 a man whose name I do not recall but whose picture was shown to me today by Mr. Shannon [the larger agent] and Mr. O'Brien [the smaller one] came into my office. . . . The purpose of turning over blueprints was to obtain contracts. . . . I have not seen this man since 1941 or 1942. . . ."

The most obvious flaw in the statement was Brothman's curious inability to remember the name of a man with whom he had dined frequently, and had business dealings for years. The agents decided to see Gold next. Gold might be having a late lunch, but he would be back at the laboratory soon, said Brothman, noting that he had missed his own lunch. The agents said they would get a bite later. Before leaving, they secured Brothman's promise not to talk to Gold about the interview or in any way to put him on his guard, if he encountered Gold before they did.

Almost an hour later, Gold arrived at the office on the way to the Engineering Society Library in New York, where he wanted to check the chemical literature on the next step in an experiment. He always stopped at the office on the way to the laboratory, to see if Brothman had any instructions for him. This time Brothman grabbed Gold's arm. "It must have been that bitch Helen," he said, so agitated he could scarcely talk.

Gold blinked. "Take it easy, Abe. What's wrong?"

"Look, Harry, look. The FBI was just here. They know everything. They know about us. They know you were a courier. They even have pictures of you and me together. They are coming to see you this afternoon. We can't get out of it."

Miriam Moskowitz suggested that they go back over the talk with the agents to see what Harry thought. "That's it, Harry," said Brothman, eagerly. "You got to cover me up, Harry. You got to tell the same story as me. Did you know John? You got to say you knew him. You got to cover me up."

Gold sat down and listened. What did the man in the picture look like? "Well, he had a wizened face, a wry grin, a baldish dome, and curly hair, what there was of it," said Brothman. "It was John, you know . . . oh, you don't know him? His real name is Gollush, something like that. Will you help me, Harry, will you help me out?"

Miss Moskowitz suggested letting the FBI go to hell. "That's no good," said Brothman. "Look, Harry, how about a book? You and me, we're writing this book on chemistry."

Gold looked pained. "I'll think of something," he said, and left amid little cries of confidence and encouragement, which did not mean quite the same thing. On the way to the laboratory in the Queens Independent Subway, Gold did get an idea or two. The FBI agents surged into the laboratory so soon after Gold's arrival as to suggest that they might have been watching the place. Gold was still chewing the incriminating sheet of paper when the agents showed their credentials. Then Miriam arrived, having come by taxi with last-minute advice. After she was shooed away, the large agent produced a picture of Jacob Raisin, alias Golos, alias John. "Ever seen this man?" he asked.

"Certainly I have," said Harry Gold. "That's Golush or Golish. What a phony-baloney he turned out to be!"

"You don't like him, eh?" purred the smaller agent. "We're making some inquiries, and maybe you could tell us what you know about him."

Gold seemed only too willing to talk. "That man promised me everything!" he exclaimed. "He promised me I would have an opportunity to no longer work in a sugar refinery or a distillery where the scope of the work was necessarily limited; that I would get into a field where I could really expand and utilize my abilities. How I had those abilities he particularly explained. I took that for just the soft soap it was. He was not the first man who ever promised me things. In fact, if the number of people who came around to me at one time or another and who promised me that they were going to make me an extremely wealthy man, or an extremely well-to-do man, or an extremely famous man, were laid end to end they would reach from here to Colorado."

"When did he make all these promises?"

"When we first met," said Gold. "He told me—"

One of the agents interrupted to suggest that a laboratory was hardly the place for a quiet talk, so they adjourned to the agents' car. There Gold sat for two and a half hours, pinned to the rear seat by the insistent probing of the agents, who were swiveled around in the front seat so as to watch every fleeting expression on his face. Without warning, it is doubtful that Gold could have matched Brothman's story and still remain within safe bounds himself. Even with the warning, he ran into sharp turns along the road which required shrewd calculation under the guise of frightened confusion.

Gold had this advantage: he had never before run into the FBI in any inquiry about espionage. There was no evidence of any kind against him except Brothman's voluntary statement that Gold had succeeded Miss Bentley as a go-between with Golos. However, Golos was no ordinary man. The FBI had their own records on him, and Miss Bentley had told how he organized United States nets; how he acted as liaison with nets in Canada and Mexico; how he served on the three-member Central Control Commission, which disciplined American comrades who got out of step ideologically; how he attended top United States Communist meetings, sitting unseen behind a black curtain; how he gave orders on occasion to Earl Browder, when Browder was the nominal head of the United States Communist party.

Though Gold was in the process of verifying Brothman's statement that he had agreed to provide documents for this sinister character, he was doing so in a way which made the imaginary relationship sound innocuous. He had an additional advantage in that he was able to pose as being completely cooperative.

The three men returned to the laboratory at seven o'clock to reduce Gold's statement to writing. Miss Moskowitz phoned at eight. "Hello," said Harry Gold. "Yes. I'm busy now. Try me again in a little while." His statement began:

> In October, 1940, I was introduced to a man by the name of John Golush or Golish by Carter Hoodless, who was a good friend of mine. The introduction took place at a meeting of the American Chemical Society at the Franklin Institute in Philadelphia. . . .

Bringing in Carter Hoodless was an inspiration. Gold really knew Hoodless, a young man of wealth and social position in Philadelphia, since he had tutored him in evening courses at Drexel Institute during the winter of 1935-37 and later had worked with him at the Pennsylvania Sugar Co. Furthermore, Hoodless could be relied upon not to question the mythical introduction to Golos at the ultra-respectable American Chemical Society meeting, since Hoodless had died in 1942.

After the meeting [Gold's statement continued], Golish or Golush and myself went to a restaurant on Broad Street where we remained until 2:30 A.M. On this occasion Golish or Golush made the following proposition to me: that I was to telephone Abe Brothman, a chemical engineer in New York City, and to make an appointment to see him; that I was to discuss two chemical processes with him and to obtain blueprints from him which I was to evaluate against the chemical soundness of the process. The two chemical processes were phenol formaldehyde resins and urea formaldehyde resins.

He stopped writing. "Do you want all this?"

"Certainly," said the smaller agent. "Are you a Communist?"

"No," said Harry Gold. "Why do you ask?"

"I'm just curious," said the agent. "You can put that answer in later. Keep on writing."

Gold wrote:

About one week after this meeting with Golush or Golish, I telephoned Brothman in New York and made an appointment to see him in about two weeks. I saw Brothman the first time in November, 1940, and obtained the blueprints. This meeting was in the evening and took place in New York City in a restaurant in the downtown section.

Gold didn't actually meet Brothman until 1941, and then by sliding into the front seat of a parked sedan and giving a recognition phrase, but who knew that besides him and Brothman?

For the next six months I made trips to New York City on the average of every three weeks and on each occasion Brothman met me and we would have dinner together and Brothman would turn over more blueprints to me. I kept those blueprints in my home in Philadelphia and I never did turn them over to Golish or Golush. I received four or five telephone calls from Golish or Golush in regard to seeing him. He kept telling me we would get together but no definite meeting was ever made. The last time I heard from Golush or Golish was by telephone in May or June of 1941. . . .

It was nearly nine when the agents left, after taking note of Harry Gold's home address in Philadelphia and the address of the room he rented but rarely used with a Queens family named Pereira. A few minutes later, Miriam phoned. Cautiously, Gold said he was through with his work at last. She said Abe's headache was better and they would be out to pick up Gold shortly.

"How did you make out with the Rover Boys?" demanded Brothman, breezily, upon arrival.

Without looking up, Gold murmured that he thought he made out fairly well.

"Oh, he was wonderful!" exclaimed Miss Moskowitz, in an attempt to bridge the unspoken antagonism between the two men. "You should have seen him this afternoon when the agents came in."

The three of them adjourned to a restaurant called Sunny of Chinatown, in Rego Park, where by mutual consent they concentrated on eating before embarking on serious talk. Returning to the laboratory around eleven, they continued to compare notes. After hearing Gold's account for the second time, Brothman said it was a very fine choice of story. Miss Moskowitz said it was grand. "I never knew you had it in you, Harry," she said, almost coquettishly.

Harry Gold coughed. "They may be back," he said. "If they ask about my using the name Frank Kessler, you can say I was doing secret work for you, Abe, and I was very much afraid that if Dr. Rich found out he would raise the almighty devil because he never permitted us to speak to anyone in the laboratory, not even visitors that came in. He was always afraid somebody was going to take one of his precious processes. He was a tremendously suspicious man, though he was a nice man, too. Dr. Rich was a friend of Dr. Kirkpatrick, editor of *Chemical-Metallurgical-*

Engineering magazine, that you used to write articles for. I was afraid those trails might cross some time, and if he found out I was working outside the distillery he would really raise the dickens. That's partly true, Abe."

"Sure enough, Harry," boomed Brothman.

"Another thing," said Gold. "Don't mention those stories about my being married, and having twins. They might check up in Philadelphia. I had to give my right address. I've always been a bachelor."

You could have tossed a half dollar in Brothman's mouth, and the look of amazement on Miss Moskowitz' face was ludicrous in the extreme. "Those stories about your brother getting killed in the war," said Brothman at last, "and your parents adopting Cousin Joe. They're all false, too? They are? Well, I'll be—"

Miss Moskowitz put her hand on Brothman's forearm. "I don't get it," he said. "He had a reason," she replied. "He must have had a reason. He'll tell us about it."

"I had to do it," said Gold. "I got started, and I couldn't stop. Sometimes I lied so much I could almost feel the steam coming out of my ears."

"Look, Harry," said Brothman. "Maybe the FBI is more interested in you than in me. Don't you think you ought to come clean about any espionage activities you haven't mentioned to me? I don't want to be tripped up by some incident I don't know anything about. It is better if I hear it from you now."

Gold shook his head firmly. "You're in deep enough," he said. "What you don't know can't incriminate you."

All along Brothman had thought of himself as a whale, and of Gold as a minnow in the seas of espionage. Now you could sense the process of readjustment in his mind. He kept eyeing Gold in a peculiar way. When Miss Moskowitz went out at 1 A.M. to a White Tower on Queens Boulevard for hamburgers and coffee, Brothman blurted out, "Listen, Harry, you're not sore, are you? Just because I gave your name to the FBI? I had to do it, Harry.

They would have run across you sooner or later, and they would wonder why I hadn't mentioned you."

Gold was leaning forward on his laboratory stool, with sleepy eyes. "They had pictures, didn't they?"

"Pictures?" repeated Brothman. "Oh, yes, a picture. They had a picture of us together at a restaurant. I told you that. Even without a picture, they would get your description. Everybody knows we're in business together."

"They didn't show me that picture," said Gold. "What did it look like?"

Brothman couldn't remember the pose. He got only a glance at the picture, he said. Their heads were close together, he remembered, on second thought, but he couldn't be sure of the restaurant where the picture was taken.

Gold didn't say it, but the obvious thought was like a drawn sword between them. If there were no picture, the FBI might not have known about him, and by his statement he might have put his life unnecessarily, in their hands. Gold fell silent. He was still sitting there, like a Buddha, when Miss Moskowitz arrived with the hamburgers and coffee. "Thanks, Miriam," said Harry, taking his. He turned to Brothman. "Even if there was no picture, we have to stay together on this."

Brothman smiled in relief. "I'm glad we're still friends, Harry," he said.

3

In order to be prepared for any further visits by the FBI, Miriam Moskowitz thought Brothman and Gold should get expert advice. The two men talked it over among themselves and agreed that might be the proper thing to do. On the last day of the 1947 Memorial Day week end, therefore, Naomi and Abe Brothman drove Gold into New York from their Sunnyside home, and parked on one of the side streets off Central Park West in front of a building where Abe said Gibby Needleman, a contract lawyer with the Amtorg Trading Corporation, had an apartment.

"Gibby's in the know," said Brothman. "Remember last summer when we were at the Amtorg office trying to negotiate a contract? Well, just before we left, Gibby took me aside and said he had full knowledge of your record. I thought I had full knowledge, too, in those days."

"Why don't you ask Gibby?" said Gold. "Maybe I will," returned Brothman. "Now look, Naomi, you and Harry watch those windows across the way while I'm inside to see if there's any signs of observation. I've been pretty careful and I don't think we've been followed."

Brothman remained inside for half an hour. Except for a man and woman who seemed to be quarreling, or making love, there had been no movement back of the window curtains across the street. Looking disgruntled, Abe came out and slid into the driver's seat alongside his wife, while Needleman got in back with Gold. They drove around aimlessly for a few minutes.

"I just wanted to repeat what I told Abe," Needleman said to Gold. "If the FBI bothers you again, throw them out of the laboratory. You don't have to talk to them. Tell them you're busy, tell them anything, but don't do any talking."

Nobody raised any argument. "Might as well let me off here," said the lawyer, indicating a corner. Brothman stopped the car as requested, and Needleman strode down the sidewalk with a wave of his hand. Brothman then drove to his $6,000 summer home up near Peekskill. On the way they talked. While he was home over the week end, in fact, shortly after he arrived, Gold said, two agents of the FBI came to the house.

"The same ones?" asked Brothman.

Gold shook his head. "These were from the Philadelphia office," he said. "It wasn't even a search. They just asked about the blueprints and I took them around the house and said there weren't any."

Brothman took his hands briefly off the wheel to make fists.

"Why did you say anything about having blueprints?" he demanded, forgetting entirely that Gold had included that statement to match his own. "You're supposed to be a quick thinker, aren't you? I don't get you at all."

Gold let it ride. Naomi began talking about the two children she had left in charge of her mother in Sunnyside. The old lady, Naomi said, had reached her late sixties, and the liveliness of a pair of youngsters, respectively six and three, left her exhausted after a day or two.

Suddenly Naomi switched to Gold's imaginary children. "You know I miss Essie and David," she confessed. "I got so fond of those kids. I find myself wanting to ask about them all the time. Why did you get rid of them, Harry?"

Gold screwed up his face. "What do you think of Needleman's advice?" he asked Brothman. Brothman said it would undoubtedly be best for both of them to continue to seem to be cooperating to the best of their ability with the FBI. Gold nodded; on that, at least, they were in agreement. They agreed on other things. The trouble was, the relationship between them had been poisoned at its sources, and now both knew it. Tension increased over week ends, when they had time to sift their grievances, but Brothman insisted they stay together. He expressed annoyance whenever Gold wanted to visit his parents in Philadelphia, though Gold had his own forms of firmness, and did not usually give way.

The blowup came unexpectedly, over Tom Black, one week end when Brothman and Miss Moskowitz were driving Gold to Penn Station so he could catch a train to Philly. Tom Black was the chemist who had introduced Gold to espionage. Brothman had learned about him in 1943, when he and Gold needed a stenographer to shape up a report on the Aerosol bomb. This was an insecticide dispenser, not a bomb to kill people, but even so, protecting soldiers from insects in the tropics had more than a little military importance.

Through Black, they secured the services of Jean (Jennie) Zawyrucha, a 17-year-old girl who had taken courses in stenog-

72

raphy at the West Side High School in Newark. Gold paid Jennie $10 or $15 each time they met, for spending two or three hours a week with him and Brothman in a room at a midtown New York hotel, usually on a Wednesday evening, and then typing out notes at home. At the hotel, Brothman would dictate and Gold would help in little ways, like writing technical words in full for the girl as they came up.

Brothman had enjoyed kidding Harry Gold about his solicitous treatment of Jennie, which included stopping at Newark on his train trip from Philadelphia, in order to escort her to New York, and escorting her back to Newark afterward. Rather stiffly, Gold said he had promised Black to take care of the girl, because she was young and innocent, and he meant to fulfill his promise. Gold used his right name in dealing with Jennie, explaining to Brothman, to whom he was still Frank Kessler, that he felt safer in giving her the name of his Philadelphia friend, Gold, even though she had no idea espionage was involved.

Brothman and Gold had a major row over Black in 1946. Brothman found Black using his Elmhurst laboratory, and showed extreme annoyance. Gold said he had previously announced an intention to get Black over for some consulting work, and that Brothman had endorsed the idea enthusiastically, but Brothman denied any prior knowledge. When Gold put in a request later for several days' pay for Black, Brothman refused in rough terms.

Apparently Abe had been reappraising past events, because on this week-end auto trip in 1947 he began growling that Gold had been willing to give his real name to Jennie when he was still keeping it secret from Brothman.

"Who's Jennie?" demanded Miriam Moskowitz. "She sounds interesting. One of Harry's girl friends, I hope. I've been hoping to meet one of Harry's girl friends someday."

Brothman snorted. "Let me tell you something, Harry. I think you made an awful mistake bringing that fellow Black into the lab."

Heatedly, Gold said Black was a good chemist, and an old friend, who had never even received expenses for coming to work at Abe's invitation.

"I never invited him," said Brothman. "Not me. I think you were playing the same trick you used to play on Dr. Rich. That's not all. I got an idea now that Black's the key figure among Americans in the net. Why in hell you'd bring a person like that around I can't understand. Didn't you realize it would attract attention? Maybe that's how the Rover Boys got wise."

Harry Gold started to say something about Helen, only to lose words in a conviction that talking did no good. Abruptly he was shivering with rage, wrestling an impulse to choke Brothman into silence. Fortunately, he was sloppy fat in those days, squeezed tight between Moskowitz and Brothman in the front seat of the car, and couldn't turn easily. Miss Moskowitz held one arm until Brothman brought the car to the curb and stopped.

Gold tried to laugh it off. "One more word, Abe," he said, a little shakily, "one more word and I would have popped you square in the nose."

"That might have been an improvement," shrilled Miss Moskowitz with a significant glance at Brothman's profile. "You know, Harry, you surprise me more all the time. I expect to find you kissing a girl almost any day now." Her laughter sounded tinny, with the two men still half-mobilized for action. "Look, boys," she said, "you're both acting foolishly. This is no time to fight. A falling out between the two of you is just what the Federal authorities want. Can't you see that?"

"O.K., Miriam," shrugged Gold, and in the process lifted his right arm over her head so as to rest on her shoulders. Brothman started the car again. Under cover of Miss Moskowitz' chatter, they reached the terminal without further trouble.

It wasn't until the end of July, 1947, eight or nine weeks after the FBI visit, that subpoenas arrived for Brothman and Gold to appear before the special New York Grand Jury investigating subversive activities. That upset Brothman all over again. First he wanted to explain his actions on the basis of a book he was writing. Next he told Miss Moskowitz mysteriously at the office that he had an entirely new story cooking in his mind. She wasted no time hustling him over to New York in the afternoon to see Gibby Needleman. That night they had dinner at Topsy's Rest in the Forest Hills section of Queens. When Brothman excused himself to go to the toilet, Miss Moskowitz took advantage of his absence to assure Gold everything was all right, since she and Needleman, between them, had persuaded Brothman to stick to his original story.

Largely to be able to mention that they had a respectable lawyer, with a respectable address, Brothman and Gold hired Thomas Kiernan, of Clearly, Gottlieb, Friendly & Cox, 62 Wall Street, to listen to a carefully expurgated version of what they planned to tell the Grand Jury. Kiernan looked skeptical at times during the recital, but he did not interrupt or accuse his clients of lying. At parting, he reminded them that the best defense was the truth.

That night, they rehearsed their lies for the final time, and gave each other courage for the morrow. For his part, said Brothman, he would neither wince nor cringe nor flinch nor beg, he would not appear abject, or show fear; if necessary, he would be defiant. He had heard the Grand Jury was stuffed to the gills with espionage stories and wanted to indict. On the other hand, in their particular cases, he believed the FBI had little real information and was just fishing around.

Gold said he would play safe. He wanted to create the impression of a somewhat timid, frightened man who found himself on the fringe of espionage and was aghast at what happened.

Mrs. Brothman and the kids were up in the country, so that night Gold stayed with Brothman in Sunnyside. Before turning in, the two men got confidential and hinted at the things which were really worrying them. Gold wondered if a man's wartime travels, say to the Southwest, could be traced through hotel and railroad reservations. Ridiculous, said Brothman, too many thousands of civilians and soldiers were on the march in those years to make tracing feasible.

In turn Brothman debated whether Helen had fully appreciated the value of the technical information she passed on to Golos. Not likely, said Gold; by Brothman's own description, the woman was a nitwit.

Gold was half asleep when Brothman stirred him to ask assurances that there were no hard feelings over mention of his name to the FBI. No hard feelings, murmured Gold. Brothman tried to return the compliment by saying he understood why Gold had to tell lies about his family. He wasn't upset about that any more, he said. Within a few minutes, he was snoring, but Gold lay there quite awhile, staring up into the darkness.

The actual performances of the two men before the Grand Jury were anticlimactic. By this time they had ironed out the wrinkles in their stories; Ananias himself would have been proud of them. Brothman slurred over his earlier inability to recall Golos by name, by asserting he was confused whether the name was John Garlis, Garlick, Garlock, or Gollock. Gold, of course, kept speaking of Golish or Golush. Even in his prime, Jacob Raisin never created such a fog.

Brothman's account of his dealings with Golos was a masterpiece of evasion. He said Golos claimed to have been fired by the Russian Purchasing Commission but to have retained contacts with "very high people" in Soviet commercial circles, including Amtorg. He believed Golos' story, said Brothman, partly because the Russian insisted on an agreement that he would receive ten per cent of all profits on contracts from Soviet sources which he was able to swing to Abe Brothman Associates.

"Golos had a nice line of chatter," said Brothman. "He was informed about a great many things and he would speak about anything and everything." Did he talk about Communism? "No, indeed," said Brothman. Was he a Russian? "He was Jewish," replied Brothman. Did he suspect Golos was a spy? He did not suspect Golos of anything, said Brothman, until the FBI men came around with that picture.

Licking his lips nervously, Gold said he was making only $50 a week when he met Golos, and he was desperately anxious to increase his income. Golos did not talk much like a technical man but he showed enough signs of an engineering background to arouse confidence, Gold said. He began to class Golos as a phony, he said, when no provision was made for meeting the expenses of his first trip to New York, amounting to $5 for train fare and a couple of dollars for food. When he heard about this, Brothman insisted on paying these expenses, Gold revealed.

For the benefit of the Grand Jury, Gold acted out imaginary phone conversations with Golos with great conviction, though he had never talked to or met the man. Golos "would say, 'Hello, Mr. Gold.' Or I think later on he used Harry. 'This is Mr. Golos.' I thought it was Mr. Golish, or Mr. Golush then. Then later I think he used just the word John because his voice was very distinctive, it was heavily accented. He would say, 'I am in Philadelphia and I have to take a train now. Unfortunately, I can't see you. I will get in touch with you within two or three weeks.' "

Toward the end of his testimony, Gold was asked by a juror, "Didn't you realize you were doing something that wasn't on the level by taking part in these conversations in New York and carrying things back and forth?"

Gold kept in character as a chemist who was academic minded but not entirely devoid of ideas as to where his bread was buttered. "You see," he said, "Carter Hoodless—he was the son of one of the two men who controlled the sugar refinery—he always told me, 'You aren't going to get anywhere here.' He said, 'Uncle Willie'—that was the general manager—'has everything here and nobody is going to get very much while he is around, and,' he said, 'if it changes hands, then all of us may go, so the best thing to do is look around, look around while you are in, Harry. Keep

The Atom Spies

your eyes open for something.' That was the reason Brothman appealed to me."

The Grand Jury which listened to this cover-up remained in session throughout 1947, checking on Bentley leads and tips from the 1946 Canadian spy exposé. There were widespread rumors of two types: (a) that witnesses had failed to come up to expectations; and (b) that political factors were blocking indictments. In the spring of 1948, the Grand Jury shifted emphasis and began to listen to voluminous evidence which resulted in the indictment of the dozen members of the Communist party's national board, or Politburo. No action was ever taken by this Grand Jury against Brothman or Gold. Without some evidence to discredit their own statements, it was hard to see how any action could have been taken against them at that time.

4. Klaus Emil Julius Fuchs

AT THE peak of his usefulness to the Soviet Union, Klaus Fuchs came close to "breaking" as a spy. He was vulnerable to exposure, he told Harry Gold, when the pair met on the outskirts of Santa Fe on September 19, 1945. In Dr. Fuchs's brief case was a detailed report on the Alamogordo blast of July 16 which served as a dress rehearsal for Hiroshima and Nagasaki. The German physicist, by then a naturalized Briton, might well have felt jubilant; here one world war was ending in total eclipse for the Nazis, whom he had opposed openly for years, and in unsuspected strength for the international Communist movement which he had served secretly for years. His mood, in fact, could only be described as exalted as he picked up Gold near a large church toward the city limits and drove to a bluff overlooking the city for a talk. It was around six o'clock, and the lights of Santa Fe came blinking on below them, one by one in the dusk, as Dr. Fuchs pointed out the possibility, now that the power in the atom had been tapped, of converting a few pounds of matter into enough energy to heat and light all the homes in a country, or destroy that country. While Gold listened with downcast eyes, the physicist went into detail about the prodigious Alamogordo blast, which had been seen and heard two hundred miles away. The natives of New Mexico, who had previously been inclined to dismiss the project as boondoggling, now regarded the scientists as heroes, said Dr. Fuchs, with a trace of cynicism, as though he were privately evaluating his own role.

As his exaltation began to ebb, Fuchs became uneasy. Several developments tended to convince him, he said, that he would not be as useful or desirable an informant for the Soviet Union in the future as he had been in the past. In the first place, there was no longer free and easy co-operation between the British scientists and their American colleagues at Los Alamos, he said; many departments formerly accessible to him had been closed. One indication of this new suspicion, he declared, was a refusal of his request to visit the plutonium plant at Hanford, Washington. Since the job was done anyhow, so far as the bomb was concerned, and the war which had given impetus to the job was now over, the leaders of the British contingent of scientists at Los Alamos considered it likely that they would have to return shortly to England.

If that were the case, said Gold politely, perhaps they should work out arrangements for a new contact when Dr. Fuchs arrived in England. This was one of the points which he had been instructed by Yakovlev to bring up, and he had merely waited for the proper opening. Fuchs also was so well trained that what he said was spoken really to Yakovlev, with Gold serving as an almost invisible intermediary. Together the pair worked out an arrangement not varying much from Yakovlev's ideas. The arrangement had to be flexible, since no date, not even an approximate date, for Fuchs's return was yet available. On the first Sunday, then, of each month after his arrival in England, Fuchs would appear at 8 P.M. at the street entrance to the Teddington station. He was to carry two books in one hand, and five books, preferably thin books of poetry bound with string and supported by two fingers, in the other hand. He was to watch for a stranger carrying Bennett Cerf's joke book, *Try and Stop Me*. When the stranger sauntered by, it would be up to Fuchs to stop him.

After the British physicist and his American chemist-courier had made notes on the agreement, Fuchs said there was something

80

on his mind he wanted to mention: he was worried over the fact that the British Army had reached Kiel ahead of the Russians. If the Russians had gotten there first, his troubles would have been over, but it was apparently fated to end the other way, he declared. Back in his student days at the University of Kiel, he said, he had been an active Communist, intriguing against the Nazis, spying on them, even fighting them in the streets. The Gestapo had compiled a thick dossier on him. Should this dossier now fall into the hands of British Intelligence, as it very well might, Dr. Fuchs said, he would come under suspicion and be forced to stop espionage work. He had another, more personal worry, he said, concerning his father, an outspoken Lutheran preacher in Germany. The Rev. Emil Fuchs was planning to visit England. He might even come to America. He was a man who said what he thought under any circumstances, and he would be likely to ask acquaintances if his son Klaus was still a Communist, or blurt out some other indiscretion with the best will in the world.

Gold promised to pass along the information. With all his early joviality gone, Klaus Fuchs drove back into Santa Fe in the darkness, dropping Harry Gold off near his bus station, after turning over to Gold his envelope of information at the last possible moment. Gold's rendezvous with Yakovlev in New York was set for the evening of September 22. They had shaved their time margin too close, and Gold arrived one hour after the rendezvous. He was unable to report on Fuchs, or even to pass on the physicist's report, until the alternative meeting on September 29, out on Main Street, in Flushing, Queens.

To Gold's surprise, Yakovlev showed not the slightest interest in Fuchs's misgivings. No evidence developed subsequently that the Russians tried to sneak the incriminating dossier about Fuchs out from under the noses of the British, or shied away to any degree from the scientist as an informant. Presumably they knew that the Nazis had turned over reports on Fuchs and thousands of others to British Intelligence during the early days of the war.

Concluding that this was a Nazi trick to label all German refugees Communists, and thus make them useless to the Allies, the British had ignored the dossiers.

Fuchs's concern over the Kiel dossiers seems to have been more of an instinctive move away from espionage than anything else. Furthermore, his father did not visit England, or the United States. Perhaps the feelings of almost godlike responsibility which had been stirred in all the participating scientists at the birth of atomic power—pride and what Dr. J. Robert Oppenheimer called a "consciousness of sin"—had something to do with Klaus Fuchs's doubts. Certainly he underestimated his stay in the United States; he did not leave for another nine months. When he did reach England, in the summer of 1946, the apparatus gave him the familiar Moscow money test, to see if his hesitations, and the break in communication, indicated ideological deviation. At his London subway rendezvous, he was offered $500 in cash for his services. Though he had waved aside $1,500 which Gold brought him from Yakovlev in Cambridge, Massachusetts, in January, 1945, when no doubts as to his course perplexed his mind, he realized this time what was at stake. After talking it over with a friend of Dr. Alan Nunn May, the British scientist working in Canada who had taken $700 and two bottles of whisky as a "token payment" for turning over to the Soviet Union uranium samples from the Argonne National Laboratory in Chicago, Dr. Fuchs decided to keep the money as "a symbolic payment signifying subservience to the cause."

Unlike Elizabeth Bentley, who had accepted $2,000 from Anatol Gromov in order to deceive him as to her loyalty, Klaus Fuchs meant what he said, at the time. He continued to pass information to Soviet couriers. Since most of the material was obtained through friends who had no sympathy for Communism, some conflict began to develop in Fuchs's mind, or at least a recognition that a conflict should have been created.

"I used my Marxian philosophy to conceal my thought in two separate compartments," Fuchs said pretentiously in 1950, when

82

he was arrested. "One side was the man I wanted to be. I could be free and easy with other people without fear of disclosing myself because I knew the other compartment would step in if I reached the danger point. It seemed to me at the time I had become a free man because I succeeded in the other compartment in establishing myself completely independent of the surrounding forces of society. Looking back at it now, the best way is to call it a controlled schizophrenia."

Seizing on "controlled schizophrenia," some of the flossiest writers on both sides of the Atlantic proceeded to embroider the notion that Fuchs was a Jekyll-and-Hyde sort of concealed lunatic. A literary cult grew up around the scientist. He was described as something new under the sun, a unique freak, like a man with three heads, a terrifying eruption of nature, worse than flood or lightning or any of the familiar cataclysms. In all this there was some confusion of thought between the awesome devastation of an atomic blast and Fuchs's role as a spy.

In the light of the evidence, what Fuchs accomplished was merely dissociation of two forms of activity which caused some friction in his mind. Trifling with his vague form of irresponsibility may have given him relief during a bitter time, but that was no reason for its public acceptance. The British scientist knew how to manage his affairs, and he perceived the nature and quality of his acts. While living in friendly equality at Los Alamos with a devoted team of scientists, he could still ponder the effect upon himself of a race to Kiel between British and Russian soldiers. While passing documents to a Soviet courier in Santa Fe, only twenty-five miles away from Los Alamos, he could still ramble on discursively about their eventual scientific significance. Klaus Fuchs was neurotic, eccentric, and somewhat infantile in his general reactions to society and politics. He had been corrupted early in life by a thorough Stalinist indoctrination. Despite these things, he was completely sane by moral and legal standards. In many ways, he was not nearly so odd a man as his American contact in atomic espionage, Harry Gold.

83

2

Repudiation of religion, after a strict religious upbringing, seems to have played a role in preparing Klaus Emil Julius Fuchs for the immoral deceptions and stealth of espionage. His father was a Lutheran preacher widely known in Germany as far back as the turn of the century. The Rev. Emil Fuchs held a grandiose conception of his obligations to God and society, and he did not neglect the constructive development of his four children. In his home, Duty, Religion, Brotherhood, Internationalism, and Peace sat down every evening as dinner guests with the rest of the family. The two boys and two girls were reared in an intellectual greenhouse; they learned a lot, but it couldn't have been much fun. Yet when he decided in 1950 to put the best face he could upon his underground work, and his earlier life, Klaus Fuchs started with the unexpected remark that he had a happy boyhood. He seemed so anxious to put this point across as to suggest some secret debate with himself. Certainly he and his brother and sisters grew up in the shadow of an egotistic, overpowering father.

The burden laid upon the four children was to accept at home and to sponsor abroad their father's idealistic and in some cases highly unpopular views. The Rev. Dr. Fuchs was among the earliest pastors to joint the Social Democratic party in Germany. Long before the first world war, he denounced the Hohenzollerns as he later denounced Hitler. When his youngest child, Klaus, was born in 1911, in the provincial town of Russelsheim, near Frankfurt, the Lutheran preacher was off touring the country with a group called the Religious Socialists. He never approved the first world war, with its U-boat sinkings of helpless merchant ships and its merciless Big Bertha pounding of beautiful Paris, and nobody could change his mind about this, even when the hardships of defeat made defeatism seem criminal in the eyes of the neighbors.

When the soldiers went off to battle, the Fuchs children were forbidden to join in the cheering. All four of them felt isolated from other children, but Klaus felt it most. He was a pale, weak boy with a somewhat bulging forehead, socially awkward, intellectually arrogant, and physically clumsy. When other boys picked on him, he tried to fight back with his father's dogmas, instead of his fists, and that didn't work. Klaus could not believe his father was wrong, since in the succession of small towns where they lived, the pastor was looked up to, on moral and intellectual grounds, even by those who did not agree with him. After the war, economic conditions in Germany became so miserable that the continuous clamor of politics reached into the primary schools. The sons of former soldiers, to whom pacifism was anathema, tended to gang up on Klaus. On one occasion, according to his own sketch of his life, he was "very brave." It seems the school had held a celebration on the anniversary of the founding of the Weimar Republic. Some of the pupils protested against the celebration by wearing the imperial badge, Klaus counterprotested by wearing a republican badge, and the others tore it off. Though his gesture did not seem particularly impressive to his schoolmates, it was highly praised at home.

Political crosscurrents in the churches led the Rev. Dr. Fuchs in 1925 to desert the Lutherans and become a Quaker. Klaus, then fourteen, was becoming doubtful about letting other people push him around. He envied the few radical boys who fought back against the tough little nationalists. Nevertheless, he joined the student section of the Social Democratic party at the University of Leipzig several years later, and duly resigned when the party supported a policy of naval rearmament for Germany, conflicting with the family feeling for pacifism.

When his father was appointed professor of religious science at a teachers training college in Kiel, Klaus shifted to the University of Kiel. He rejoined the Social Democratic party there, only to slip away after awhile and offer himself as a speaker for (though not immediately a member of) the noisy and growing Young Communist League. The death of his mother in 1931 removed a quietly restraining influence. Mealtimes at the Fuchs home became stormy, as Klaus began to reject the guidance of his father in politics or anything else.

Along with other Social Democratic rebels, Young Fuchs joined a group of Communists in a dangerous game of fraternizing with Nazi students who were believed to be possible converts for the Left because of their "sincerity." It was during this seminar in double-dealing that Klaus Fuchs, according to his self-serving 1950 story, began to work out his technique for hiding unpleasant facts from himself. He exposed several neo-Nazis, he said, for a course of action which they had discussed with him but not quite put in action. Unhappy at first about his own unscrupulousness, Klaus decided finally that the ethics of politics had nothing to do with the ethics of personal relationships, and need not be considered together. From this position, he did not have to travel far to reach the Communist belief that in the class struggle all weapons were allowed, and that the only permissible use of bourgeois morality was to take advantage of it.

At a time when only a common front with the Social Democrats decided to concentrate its fire on the Social Democrats. Its fantastic assumption was that if Hitler got on top, he would immedi- could have stopped Hitler, the Communist party in Germany ately topple off, or be overturned by a Communist-led revolution. Fuchs joined in the sport of weakening the Social Democratic party, then withdrew from that Party on the ground that it lacked strength, and joined the Communist party.

During his undergraduate days, Fuchs showed considerable skill in the experimental and analytical techniques of science. In his swing away from the moral measuring rods used by his father, he adopted an extremely materialistic philosophy. Then in the name of the Communist party, he accepted all the shoddy premises of Stalinist propaganda on the basis of faith and good works. He examined nothing, not even the Communist claim that science was one of the class weapons, that the true believer in those fields must be a soldier among soldiers, that there was no such thing as objective truth, even in the laboratory.

On the practical plane, Klaus took a mistress from Party circles, while still living at home. He dressed in what he considered a proletarian style, and spent his spare time in street agitation. He became head of the Party cell at the university and from that was promoted to conspiratorial work. He found this gratifying to his ego (since he could assure himself he was smarter and more important than people suspected) but rather wearing on his nerves. He was running secret errands for the Party even before the Nazis gained power in 1933. When the Reichstag went up in smoke and an organized hunt for dissenters began, young Fuchs was on a train bound for an underground conclave of student leaders in Berlin. He left home, and established a ménage with his mistress. According to Kurt Singer, a Viennese-born writer now living in the U.S. whose latest book on espionage, published in 1951, was *The World's 30 Greatest Women Spies,* Klaus's woman was called Hilda Brandt in the Party, Brandt being German for fire, though she also used the names Heiss, Warm, and Kalt, German terms for hot, warm, and cold, during her later underground work in Europe and America.

Since warrants of arrest had been issued for the leaders of the Kiel University Communist cell, Klaus Fuchs remained in hiding in his room for months with his mistress, who would slip out occasionally to buy food with money begged from suspicious and begrudging relatives. Klaus played solitaire by the hour, read endlessly, and brooded over the future. The strain of waiting for orders told on them both, and they quarreled a good deal. The whole Fuchs family meanwhile was feeling the weight of persecution. One of Klaus's sisters, an artist, jumped to her death in front of a train as she was about to be arrested. Another relative had a nervous breakdown. Disdaining concealment or subterfuge, the Rev. Dr. Fuchs went proudly to a concentration camp for nine months.

Dr. Fuchs had sent a message to Klaus urging him to leave the country, on the ground that the boy was not equipped, nervously or physically, for underground work. "As for me," the doughty fighter for lost causes had declared, "my place is here in Germany,

87

fighting Hitler!" Klaus rejected the appeal of his father indignantly. Then the Party, recovering from its early paralysis under Hitler, ordered him to leave, to prepare himself as a future scientific leader of an eventually Soviet Germany. Hilda did not like the order, which did not include her. In obeying the Party, Klaus had some obligation to her, to prove he was doing the right thing, but he had a greater obligation to his father. If Klaus Fuchs's place were not in Germany, he had to justify his absence in the form of future Party service.

More than that: since the relationship with his father played a key psychological role in his life, Klaus Fuchs had to prove that obedience to his material substitute for religion would lead to greater concrete results for Germany than his father's Quakerism.

After receiving shelter for a while in France, the doubly dedicated young Communist was transferred to England by the Society for the Protection of Science and Learning, a non-Communist organization which was being infiltrated to some extent by Communists. Fuchs attended Bristol University, where with direct and indirect financial help from the Party he was able to win his Ph.D. in mathematics and physics, and then Edinburgh University, where he received his doctorate of science and earned a Carnegie research scholarship. During those early years in England, from 1933 to 1939, Fuchs associated almost exclusively with Communists, and chiefly foreign Communists, but he did not apparently engage in espionage. For one year he is said to have paid dues to the British Communist party. He was so far from hiding his political feelings that when war broke out between Germany and Britain, he appeared before the British aliens tribunal and presented membership in the Communist party as proof that he was anti-Nazi. Under the liberal illusion about Communists, which was as prevalent in the British Isles as in America during this period, this was interpreted tentatively as loyalty to Britain.

After awhile, as a precaution, the British interned Fuchs and other German refugees on the Isle of Man. Was this a severe, excessively suspicious act on the part of the British? Klaus Fuchs seemed to think so. In his 1950 statement, among other bland excuses for betraying the country which gave him refuge and a place in the scientific sun, Fuchs expressed significant regret that he had not been privileged to watch the rank-and-file bravery of Britons facing invasion.

When the *Panzers* tore through the Low Countries and France, and a Nazi attempt to leapfrog the Channel seemed imminent, Fuchs along with other aliens was shipped to a camp in Canada. Fuchs concluded that this failure to appreciate him proved the British were a Fascist people. He was particularly annoyed over a ban on newspapers at the camp. In his 1950 confession he implied that if he had been permitted to read of England's day-to-day gallantry in the face of odds, things might have been different. (The man apparently never realized that the purpose in keeping newspapers out of the camp was to prevent Nazis and anti-Nazis from fighting over day-to-day turns in the fortunes of war.)

The British had to be alert to the possibility of Nazi spies masquerading as refugees. Fuchs's claim of Communism provided no absolute guarantee. Hitler and Stalin had signed a pact in 1939, allowing their countries to work, temporarily at least, along nearly parallel lines. Who could tell then whether Germany and Russia would become outright allies, or betray each other? Under the circumstances, it was expecting rather too much of the British to hand Fuchs a free ticket to a grandstand seat on the cliffs of Dover.

Following the invasion of Russia by Germany in June, 1941, Klaus Fuchs was allowed to return to Britain, where a non-military position was awaiting him at Glasgow University. There have been hints from authoritative quarters that quite innocent German refugee scientists in the United States were used by the Communist party to point out Fuchs's availability for scientific work. Prof. Rudolph E. Peierls, an outstanding German refugee physicist in England, heard about Fuchs, and asked him to help in some war research at Birmingham University. Fuchs did not

know in advance that the work involved nuclear fission, but he
would have accepted anyway, and his subsequent actions would
have been the same regardless of the nature of the war work, he
has said. How Fuchs found himself at the very heart of basic
research for a new and revolutionary weapon was defined by
Statements Relating to the Atomic Bomb, British counterpart of
the American Smyth Report, published in 1945:

> The first step to be taken was to establish the nuclear data on
> which depended the possibility of an atomic bomb and which
> determined its size. This work had already begun at Liverpool
> early in 1940 under Professor Sir James Chadwick and it was now
> pushed on more rapidly. . . . The many theoretical aspects of the
> problem were investigated by Professor Peierls, assisted by Dr.
> Fuchs and others. They used the experimental data provided by
> Liverpool and Cambridge to calculate the critical size of the bomb,
> they examined the mechanics of the reaction, and calculated the
> amount of energy likely to be released in an atomic explosion. . . .

Klaus Fuchs, thirty in 1941 and still a bachelor, came to live
with Professor Peierls and his family in a rambling frame house
in Birmingham. He got along particularly well with the professor's
children. Among unattached women on the campus, he caused
something of a flurry, though he developed no exclusive attachment. Women of a maternal type seemed to like him best. Unlike
Harry Gold, Fuchs did not shy away from normal social contacts,
nor did he work conspicuously long hours in the laboratory. He
was frequently preoccupied, but not furtive. Other scientists regarded him as a competent theoretical physicist who was not
above the mild gossip of the faculty club. People generally
thought of him as conscientious, sensible, and a little dull.

In 1942, Klaus Fuchs became a naturalized Briton. That same
year he approached a British Communist of his acquaintance
with an inquiry about the Soviet espionage apparatus, and a contact was duly arranged in London with a courier. He did this
because he believed one of the least believable of the Soviet propaganda themes of the period, "that the Western Allies were de-

liberately allowing Germany and Russia to fight each other to death."

Was there no excuse for Britain's carelessness? There was the obvious fact that the empire was fighting a critical war in the present, not a possible war in the future. There was a great flaring of interallied sympathy, in response to the sacrifices of the Russian people and the heroism of the Russian soldiers at Leningrad and Stalingrad. For the moment, almost anybody willing to work wholeheartedly for the overthrow of the Nazis was being used, without too many questions.

Fuchs's Party past was known to members of the British security police, agents of Scotland Yard and the Army's counterintelligence corps. At each of several changes in his scientific assignment, he came under fresh security. How did he keep his job? Was the situation as simple as his defense attorney, Derek Curtis-Bennet, suggested at his trial? "Anybody who has read anything about Marxist theory must know that a man who is a Communist, whether in Germany or Timbuktu, will react in exactly the same way. When he gets information, he will automatically and unhappily put his allegiance to the Communist idea first." After his initial espionage contact in London, of course, Fuchs was no longer an open Communist. No stray remark or surface clue connected him with the Party, much less with subversion. He avoided British Party members and concealed his rare contacts with Soviet couriers. In the war effort, he was making an increasingly valuable contribution, and each degree of progress in atomic research added to his value.

Americans need feel no smugness over the failure of British counterintelligence to expose Fuchs during this period. When he did arrive in the United States in the next-to-the-top layer of British experts, he was accepted automatically on Britain's recommendation. The FBI got around later to its own screening, according to Kurt Singer, and also passed Fuchs. It would have required damning evidence to upset his status. In those days, any open challenge of Fuchs, or of Alger Hiss, to take an American example, would have amounted to an open challenge of all those who had previously vouched for him, innocently or not. It would have been considered a crippling blow to interallied unity.

3

The Allies were underdogs in the scientific struggle to produce an atom bomb; almost everybody expected the Nazis to win. A trace of awe touched Winston Churchill's Introduction to the British *Statements Relating to the Atomic Bomb,* released in 1945 to celebrate the surprising Allied victory. "By God's mercy," said the Prime Minister, "British and American science outpaced all German efforts. These were on a considerable scale, but far behind." At the start of the war, it was estimated that the Nazis had a two-year advantage in nuclear fission research over the British, and that the British were ahead of the Americans. As the war progressed, it was obvious that the Germans, if they were maintaining, not increasing, just maintaining their initial advantage, were the chief and conspicuous target for espionage. In point of fact, the first effective program of spying, and sabotage in this field was carried out by the Anglo-Americans.

Conscious of being behind in the race, the British were reluctant to reject brilliant theoretical physicists like Klaus Fuchs merely because of a tincture of Red in their political past which might have faded with time. Fuchs benefited indirectly from a world-wide veneration for German science. Many of the best Allied scientists owed to Germany part of their technical training, or, if they were refugees, all of it. They could scarcely visualize any country surpassing Germany in a laboratory war. Keeping within reach of Germany in the production of new weapons would have satisfied most of them.

There was Einstein. The shaggy-haired, gentle German mathematician had expressed the relation between mass and energy in his historic 1905 formula, which lacked proof for many years because of the immense disproportion between its two chief factors. According to his theory, a one-ounce mass, if entirely transformed into heat energy, would be able to convert a million tons of water into steam.

There was Otto Hahn. This German chemist, working at the Kaiser Wilhelm Institute in Berlin, discovered in December, 1938, that bombardment of uranium with the emissions from radium produced two elements—krypton and barium—with roughly half the atomic weight of uranium. Finally there was Lise Meitner, half-Jewish scientist fleeing Germany because of Himmler's religious exclusion laws, who collaborated in England with O. R. Frisch, another German refugee, on a guess that stabbing a uranium nucleus with a neutron would split the nucleus in half and thereby release one hundred million times more energy than in ordinary burning.

Einstein himself, in his 1950 volume of collected essays, entitled *Out of My Later Years,* put the thing in perspective with a simplicity only possible with complete understanding.

> I do not consider myself the father of the release of atomic energy [he wrote]. My part in it was quite indirect. I did not, in fact, foresee that it would be released in my time. I believed only that it was theoretically possible. It became practical through the accidental discovery of chain reaction, and this was not something I could have predicted. It was discovered by Hahn in Berlin, and he himself misinterpreted what he discovered. It was Lise Meitner who provided the correct interpretation, and escaped from Germany to put the information in the hands of Niels Bohr.

In his modesty, Dr. Einstein neglected to tell the other half of the story of the gigantic focusing of material and intellectual resources which produced the bomb. Early in 1939, Dr. Bohr, the Danish physicist, crossed the Atlantic to bring the Meitner-Frisch hypothesis to the attention of Einstein, who had found refuge at the Institute for Advanced Study, Princeton, New Jersey. The resulting discussions stirred American scientists (including Enrico Fermi from Italy, Leo Szilard from Hungary, and scores of

The Atom Spies

others with foreign-sounding names and diverse origins) to feverish experimentation. Then Einstein wrote President Roosevelt,
making these points: "Some recent work by E. Fermi and L.
Szilard . . . leads me to expect that the element uranium may be
turned into a new and important source of energy in the near
future. . . . It may become possible to set up a nuclear chain reaction . . . by which vast amounts of power and large quantities of
new radium-like elements would be generated. . . . This new
phenomenon would also lead to the construction of bombs. . . ."

Since Einstein believed he was too unimportant to obtain a
personal appointment with the President, his friend Alexander
Sachs, an economist, carried the letter to the White House. FDR's
reaction reflected the prevailing view in those days that the
Yankee best in science would probably not measure up to ordinary Teutonic efficiency. "You want to make sure the Nazis
won't blow us up?" the President said, with a grin, and Sachs
nodded. Not until 1940, following an additional Einstein note
stressing underground reports of intensified atomic research in
Germany, did the United States approve its first transfer of funds
($6,000) for a project which eventually cost billions.

Einstein, like Klaus Fuchs's father, was a lifelong pacifist, but
he felt a primary personal and scientific obligation to the country
which had given him a place to live and work away from Nazi
persecution. In England, too, refugees were conspicuous in the
clamor for atomic action. Professor Peierls was one of the five
British scientists selected in 1941 to head up the deceptively
named Tube Alloy Project. He and Fuchs conferred with a United
States atomic mission which crossed the Atlantic in November of
that year, and in 1942, Peierls went to the United States with a
British delegation to make contact with the scientists working on
the Manhattan District Project. Fuchs reached America in December, 1943, with other ranking British scientists, for a close-
knit laboratory effort which culminated in the Alamogordo blast
nineteen months later. The fact that Fuchs was one of a sizable
contingent of anti-Nazi refugee scientists, who were immensely

94

valuable and generally reliable, tended to dissipate any suspicion that he continued to cherish any private allegiance to Communism.

Fuchs may have fared better as a refugee in the West than he would have in the East. Quite a few anti-Nazi scientists, Jews and non-Jews, left Germany for Russia during the early thirties. Those who were Communists were largely wiped out during the tremendous Stalinist purges of the late thirties, when some eight million persons were arrested over a two-year period. Surviving German scientists were handed over by Stalin to the tender mercies of the Gestapo as a gesture of friendship at the time of Soviet-Nazi pact. The deportation order did not include a few important German scientists like Lange, the physical chemist who became famous for catching lightning in the mountains of Switzerland to obtain high voltages. Having come to Russia from Germany way back in the twenties, he had acquired Soviet citizenship and was therefore able (or forced) to remain at his post.

Both Fuchs and Gold found excuse for treachery in the fact that Russia remained apart from the Allied atomic effort. In their confessions, which differed widely in many respects, they both expressed the opinion that the Soviet Union should have been invited to join the Allied team. Of course, during the 1939–41 pact with Germany, Russia was obviously disqualified, and for a while after the Nazi invasion, its hands were pretty full with the problem of survival. No evidence has ever been produced to show that Russia would have joined an atomic coalition, if invited, or would have played fair if it joined. Attempted collaboration in other fields during the war proved pretty much of a disillusioning one-way street. After receiving all sorts of secret military information, and military supplies from the Allies, the Russians were still refusing to allow Americans to inspect their tanks in use on the Western front toward the close of the war. A deep-seated, almost paranoiac distrust of the rest of the world made Russia an uncomfortable partner at best, and a deadly one at worst. Harry Gold believed that Russian participation would have speeded up development of an atom bomb, but it might have slowed down the work instead, through the introduction of different standards as well as distrust in what was an unusually harmonious atmosphere. What set Stalinist scientists apart, as it set Nazi scientists apart, was the necessity of anticipating possible political interpretations of objective scientific truth. Fuchs and Gold might well have been cured if they could have been sent for a year's work in a Soviet laboratory.

Despite this handicap, Russia possessed considerable scientific resources before the war. The world center of atomic research in the early thirties was probably Lord Rutherford's laboratory at Cambridge, England. His laboratory assistants included Peter Kapitza, a Soviet citizen, who had the run of the place. One day Kapitza went home on vacation; he never returned to England. He had been chosen to head up atomic research in the Soviet, along with two other native Russian scientists. It was Kapitza who later developed, according to Soviet sources, an impulse dynamo which obtained the highest magnetic field strength ever produced. It was Kapitza also who illustrated the cancer at the heart of Soviet research. In 1951 he was removed from his post as a "poor security post," Victor Cohn revealed in the *Minneapolis Tribune* in April of that year, because of a speech delivered by him at the 220th anniversary of the Soviet Academy of Sciences declaring: "There is really no such thing as socialist science or British science. There is only one science devoted to the betterment of human welfare. Science must therefore be international."

Unlike the British and the Americans and the Canadians, the Russians never published a formal report on their progress in atomic matters. According to an article by Dr. Gerald Oster in the February, 1946, issue of the *American Review of the Soviet Union*, they had three major institutes carrying on nuclear research as far back as 1932. They began to build cyclotrons in the early thirties immediately after Prof. Ernest O. Lawrence of California designed his first machine to experiment on atomic nucleuses, and they pioneered, Dr. Oster said, "in the splitting

96

of nuclei by cosmic rays." Cosmic rays fascinated the Russians. In 1944, they set up a State Commission under the Armenian physicist, Artyom Alichanian, to construct permanent laboratories on high mountain peaks, doing nothing but cosmic ray research. In 1948 Alichanian and his brother Abram received the Stalin prize, first class, worth two hundred thousand rubles, for a discovery that cosmic rays contained particles called varitrons, having masses greater than electrons.

The Alichanian discovery provided a new picture of the fundamental building blocks in nature. The only trouble with it was, according to non-Russian scientists, that varitrons were strictly imaginary. Soviet propagandists puffed up the discovery over the years, nevertheless, as proof of the superiority of Communist science over bourgeois science. Then in one of those unexpected turnabouts which make analysis of the Soviet Union difficult, the Alichanian brothers were repudiated in the winter of 1951–52 by the Soviet Academy of Sciences, which asserted what the rest of the world already believed, that varitrons did not exist.

When the German armies drove deep into Russia early in the second world war, Soviet laboratories engaged in experimental work on uranium and heavy water at Dnepropetrovsk, Leningrad, and Kharkov were shifted to Siberia, but the work never stopped entirely. According to Dr. Oster's article, a member of a Soviet commission appointed in 1937 to study isotope separations, kept trying in 1942, in his transplanted laboratory in Siberia, to get U 235 by thermal diffusion of a hexaflouride of uranium, though he did not succeed. Certainly quite a few time-wasting and expensive experimental dead ends should have been avoided in Russia by the acquisition of secret Allied atomic data through espionage. The fact remained that no country could make an atom bomb, not in one year or in ten, regardless of how many secrets it stole, unless it possessed considerable scientific know-how, engineering capacity, and industrial strength.

Before the war, the Russians had no need of atom spies. The free exchange of scientific information throughout the world kept them up to date on basic research. France's foremost nuclear physicist, Dr. Frédéric Joliot, who served as a Western European outpost of Communism in scientific circles, did react somewhat strangely in the spring of 1939 to a suggestion by Drs. Bohr, Szilard, Fermi, and others that all anti-Nazi scientists stop publication of their papers on atomic studies. On the pretext that a letter by him, submitted before all the U. S. scientists agreed to the idea, had been published by the *Physical Review* in the United States, Joliot balked at secrecy and managed to block any agreement for another year. This did not affect the Germans, since they were ahead in atomic research at the time and knew it, but it did give the Russians an extra year of access to Western progress in the field.

Joliot-Curie, as he called himself after marriage to Marie Curie's daughter Irène, kept working in his Paris laboratory on uranium experiments during 1939 and through the spring of 1940. He made significant contributions in this field. When France toppled, he decided to remain in the country to give secret assistance to the underground. He instructed his coworkers, H. H. Halban and L. Kowarski, to smuggle 165 liters of heavy water—useful in slowing down neutrons so that they could be handled in a chain-reaction pile—out of France to England. The 165 liters, acquired from the Norsk Hydro Co. of Norway just before the Nazi invasion of Norway, constituted just about the entire stock of heavy water available in the world at the time. It gave British science a chance to take a long stride toward overtaking the Nazis in atomic research.

Why did Joliot-Curie do it? Why didn't he send the precious heavy water (for the discovery of which Prof. Harold C. Urey of Columbia University won a Nobel prize) to the Russian laboratories, or if that was impossible, destroy it? It was likely that he had received no Soviet instructions, in those hectic days when the Nazis were preparing to turn against their friends, the Russians, and he did what seemed best in the emergency. Lack of heavy water certainly infuriated the Germans when they took over

Joliot-Curie's laboratory, and they decided to carry on his experiments with their own physicists, to save time, instead of moving the cyclotron and other equipment back to Germany.

The curious crisscrossing of international loyalties during those days was illustrated by the two French scientists who took Joliot-Curie's heavy water to England. For a while they continued heavy water experimentation at the Cavendish Laboratory in Cambridge, England. Dr. Halban joined the directorate of Britain's Tube Alloy Project, and served as the first chief of an atomic research group at Montreal composed of American, English, and Canadian scientists. Dr. Kowarski returned to France from England after the war to serve as second in command of the French Atomic Energy Commission, under Joliot-Curie, until Joliot-Curie was finally fired by the French for his Communist views in 1950. Kowarski then became second in command under Dr. Jean Perrin, who was named to succeed Joliot-Curie. In 1951, Kowarski was refused a United States visa to attend a nuclear physics conference in Chicago, to the annoyance of various non-Communist European and American scientists who expressed a belief that he had no Communist sympathies.

Congressional efforts to identify the chief postwar Soviet atom spy in the U.S. culminated in the 1949 testimony of General Modelski, a Polish military attaché in Washington who had broken with his government, that this was the secret role of Ignace Zlotowski, who had entered the country as an alternate delegate to the UN. Zlotowski skipped back to Poland before he could be questioned. His record revealed that he had received prewar training in nuclear physics at Joliot-Curie's laboratory in Paris. It is perhaps worth noting, in passing, that Bruno Pontecorvo, perhaps the most important atom spy of all, was also a Joliot-Curie laboratory alumnus.

Niels Bohr, who had done so much to push the United States into the atomic race, had to stop laboratory research in Denmark when the Nazi storm troopers appeared in April, 1940. He kept his personal supply of heavy water in a large beer bottle in his refrigerator, to hide it from the Germans. Later he fled from Denmark in a small boat, clutching the precious bottle to his bosom, only to discover when he reached Sweden that it really contained beer. In his hurry he had left the fake beer bottle behind. An anguished appeal to the Danish underground resulted in liberation of the heavy-water beer bottle.

In May, 1940, when the Nazis rolled up Norway, one of the first things they did was to order Norsk Hydro (the only place anywhere at that time which made heavy water in quantity) to raise its heavy water production to three thousand pounds a year. In 1942, they boosted the rate to ten thousand pounds a year. British Intelligence decided that the heavy-water plant at Vemork had to be put out of action at any cost. In two desperate and bloody attempts, British commandos working with Norwegian underground fighters managed to blow up the plant, as well as three thousand pounds of heavy water being stored there.

Since by this time considerable supplies of heavy water were available to Germany elsewhere, these raids did not stop the Germans. They did give the Nazi leaders indirect comfort by convincing them that German research must be far in advance of the Allies, since the Allies went to such extremes to hamper it. The Germans rebuilt the Norwegian plant in record time, thus convincing the Allies of the high priority of German uranium work. The next Allied step was to unloose American bombers under Bernt Balchen. The hammering from the air did so much damage at Vemork that the Nazis decided to dismantle their remaining Norwegian heavy-water installations and send them to Germany, along with some three thousand pounds of heavy water. The heavy-water containers were loaded on the Lake Tinnsjo ferryboat *Hydro* for shipment, and the *Hydro* was promptly blown up by Norwegian underground fighters who crawled into the holds to leave high-explosive charges.

Meanwhile both the Americans and the British had developed special intelligence groups, military and civilian, to keep track of what was being done in the various Nazi atomic experiment centers. Through bombing, the German scientists were kept on the run, moving their battered equipment from one place to another, but never quite getting out of range. Allied espionage in this respect was so thorough that toward the end of the war, the Allies had the street address of every single atomic installation in Germany.

From 1943 on, espionage reports indicated that the Nazis were not progressing as rapidly in nuclear matters as expected, not as rapidly, in fact, as the Anglo-American effort, in which the Canadians were now sharing.

These reports were precise and accurate, as it turned out, but they were not believed. So invincible was the myth of German scientific supremacy that the information was interpreted as proof that the Nazis had somehow eluded observation and were proceeding somewhere along new lines in impenetrable secrecy.

Apprehension reached new heights in Anglo-American scientific circles toward the close of 1943. The Allied scientists argued that the Germans might not have a bomb yet, but they must have chain-reacting piles, and the piles must be producing great quantities of artificial radioactive materials. What would prevent them from slaughtering city populations by means of unseen radiations, or poisoning urban supplies of food and water? According to Dr. Samuel A. Goudsmit, a Dutch-born physicist who became a professor at Northwestern University, some American scientists figured that Hitler, with his flare for the dramatic, would choose Christmas Day to drop radioactive substances on Chicago, then the hub of Allied nuclear research. Several men engaged in the project were sufficiently worried to send their families to the country, and scientific instruments were readied to measure the radioactivity when and if the Germans hit Chicago.

Toward the end of the war, the United States dispatched one super-secret intelligence outfit to Europe under Dr. Goudsmit, called the Alsos Mission. The Mission was to accompany the advancing armies and do nothing but ferret out hidden atomic secrets in Germany. By picking up and interviewing, one by one, the Nazi experts, starting with Otto Hahn and Werner Heisenberg, the Allied intelligence experts made the almost incredible discovery that the Nazis had missed the whole principle of the bomb. They didn't even know about plutonium.

Most of the captured Nazi scientists were interned in England by the time of the first broadcast about the dropping of the bomb on Hiroshima. They laughed at the idea; they had tried, it couldn't be done, at least not right away. When more details became available, the Nazis concluded that an atomic pile had somehow been dropped, though such a pile, if droppable, would have fizzed rather than exploded. It took additional days for the deflated Germans to realize that the Allies had used an atomic pile only to make plutonium and had fashioned the bomb out of plutonium. Overwhelmed by feelings of failure and remorse, two of the Nazi scientists attempted suicide. Others fell into deep depression and worried about their eventual reception in Germany at the hands of fanatical nationalists. Finally, some of the younger German scientists worked out a defense for home consumption: they were not really aiming at a nasty thing like a bomb, they were just working on an atomic machine, "for peaceful purposes, not for purposes of destruction." This propaganda line worked so well, despite its transparent falsity, that the Russians picked it up years later. The Russians also picked up an impressive flock of German nuclear physicists. In June, 1945, they extended formal and highly flattering invitations to several German experts on the separation of U 235.

Later, half a dozen lesser Nazi nuclear specialists were reported to have slipped behind the Iron Curtain and to be living, first in the Crimea, and then in the Urals. Russian propaganda was quick to capitalize on the bitterness and frustration of many of the defeated German scientists.

Less alert, perhaps, in reversing an alliance than the Russians, the Allies nevertheless obtained, through the Alsos Mission, a comprehensive explanation as to why German atomic science failed so miserably. The disintegration began in the early thirties, when the Nazi leaders pigeonholed physics as one of the abstract or non-Aryan sciences, whatever that meant to them. According to Goudsmit, who wrote about his atom-spying experiences in a dramatic book called *Alsos*, scientists were generally suspect in Germany during the prewar period, because they proved to be overwhelmingly anti-Nazi, though divided in categories ranging from reactionary to liberal, from Freemason to Jew, and from pacifist to Communist. A "purification period" lasting from 1933 to 1937 resulted in at least two out of every five professors losing their jobs. Teaching staffs in the universities could not be replenished for lack of substitutes. When the war came along, indiscriminate drafting of scientists added to a condition which allowed a second-rate chemist to be elevated to chief of civilian research because of his political virulence, and made him complain about "scientific chaos" in a secret report unearthed by the Alsos Mission.

The German Army placed a man named Schumann, a descendant of the composer and a former director of military music, in charge of its research. Other incompetents and political hacks in positions of responsibility weakened the fiber of effort among those they directed. Scientific meetings of German atomic experts degenerated into meaningless wrangles over Einstein, a scientific giant who could not be overlooked, and yet who had to be overlooked, because he was a Jew.

One reason why the Nazis, by 1945, had not passed the stage of atomic development reached by the Allied scientists in 1941, was that the military could not get along with the scientists, and especially vice versa. Inadequate funds were advanced at first for atomic research, and when more funds were procured, nobody seemed to know what to do with the money. Instead of sharpening their wits on each other's hypotheses, the German scientists broke up into competing, seclusive groups. Werner Heisenberg, the foremost German nuclear physicist, for example, never hit on the idea of using plutonium, because it was suggested in a secret report by his colleague Houtermans, who was not a member of the inner Heisenberg clique.

In this atmosphere of mutual contempt and political jockeying, spectacular crackpot ideas thrived. One plan, to use betatrons, the high-voltage machines invented in America, to burn the crews out of Allied bombers in flight with X rays, attracted Air Marshal Milch and resulted in the diversion of important apparatus from the uranium research project. Another project, which some competent German physicists went along with as a sort of joke, was designed to explode the bomb load of Allied planes by making two infrared rays intersect in the sky.

Plenty of money was always provided for the amusement of what might be called the psychopathic wing of Nazi science. Notable in this field were the infamous experiments by Dr. Rascher at Dachau to determine the conditions of survival after long exposure to extreme cold, experiments which had support from the Air Force.

Compared to this sort of thing, the Allied atomic effort during the war was magnificent, and comparatively free from basic mistakes. It didn't quibble over a scientist's religion or his race or his national origin. It concentrated on getting the most efficient men available, and it came pretty close to getting all of them. Co-operation between groups of scientists, and between the scientists and the military, was on the whole excellent. Personal favoritism and jockeying for prestige among the experts seems to have been held to a minimum.

Certainly the refugees justified their inclusion in the combined Tube Alloy and Manhattan District projects. Without them (always including Einstein) it is unlikely that an atom bomb would have been produced at all. The political screening on the projects did not prove adequate. If a man like Klaus Fuchs, a refugee from Germany's political lunacy as well as its scientific chaos, managed to slip into a position where he could betray the whole setup to the Russians, that was only the other side of a procedural coin which seemed at the time to have considerable merit.

5. A Net is Torn

SINCE spies never work alone, exposure of a single agent creates an immediate emergency for both sides. This applies in peace as well as in war, and to spying among supposed allies as well as among acknowledged enemies. Things may have been moving along in an orderly, almost businesslike manner: espionage and counterespionage, thrust and counterthrust, parry and riposte. Suddenly there is an anguished flurry, and perhaps the flow of blood. Those being spied upon have a chance to "play back" an alien apparatus, to eliminate or control it. Those doing the spying, if they are smart enough or lucky enough to learn quickly which one of their operatives has been "blown," may be able to replace the lost link in the chain of contact and carry on as usual. Speed and ingenuity, more than force, usually settle the issue.

During World War II, George and Joanna Wilmer, a suave husband-and-wife team of Soviet operatives with previous service in America, were ostensibly part of the Rado-Foote spy ring working for the Russians against Germany from Switzerland. Actually, they had sold out to the Nazis.

Sensing the danger at once, one of the spy-ring leaders recommended dropping of the Wilmers as untrustworthy, but Moscow ridiculed and rejected the idea that such a pair of veteran spies could renege. The emergency thus prolonged was resolved in slow motion. The Wilmers tried first to lure away the acting director of the Soviet ring in the hope of capturing the code book and the apparatus. This attempt failed. Next the Wilmers concentrated on uncovering the identity of the other members of the Rado-Foote ring. This succeeded. The Nazi secret police were then mobilized for decisive action. By what might be termed a sexual diversion (one Abwehr agent became the lover of a key Russian woman spy), by kidnaping, by intrigue, and by concealed denunciation to the Swiss police, the Nazis managed to knock out the major elements of the ring and silence its three "music boxes," as the vital radio sending sets were called in code messages.

Other examples can be cited, but the most reverberating explosion of a single agent in the twentieth century was provided, of course, by Igor Gouzenko, the twenty-six-year-old cipher clerk at the Soviet Embassy in Ottawa. When he decided that he preferred the temperate climate of democracy to the rigors of totalitarianism back home, and strolled out of the Embassy on the evening of September 5, 1945, the documents he took with him did much more than expose two of the five Russian spy rings operating in Canada at the time. Those documents marked scores of espionage trails to be followed down through the Western Hemisphere and particularly into various odd corners of the United States.

To an extent not realized, unfortunately, for fully five years, the Gouzenko documents blew the lid off Soviet underground efforts in America and Europe to gather up every last bit of secret information about the atom bomb.

Gouzenko had a fair appreciation of the size of the stakes. He figured that the Russians would kill him and his wife to prevent the documents from reaching the authorities. On September 6, he tried vainly to sell his story to a Canadian newspaper; in nightmarish fashion he went from editor to editor without reaching anybody who would take him seriously. That evening he noticed Soviet agents lurking outside his apartment house. He asked a Canadian Air Force officer who lived in an adjoining apartment to take in his little boy overnight so that one of the family would survive. The R.C.A.F. man responded boldly by turning over all the Gouzenkos to another neighbor and going off on his bicycle for help. When he and the police returned, they found the Canadian head of the dread NKVD (the Russian secret political police formerly known as CHEKA and OGPU and now known as MVD) and three other burly Russians prowling through the Gouzenko apartment, which they had entered by the simple expedient of breaking down the door.

The Gouzenkos and their documents were taken into protective custody the following day. That set the stage for the acute espionage emergency for both sides. The person most immediately affected was Colonel Zabotin, the Soviet Military Attaché who had brought Gouzenko to Canada with him in 1943, and on whose staff Gouzenko had served.

Zabotin explained his ruthless wartime spying against Canada and the United States in these words: "Today they are allies; tomorrow they will be our enemies." He provided Moscow with what was probably its first bird's-eye view of the Manhattan District Project, listing military officials from General Groves down, as well as leading scientists and describing United States installations at Chicago, Oak Ridge, Hanford, and Los Alamos. Through his assistant, Lieutenant Colonel Motinov, he sent samples to Moscow of U 235 enriched, and U 233, which had been obtained from Dr. Alan Nunn May. For his espionage coups in the field of nuclear fission, Zabotin received, to his great delight, the Order of the Red Banner and the Order of the Red Star. "Now I have nothing to be afraid to go to Moscow," he told his colleagues. When Gouzenko torpedoed his apparatus, Zabotin scurried from Canada without notifying the Canadian government. In December, 1945, he departed on the Soviet vessel *Alexander Suvorov,* which sailed late at night from New York without complying with port regulations. According to the *New Leader,* an informative and valuable United States Socialist weekly, Zabotin was reported dead four days after his arrival in Moscow. His death was attributed to heart failure.

Pravda said editorially that the Canadian government was trying to harm the Soviet Union by instigating an unbridled anti-Soviet campaign. Volunteers might have turned over data here and there, the Russians announced, but it was "ridiculous to assert that the communication of such insignificant secrets could create any danger whatsoever for the security of Canada."

With an implied glance at the United States, toward which, of course, the Zabotin net was really directed, *Pravda* concluded with a statement that all the information acquired could be found "in the published works of the American Smyth"—the *Smyth Report on Atomic Energy*. This statement was about as true as Moscow's claim some years later that it had never heard of Klaus Fuchs.

The Royal Canadian Mounted Police rounded up, on February 16, 1946, some twenty-two persons tied into Soviet espionage activity by Gouzenko and his documents. Just before the roundup began, George N. Zarubin, the Russian Ambassador to Canada, returned to Moscow. He was a peculiar diplomat, this Zarubin, a man with an iron face who had served the NKVD for years. In the thirties his job had consisted of watching, and occasionally liquidating, Russian Communists who broke with the government and tried to stay in a foreign country. Zarubin went to Germany in the late thirties, using the cover name of Rudolf and a fake United States passport, and was reported to have brought back to Russia Hitler's first tentative feelers which resulted in the Hitler-Stalin pact of 1939.

In the wake of Zarubin's disappearance, which hardly supported the claim of innocence advanced by his government, rumors spread that the entire Soviet intelligence system was receiving a house cleaning. No doubt that was true. The most important shifts were those designed to meet the immediate emergency, to cover the exposed nerve ends of Soviet espionage, particularly in the United States.

Among the first to go was Lieutenant Colonel Motinov, who as Zabotin's assistant had been field director for Russian military intelligence in Canada. He moved to New York, as a member of the Soviet staff at the United Nations, and lived there quietly for more than a year, without any protest from anybody. Since his Canadian assignment had included liaison with Soviet spies in the United States, it might be assumed that he used his new position to cover up agents in danger of exposure. The two chief recruiting officers of the Zabotin net were Fred Rose, Communist member of Parliament, who kept in touch with J. Peters, alias Alexander Stevens, Whittaker Chambers' underground boss in the United States; and Sam Carr, national organizer of the Labour-Progressive (Communist) party in Canada, who maintained a correspondence with Jacob Nathan Golos. Both Carr and Rose were subversive experts with special Moscow training. Rose stayed to face the music after the Gouzenko revelations, but Carr became a fugitive. He went to New York, where he lived under his own name, unmolested, with his wife, at 115 West 74 Street, until he was picked up in January, 1949, and returned to Canada for trial. His activities during those three years in patching the torn hemispheric web may be conjectured.

The *Report of the Royal Commission to Investigate the Facts Relating to and the Circumstances Surrounding the Communication by Public Officials and Other Persons in Trust of Secret and Confidential Information to Agents of a Foreign Power* was published in June, 1946. This 733-page Canadian analysis of the Gouzenko revelations remains one of the great historical documents in espionage. It left behind a puzzle, still not fully solved, which for years has intrigued and fascinated *aficionados* who regard spying as a sort of cops-and-robbers game without sociological or political overtones.

The mystery centered around four superspies working with Zabotin, whose cover name was Grant, under cover names begining with G: Golia, Galya, Gini, and Green. Who were the four Gs? Gouzenko didn't know. Zabotin had paid the Stalinist penalty for failure. Rose, with whom they had underground dealings, went to the penitentiary for six years rather than identify them. These were the only four cover names in the Gouzenko documents which were listed as "unidentified" in the Canadian Report. In one document, they were referred to as Montreal activists, a phrase which might have been interpreted as a reference to the Montreal group of United States, Canadian, and British scientists doing research on an atom bomb. Galya was listed as a "housewife," occupying an "apartment" next to "Davie." Davie meant Major Sokolov, the Commercial Attaché at the Soviet Embassy in Ottawa. Could the "next apartment" mean "next country"—the U. S.?

Green had a "key position" as "assistant to the superintendent of the section on contracts" in a government department of some kind concealed under the code name "locomotive." He gave information on certain things only, one Gouzenko paper stressed. Did this description suggest somebody of strategic importance in the United States State Department?

Gini and Golia were in a special "auxiliary group." Gini, identified as "Jew" in the Gouzenko documents, had a "photo-laboratory" and Golia, "a young artist," worked "at his place." To those familiar with Soviet espionage double talk those descriptions could be stretched to mean that Golia was a young nuclear physicist working in a laboratory in close contact with Gini.

Not until 1950 was there any progress beyond these original and unofficial guesses. Then, in the wake of the Fuchs revelations, French reporters with supposed pipelines under the Channel into British counterintelligence asserted that Klaus Fuchs had been identified as Golia.

Inspector Leopold, Canadian investigator of the Gouzenko documents, had crossed the Atlantic to work on the Fuchs case with Commander Burt of Scotland Yard and Inspector Whitehead of the Special Intelligence Services. The three men had found some intriguing papers at Fuchs's home, according to the stories in the Parisian newspapers. Not only had Fuchs been established as one G, but another Briton had been more than tentatively placed as a second G. A joint Anglo-Canadian intelligence report had gone secretly to FBI Director Hoover, mentioning the two British

Gs, and suggesting that American sources might well round out the solution by spotlighting the two American Gs, about whom some shrewd guesses could be made from as far away as England. No immediate reaction was received from the FBI.

The French journalistic specialists in espionage cited two curious by-products of the Leopold-Whitehead-Burt collaboration. One was an explanation for some recent instances of atomic sabotage in the United States—embodied in the secret report to Hoover—and the other a conclusion that Allan Nunn May had been a far more important spy than he seemed at the time of his arrest.

2

Formal and informal appraisals of Allan Nunn May are now available from Canadian, American, and British sources. Not unnaturally, each country has been somewhat reluctant to stress the full extent of his penetration of secrets in its area. Crosschecking of the accounts lengthens May's shadow beyond any doubt. It seems logical to believe that he had a relation to the mysterious acrostic of the four Gs. He may well have been the Soviet superior, or director in espionage, of Fuchs himself.

May was a native of England, born in 1912, which meant that he reached manhood in the early thirties, that period of turmoil and depression which helped to fashion Gold and Fuchs. He became a Communist in youth, then a secret Communist, presumably a Soviet agent, since the Canadian Report said he was "known" in Moscow before he left England. A physicist, with a Ph.D. from Trinity College, Cambridge, he was recruited in May, 1942, for early research on the hush-hush Tube Alloy Project. Under the direction of Sir Wallace Akers, various teams of experts were then following separate leads at different university and industrial laboratories. May's team was using the Cavendish laboratory in Cambridge.

The Atom Spies

The first biographical reference to May in the Canadian Report read as follows:

> In July, 1944, Dr. Cockcroft, who holds the chair of Jacksonian Professor of Natural Philosophy at Cambridge, England, and who is a scientist of international reputation, had been made director of Atomic Energy Project, Montreal and Chalk River, and worked in collaboration with Canadian scientists at the Montreal Laboratory of the National Research Council. Dr. Allan Nunn May, a British temporary civil servant, formed part of the research group that came over to Canada and was at the Montreal Laboratory as a group leader under Dr. Cockcroft.

From this, one might infer that May did not reach Canada until the summer of 1944. Actually, he arrived in January, 1943, with a contingent of British scientists under Dr. Halban, Joliot-Curie's former colleague, who resigned eighteen months later and was succeeded by Dr. Cockcroft. "Not long after his arrival," according to the Canadian Report, May was claimed by Zabotin's military intelligence outfit in Ottawa, on specific instructions from the Spy Center in Moscow. This meant that May was spying in the Western Hemisphere eleven months before Fuchs showed up, and did not follow Fuchs across the Atlantic, as many persons assumed. It provided a long undisturbed interval for May to build up an atomic spy net.

The earliest references to May in the documents stolen from the Soviet Embassy at Ottawa by Gouzenko are dated 1945. They show May, then using the cover name of Alek, providing a steady flow of atomic information for Lieutenant Angelov, one of Zabotin's assistants, who was given the cover name of Baxter.

Long before 1945, May had established himself as an authority on the United States phases of the nuclear-fission research. He had some claim to do so as senior in the nuclear-physics division of the British effort at Montreal, and as a member of two highly important Allied committees. With a dozen other British scientists, he made his first visit to the Metallurgical Laboratory at the

University of Chicago in January, 1944. It was during this visit that he met and impressed Maj. Gen. Leslie R. Groves, who had just been put in charge of the entire Manhattan District Project. Groves later recalled May as a reliable scientist (reliable because cleared by British Intelligence) and a mature one, around forty, though May was almost ten years younger than that.

For two weeks in April, 1944, May worked on a minor experiment at the Argonne Laboratory in Chicago where the original atomic pile using graphite was located, as well as a later pile using heavy water as a slowing-down material. Toward the end of August, May conferred for three days with officials of the Chicago laboratory on setting up of the Montreal pile.

During his fourth visit to the United States, from September 25 to October 30, 1944, May carried on extensive research with American scientists "in a highly secret and important new field"—so secret, apparently, that even now the details are not available. During his earlier visits, May stayed at a hotel in Chicago. This time he lived in the Argonne dormitory, except for week ends which he spent with an American scientist in the apartment of another scientist who was temporarily out of town.

In a letter sent to Senator Hickenlooper (R-Iowa) in 1946, and later read on the Senate floor, General Groves revealed he had a hunch about May in 1945, before May was exposed. "May had spent more time and acquired more knowledge at the Argonne than any other British physicist," the General wrote. "Although I had no reason to suspect him, I did not like to have him acquire such a wide knowledge of later developments. It is for that reason that in the Spring of 1945 I declined to approve a proposed fourth [Note: really fifth] visit of one month's duration. May never returned to the Chicago laboratory and never visited any other Manhattan District installation."

General Groves added a perfect example of retroactive wishful thinking. "It is very doubtful if May has anything but a general knowledge of the construction of the atomic bomb. He would not have been able to secure any such knowledge through legitimate channels. . . ."

It is true that the bomb assembly was handled in Los Alamos, yet the freemasonry among scientists, noticeable even under strictest rules of secrecy, might well have operated in the Argonne dormitory and at that week end hangout of the scientists. Anyway, why should a spy worry about legitimate channels?

On August 9, 1945, two days after President Truman announced dropping of the mushroom on Hiroshima, Zabotin wired the Director of the Center in Moscow, describing among other things, the rate at which the Americans were turning out plutonium, or U 235, at the Clinton Engineer Works (Oak Ridge) in the Tennessee Valley and at the larger Hanford Engineer Works on the Columbia River in the state of Washington. The telegram read in part:

FACTS GIVEN BY ALEK: (1) THE TEST OF THE ATOMIC BOMB WAS CONDUCTED IN NEW MEXICO (WITH "49," "94-239"). THE BOMB DROPPED ON JAPAN WAS MADE OF URANIUM 235. IT IS KNOWN THAT THE OUTPUT OF URANIUM 235 AMOUNTS TO 400 GRAMS DAILY AT THE MAGNETIC SEPARATION PLANT AT CLINTON. THE OUTPUT OF "49" IS LIKELY TWO TIMES GREATER (SOME GRAPHITE UNITS ARE PLANNED FOR 250 MEGA WATTS, I.E., 250 GRAMS A DAY. . . . (2) ALEK HANDED OVER TO US A PLATINUM WITH 162 MICROGRAMS OF URANIUM 233 IN THE FORM OF OXIDE IN A THIN LAMINA. . . .

This was not the first souvenir acquired by May. Back in April of that year, according to a handwritten entry by Angelov in a notebook taken by Gouzenko, May handed over a sample of plutonium, and was rewarded by $200 and two bottles of whisky. He got $500 for the second sample. Both samples were flown immediately to Moscow. Where did they come from? The Canadian Report refused to guess. The samples might have come from Montreal. General Groves conceded they might more easily have come from Chicago.

According to the Smyth Report, the Metallurgical Laboratory in Chicago contributed more toward the eventual bomb than any other United States installation. Its role was to prepare plans for the large-scale production of plutonium, and the use of plutonium in bombs. This required (a) finding a system using normal uranium in which a chain reaction would occur; (b) showing that in such a chain reaction plutonium could be separated chemically from other material; and (c) figuring how to manage an explosive chain reaction using U 235 or plutonium. May's 1945 report on production was so accurate that when *Life* magazine, in 1951, wanted to make a chart of fissionable materials production, it used May's figures as a base. By extension, May must have found ways to dig out other basic secrets in Chicago.

Masterminding a net from an adjoining country is an axiom of Soviet espionage, Alexander Foote pointed out in his authoritative *Handbook for Spies*, which describes his actual experiences. This principle assures "the maximum degree of efficiency with the minimum danger of compromise," he noted. Assuming that as resident director in Canada for Soviet military intelligence, Zabotin was concentrating on the United States, what was surprising was the way he cleaned out the atomic kitchen and pantry in Canada itself. He may have felt that the rules did not need to be followed too closely in a case of improvised wartime spying against allies.

Back in 1944, a site was selected on the Chalk River, near Petawawa, Ontario, for the construction of a pilot plant, or small-scale atomic pile taking advantage of Canadian supplies of uranium and using heavy water from the United States as a slowing-down medium. This important and in some ways unique installation grew rapidly. Since it was guided from Montreal, May had no trouble insinuating himself there. Zabotin was sufficiently impressed by hush-hush reports about Petawawa to pay a social visit, in the summer of 1945, to a friend living near Chalk River, and subsequently to cruise along the river in a motorboat with the

The Atom Spies

sole purpose of wiring the Director of the Spy Center in Moscow a description of what the plant looked like from the outside.

As atomic research reached its climax, Soviet espionage worried over developing new links at the Chalk River plant, in Montreal, and elsewhere as soon as May was ordered back to England. A wire from Zabotin to the Director in Moscow, dated August 9, 1945, conveyed excellently the implication, running through their correspondence, that May possessed a rare degree of autonomy among spies. It read:

> ALEK REPORTED TO US THAT HE HAS MET NORMAN V . . . [HE WAS AT HIS HOME]. V . . . WORKS IN THE LABORATORY OF THE MONTREAL BRANCH OF THE SCIENTIFIC RESEARCH COUNCIL. . . . HE ASKED THE OPINION OF ALEK: IS IT WORTH WHILE FOR HIM [V . . .] TO HAND OVER INFORMATION ON THE ATOMIC BOMB. ALEK EXPRESSED HIMSELF IN THE NEGATIVE. ALEK STATED THAT V . . . OCCUPIES A FAIRLY LOW POSITION AND KNOWS VERY LITTLE. . . .

After they had been cultivated with cash and established (in the sense that rosebushes are established), Soviet spies are directed here and there, and may be ordered to switch jobs, if necessary. May, however, was always handled with deference. On one occasion in 1945, the Director in Moscow wired Resident Director Zabotin in Ottawa:

> DISCUSS WITH HIM [ALEK]: DOES HE THINK IT EXPEDIENT FOR OUR UNDERTAKING TO STAY ON THE SPOT; WILL HE BE ABLE TO DO THAT OR IS IT MORE USEFUL FOR HIM AND NECESSARY TO DEPART FOR LONDON?

After the dropping of an actual bomb, Canadian and British contributions to the joint atomic project began to dwindle. Zabotin replied:

> HE CANNOT REMAIN IN CANADA. AT THE BEGINNING OF SEPTEMBER HE MUST FLY TO LONDON. BEFORE HIS DEPARTURE HE

WILL GO TO THE URANIUM PLANT IN THE PETAWAWA DISTRICT WHERE HE WILL BE FOR ABOUT TWO WEEKS. HE SAID HE MUST COME NEXT YEAR FOR A MONTH TO CANADA.

May appears to have been visiting Petawawa when Gouzenko strolled from the Soviet Embassy. Like Zabotin; like Carr, the spy recruiter; like Nikolai Khevinov, the *Tass* correspondent who played a considerable role in the ring under the cover name of Martin; May wasted no time in leaving Canada.

Long before he left, May arranged, through Zabotin, about meeting a new contact in London. He was to walk in a specified direction in front of the British Museum at a specified time on October 17, carrying *The* [London] *Times* under his left arm. His new contact would approach, holding the *Picture Post* in his left hand, and say, "What is the shortest way to the Strand?" May would reply, "Well, come along, I am going that way," and after an interval, "Best regards from Michael."

British counterintelligence may or may not have been alerted soon enough to post an observer outside the British Museum on October 17, because considerable time and patience were required to interpret, classify, and check the Gouzenko documents. The Canadian Report declared: "The evidence before us does not reveal whether the contact . . . was made."

Dr. May had five months to prepare. (In the Zabotin wires it had been specified that he would be lecturing in physics again at King's College, and that he could be reached there by phone in case of an emergency; one of the first steps to repair the dikes broken by Gouzenko must have been to make such a phone call.)

On February 15, 1946, the same day on which the general roundup of Gouzenko suspects began in Canada, Lieutenant Colonel Burt, counterintelligence head at Scotland Yard, came around to see Dr. May at Shell-Max House in London, where he was working. Colonel Burt inquired whether there had been any leaks in nuclear matters during May's period in Canada. "That's the first I heard of it," said May, with some brusqueness. May denied he had been approached by Soviet agents in Canada, and refused to answer further questions.

Five days of close surveillance followed. May betrayed nothing. Additional information from Canada having been received during this interval, Colonel Burt came around again. The counter-espionage chief said he knew May had been supposed to meet somebody near the British Museum, but had failed to keep his appointment. This was true, May agreed. "I decided to wash my hands of the whole business," he said.

Before anybody could arrest him, May said he wanted to confess. He quickly wrote out a statement and signed it. Like the fairy tale produced by Harry Gold for the beguilement of the 1947 New York Grand Jury investigating subversion, May's statement had the effect of sweetening up any facts which could not be denied, and of avoiding any new revelations. Presumably by this time Soviet Intelligence had figured out what was missing from the Ottawa files, and had decided that May could not be salvaged. In any event, here is how the confession went:

About a year ago whilst in Canada, I was contacted by an individual whose identity I decline to divulge. He called on me at my private apartment in Swail Av., Montreal. He apparently knew I was employed by the Montreal laboratory and he sought information from me concerning atomic research.

I gave and had given very careful consideration to correctness of making sure that development of atomic energy was not confined to U.S.A. I took the very painful decision that it was necessary to convey general information on atomic energy and make sure it was taken seriously. For this reason I decided to entertain propositions made to me by the individual who called on me.

After this preliminary meeting I met the individual on several subsequent occasions whilst in Canada. He made specific requests for information, which were just nonsense to me—I mean by this that they were difficult for me to comprehend. But he did request samples of uranium from me and information generally on atomic energy. At one meeting I gave the man microscopic amounts of

U. 233 and U. 235 (one of each). The U. 235 was a slightly enriched sample and was in a small glass tube and consisted of about a milligram of oxide. The U. 233 was about a tenth of a milligram and was a very thin deposit on a platinum foil and was wrapped in a piece of paper. I also gave the man a written report on atomic research as known to me. The information was mostly of a character which has since been published or is about to be published. The man also asked me for information about the U.S. electronically-controlled A.A. shells. I knew very little about these and so could give only very little information.

He also asked me for introductions to people employed in the laboratory including a man named V . . . but I advised against contacting him. The man gave me some dollars (I forget how many) in a bottle of whiskey and I accepted them against my will.

Before I left Canada it was arranged that on my return to London I was to keep an appointment with somebody I did not know. I was given precise details as to making contact but I forget them now. I did not keep the appointment because I had decided that this clandestine procedure was no longer appropriate in view of the official release of information and the possibility of satisfactory international control of atomic energy.

From this unapologetic apology, Allan Nunn May emerged "as a man of honor who had only done what he believed to be right," his lawyer argued later in court. Actually, the statement was a tissue of evasions and distortions, starting with the fact that May received $700 *and* two bottles of whisky, not an unknown number of greenbacks *in* a bottle.

The new antiaircraft shells developed by the U. S. Navy for use against Jap suicide fliers in the Pacific were so secret at the time when Dr. May dug out the details for his Soviet superior that they had not yet been shared with the British. May had to make some admission in this field, because of references in the Gouzenko documents, even though the admission riddled his pious talk about spying solely to safeguard humanity against A-bombs. In point of time, the antiaircraft spying indulged by May followed publication of the Smyth Report on atomic energy which he claimed dissolved his own intentions of espionage.

One continuing Soviet objective in atomic matters has been to sow suspicion among the three nations which created the bomb. Dr. May contributed to this by subtle appeals to anti-American prejudice in England. To insiders, his admission about a precisely arranged rendezvous with a stranger on another continent, his careful forgetfulness as to who did the arranging, and how, his whole procedure, in fact, suggested a disciplined agent acting under orders. So did his statement, which protected Russia, Soviet officials in Canada, Communist parties in three countries, and then himself, almost in that order.

Quite transparently, the statement was an exercise in counterespionage, designed to protect the exposed Soviet apparatus in the Western Hemisphere. It could have been, perhaps was, worked out at Znamensky 19, Red Army General Intelligence Headquarters, in Moscow.

The prosecution of Allan Nunn May proceeded in an atmosphere of offhand vagueness which later characterized the trial of Klaus Fuchs. At the arraignment on March 20, 1946, Gerald Gardiner, Dr. May's lawyer, asserted that Commander Burt had told the physicist there was a lot of information about his spying, and that he was thoroughly implicated. Commander, or Colonel Burt replied he had not been in any position on March 20 to accuse May of anything. The counterintelligence chief did say he appreciated May had not done his spying for money, Gardiner insisted. "Oh, no," said Burt. "That was contrary to my instructions, which were that the question of gain had entered into it."

Taking full advantage of the protections of Anglo-Saxon law which do not prevail in the country for which he did his spying, May demanded a trial by jury. He got it on May 1, 1946. After the trial began, May pleaded guilty, thus getting maximum leverage out of his supposed confession and avoiding a presentation of the evidence against him.

When defense attorney Gardiner remarked that May had told him the person to whom he gave information was a Russian, the Attorney General, Sir Hartley Shawcross, replied in a shocked tone, "There is no kind of suggestion that the Russians are enemies or potential enemies. The court has already decided that this offense consists in communicating information to unauthorized persons."

Justice Oliver, in imposing sentence, told May, "Whether money was the object of what you did, in fact you did get money for what you did. It is a very bad case indeed. The sentence upon you is one of ten years' penal servitude."

This sentence was four years longer than any other imposed on a member of the Soviet underground in America exposed by the Gouzenko documents. The Association of Scientific Workers of Great Britain protested vehemently and sent copies of its protest to similar bodies in the Western Hemisphere, arguing that the punishment was out of proportion to the offense. However, if Allan Nunn May failed to earn fully his decade of incarceration in Wakefield Prison in Yorkshire, by his espionage work in the United States and Canada before exposure, he certainly earned it by his performance after exposure.

3

Dr. May was by no means the only scientist spotlighted as an atomic spy by the Gouzenko revelations.

Some of the earliest tips received by Stalin about the gigantic Anglo-American gamble on the explosive instability of uranium came from Raymond Boyer, an internationally known chemist at McGill University. Boyer was born in Montreal. He received his Bachelor of Science degree in 1930 and his Ph.D. in 1935 from McGill, did postgraduate work at various times at Harvard and in European universities.

A fellow traveler or Party member from youth, Boyer was sufficiently excited about the Soviet experiment before the second world war, to take lessons in speaking Russian. An independently wealthy man, he offered in the fall of 1939 to travel to Moscow, without pay or diplomatic status, to investigate for Canada "Russia's real attitude toward the war." This offer was not accepted by the Canadian government.

As a valued senior worker with the Canadian National Research Council, Boyer had access to general atomic developments in the United States as well as to the work in Montreal and at the Chalk River plant in Ontario. Under the appropriate cover name of "The Professor," Boyer provided regular espionage reports for Zabotin through Fred Rose. He also rendered various indirect services to the movement. He had his wife, Anita Cohen Boyer, who later became the third wife of Frederick Vanderbilt Field, offer the use of their luxurious Montreal home for the informal meetings which led to the organization of the Canadian Association of Scientific Workers.

Dr. Boyer became the first president of this valuable front, behind which espionage prospects were evaluated, approached, and conditioned. Allan Nunn May, Norman V . . . . , and several others mentioned in the Gouzenko documents held official positions in the CASW.

Various other organizations in which Communists maintained strong, concealed positions howled over the Gouzenko case prosecutions on the ground that the defendants were interested solely in seeing atomic energy shared by the world. Yet Boyer was spying for the Russians, as were others in the ring, long before there were any assurances of an A-bomb. Furthermore, Boyer did not confine his spying to nuclear fission by any means, as the following appraisal written by Zabotin in his own hand in a notebook shortly after he reached Ottawa in 1943, revealed:

Professor

Frenchman. Noted chemist, about 40 years of age. Works in McGill University, Montreal. Is the best of the specialists on

VV on the American continent. Gives full information on explosives and chemical plants. Very rich. He is afraid to work. (Gave the formula of RDX, up to the present there was no evaluation from the boss).

Gave about OV.

Boyer was tried twice for conspiracy to violate the Official Secrets Act. In the first case, the jury disagreed. He was convicted by the second jury, and sentenced to two years in prison.

How idealistic scientists, conditioned to an ethic and manner of conspiracy by Communist-controlled political "study groups," were converted quickly into spies in Canada was perhaps best illustrated by that portion of the exposed atomic network headed by David Gordon Lunan.

Lunan was a Scotch journalist, in Canada since 1938, who had signed up with the Labor Progressive party. After serving as a captain in the Army, Lunan became editor of the military journal, *Canadian Affairs*. On a train trip, he talked at length with Fred Rose, who expressed delight over the similarity of their views. Rose said mysteriously he had somebody he wanted Lunan to meet. Several days later, when Lunan arrived at his office in Ottawa, he found on his desk an anonymous note inviting him to meet an unidentified person at a corner of Rideau Street. Lunan went there at the specified time, and talked for twenty minutes with an individual calling himself Jan.

After some puzzling but not impenetrable conversation, Jan informed Lunan he would head up a group of four, all of them with covering names beginning with B. Instructions in conspiracy and initial assignments for the conspirators were duly provided. In parting, Jan handed Lunan an organizational chart of the four Bs, to be burned after memorizing. Lunan obeyed instructions, and destroyed the chart, which became public knowledge only because Gouzenko walked out of the Soviet Embassy with a duplicate. Lunan served three months in jail for contempt of court arising out of his refusal to testify at the trial of Fred Rose.

He was later convicted of conspiracy, but the conviction was upset on appeal. The organizational chart defining Lunan's place in the net looked something like this:

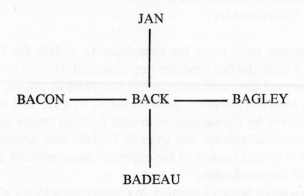

It was scrutiny of this organizational chart which originally stirred speculations about Allan Nunn May's role. Presumably a similar organizational chart existed for other letters in the alphabet— A, C, D, E, F, G . . . May had the cover name of Alek; was he the strategic nuclear physicist through whom three other nuclear physicists with cover names starting with A cleared? What about the four Gs, Golia, Galya, Gini, and Green? Could May possibly have the organizational place among the Gs which Jan had among the Bs? For want of clear answers, speculation had to be deferred.

Nobody had any difficulty figuring out the identity of the four Bs, operating with Jan (Lieutenant Colonel Rogov, a Zabotin assistant). Back was Lunan. Bacon meant Israel Halperin, a professor of mathematics from Queens University, Kingston, Ontario, who had become an artillery captain assigned to research. Badeau and Bagley were Durnford Smith and Edward Mazerall, graduates respectively of McGill and the University of New Brunswick, who were currently working for the Canadian National Research Council.

Of the three Montreal scientists assigned to him, Lunan knew only Badeau (Smith) at first, but he was assured by Rogov that the other two, Bacon (Halperin) and Bagley (Mazerall), were Communist sympathizers who had been prepared psychologically for the step. Rogov provided case histories of the scientists, as well as some hints on handling them. Lunan had his troubles, but he managed to secure a degree of co-operation from all three within an amazingly short period of several weeks.

In his first report to Rogov, Lunan said: ". . . Badeau informs me that most secret work at present is on nuclear physics (bombardment of radioactive substances to produce energy). This is more hush-hush than radar and is being carried on at University of Montreal and at McMaster University at Hamilton. Badeau thinks that government purchase of radium-producing plant is connected with this research." Halperin, he reported, lacked a conspiratorial touch and considered "most so-called secret work a joke," whereas Mazerall lived out in the country with a wife who distrusted political co-operation.

A month later, Lunan was asking his three scientists to keep their eyes open for any stray samples of U 235. Durnford Smith said he had no access to such samples, but suggested that he might transfer to atomic research, if that was considered advisable. Halperin balked. "It has become very difficult to work with him, especially after my request for U 235," Lunan reported to Rogov. "He said that as far as he knows, it is impossible to get it. I think that at present he has a fuller understanding of the essence of my request and he has a particular dislike for them." As for Petawawa, Halperin said flatly he knew nothing about it.

Pressure was being exerted steadily from Moscow for fuller information on nuclear fission. One wire from the Director of the Center to Zabotin at this time read:

TAKE MEASURES TO ORGANIZE ACQUISITION OF DOCUMENTARY MATERIALS ON THE ATOMIC BOMB! THE TECHNICAL PROCESS, DRAWINGS, CALCULATION.

Unfortunately for Lunan, his three research scientists were not close enough to the work in uranium, and there was no prospect of getting them close enough in time to be useful. Durnford Smith was not shifted to atomic work, but he was rewarded for initiative by being put in direct contact with Rogov, who knew more about science than the journalist, Lunan. Smith made occasional trips to the United States, particularly to the Massachusetts Institute of Technology, to confer with American scientists. He was able to turn over to Rogov important American, as well as Canadian, developments in radar and explosives. Mazerall contributed recent improvements in military radio. Halperin made some verbal reports, of debatable value, in the field of ordnance. All three became upset when offered cash rewards.

"Badeau (Smith) was very disturbed when I brought up the subject of payment," Lunan reported to Rogov on one occasion. "I think he felt it brought the subject of his work into a different and more conspiratorial focus."

At their trials, Smith, Mazerall, and Halperin denied taking money, though Rogov's record showed they accepted small sums, ranging from $30 to $100 each. The research men insisted they were not inspired by pecuniary motives, which might well have been true without proving that they persisted in refusing the money, any more than Klaus Fuchs or Allan Nunn May did.

Smith and Mazerall were convicted of stealing military secrets, and were sentenced to five and four years in jail respectively. Halperin was tried and acquitted. That would just about end the significance of this trio of comparative neophytes (so far as atomic espionage was concerned) except for Halperin's American connections, and his incautious habit of jotting down names of persons who interested him.

Though he was born in 1911 in the Province of Quebec, Halperin secured some of his scientific and cultural training in the United States. The FBI agents who swarmed into Canada in the wake of Gouzenko revelations, so as to check immediately on United States angles, did not neglect this phase of Halperin's life. How thorough they were was brought home to me in Washington in 1948 when Dr. Edward U. Condon, then Director of the National Bureau of Standards, mentioned in a private conversation that a government scientist known to him had just been suspended from his job as a person of doubtful loyalty on the sole ground that he contributed to Halperin's legal defense fund. It seems this scientist had known Halperin at Princeton in the early thirties. At a scientific meeting at Harvard in 1946, American scientists (including this particular one) got talking about the plight of Halperin, who was described as having a wife and three children and no money to pay a lawyer. The hat was passed among those who had known Halperin in the United States, and the American scientist in question, the son of a former chief metallurgist for one of the big copper companies, chipped in $100.

Except for that 1946 contribution, the American scientist had no connection whatever with Halperin since their days together at Princeton, Dr. Condon said. There was considerable loose spy talk in Washington during this period, and the action against the scientist seemed unnecessarily harsh, assuming that there was nothing below the level of the facts as stated. Certainly the story revealed that the FBI had gone over Halperin's American contacts with considerable care.

In 1950, a month after Fuchs was sentenced, the British authorities revealed that Fuchs's name had appeared in a 1945 notebook kept by Halperin, along with such names as Eric Adams, a former New York engineer who was sentenced to three months in jail in Canada for refusing to testify against Rose; and Squadron Leader M. S. Nightingale, of the R.C.A.F. and the Bell Telephone Co., Montreal, who also received a three-month sentence for protecting Rose.

"I wish to correct a point of fact," declared Viscount Jowitt, the Lord Chancellor, in the House of Lords on April 5, 1950, "arising out of a speech which I made last week on the motion of the noble lord, Lord Vansittart. I then said there was no truth in certain statements which had been made in the press about the Fuchs case. The fact is that in a notebook belonging to a man who was one of those examined by the Canadian Royal Commission there did appear . . . the name of Klaus Fuchs. This notebook, together with all other relevant material, was promptly made available to us by the Canadian authorities. Subsequent events have, of course, attached a significance to that name which it did not then bear. . . ."

The notebook had also been made available to the FBI, which might have been expected to show greater interest than Scotland Yard since Fuchs was still at Los Alamos in 1946, getting ready to conclude a three-year visit to the United States.

The Canadian Report, still insufficiently appreciated in the United States, gave some revealing glimpses of the long-term professional Soviet espionage net with which gifted part-time amateurs like Fuchs and May co-operated. It disclosed how Colonel Milstein, alias Milsky, Assistant Chief of First Intelligence at Moscow, was more interested in obtaining for his agents new shoes (fake documents, particularly passports, enabling travel from one country to another) than anything else when he made a Western hemispheric checkup toward the close of World War II. The first item on the agenda of a formal discussion arranged with Sam Carr, who was the spokesman for the Canadian Communist party, was: "Who prepares passports, i.e., what kind of people are they? Are they not the old shoemakers who a few years ago fell through?"

After assurances were given at the meeting that the Party's new shoemakers were reliable fellows, Milstein revealed he was concerned specifically with protecting an agent of great importance who was then masquerading as a student at a Los Angeles university. On August 29, 1945, only a week before Gouzenko made his break, Zabotin wired Colonel General Kouznetsov, Milstein's boss in Moscow, that "the fairly complicated task of obtaining a passport for our man in America" was finally being achieved.

The complicated task left a lot of clues. When Carr was picked up in 1949, after three years of concealment in New York, and was returned to Canada for trial, the charge on which he was convicted and sentenced to prison for six years was not stealing secrets, but shoemaking.

"Our man in America" reached the port of New York on September 2, 1938. He was meekly carrying a passport issued originally to Ignacy Witczak, a naturalized Canadian farm laborer, who had gone to Spain in 1937 to fight with the Loyalists against Franco. However, he was not Ignacy Witczak. The real Witczak had already returned to Canada, without his passport; this had been lost, he said, while he was swimming a river near Helicoursi, Spain. Actually his passport and those of many other members in the McKenzie-Papineau battalion of the International Brigade had been lifted on one pretext or another, and not returned, precisely so they could be used to outfit Soviet spies. The real Witczak was a bachelor; the spurious one arrived in New York with a wife named Bunia. The Witczak passport expired in 1942, but it could be renewed up to 1947. Sam Carr's task was to obtain the proper Passport Office file, then substitute a forged 1937 form containing a description and picture of the phony Witczak and his beautiful Bunia in place of the real but solitary Witczak, so that an application for renewal would jibe with the records. Carr began to fret at one point over the possibility that the real Witczak would get the itch to travel again, but Moscow assured him, quite falsely, through Zabotin, that the Spanish War veteran had drowned in the same river where his passport was supposed to have vanished.

The signature on the phony Witczak papers had to be forged at the last minute, because Moscow decided not to delay long enough to send out to California. It was a tough, grueling assignment for Carr, complicated by refusal of his superiors to pay $5,000 in promised bribes. But eventually the job was wrapped up for a mere $4,000. Very little was ever revealed about the phony Witczak by the United States authorities. He is said to have operated in Washington and Detroit as well as in Los Angeles.

He was actually in Washington when Gouzenko broke. He crossed the continent hurriedly to rejoin his wife Bunia and their American-born son. Then the FBI got on his trail, and abruptly, the Witczaks disappeared, all three of them, not to be traced again in the United States.

Alexander Foote, a Briton who served in Europe as a Soviet spy during the war, was being groomed in Moscow early in 1946 to take over a new net directed against the United States. Like all resident directors, he was scheduled to live outside the United States, in order to operate with greater impunity. Mexico was chosen as his base, but at the last minute Mexico became impractical, Foote wrote in *Handbook for Spies,* because the Gouzenko revelations had destroyed any chance of getting a fake Canadian passport.

It is difficult to isolate any one person as commander in chief of Soviet atomic espionage during the war. As the Canadian Report showed, the Russians were using at least five separate nets throughout the world: Military Intelligence (which may have had two distinct branches), the secret police or NKVD-MVD system, Naval Intelligence (comparatively unimportant), a commercial system, and a political setup. Presumably the phony Witczak handled Red Army intelligence work on nuclear fission. For the NKVD-MVD, the chief agent seems to have been a Bolshevik veteran who entered the United States in 1938 from Canada with a fake Canadian birth certificate. This man of many aliases was known chiefly as Arthur Alexandrovich Adams. Infirm rather than elderly, he blamed his ailments on cruel beatings received during the abortive 1905 uprising in Russia. He had rheumatic trouble; sometimes he would sit motionless and in pain, for half an hour at a time; in the morning, it might take him a full hour to get out of bed. Yet this half-crippled spider of a man could be amazingly energetic, when he had to be, and he was not, as it appeared, any stranger to the country. Arthur Adams had arrived in New York for the first time in 1921, as an engineering adviser to a Bolshevik commission of some sort. He stayed about a year. In 1927 he returned briefly in the guise of a Soviet auto expert, getting advice on setting up the first plant to make autos in Russia. In 1932 he materialized again as a purchaser of Curtiss-Wright fighters for his country's aviation trust. Each of these was an open visit, but according to American relatives of his wife, he always possessed hush-hush powers and responsibilities extending far beyond his official ones.

So perfectly masked was his 1938 arrival from Canada, that the United States counterintelligence people had no notion, until the fall of 1943, that Adams was in the country. Then he popped up at the Chicago Metallurgical Project, atomic center of centers at the time, in intimate association with an American scientist who was being shadowed as a possible spy.

At this point of detection, the Adams trail diverged: north to Alaska, where an alleged transfer of secrets was intercepted; east to a maze of business fronts in New York; south to Oak Ridge; and west to an attempt in California to subvert the highest leadership of the Manhattan District Project. Out of the resulting hodge-podge of espionage and counterespionage came oddly inconclusive results. Perhaps it was only in spy fiction, like *Ashenden: the Secret Agent,* that episodes were rounded off with climactic victory or defeat. These particular events, so far as American knowledge goes, tended to result in small advantages or stalemate.

6. Chicago and Berkeley

COMMUNIST scientists, and even non-Communist scientists accustomed to an ethic and an atmosphere of conspiracy by secret Marxist study groups and similar devices, were brought into contact with Soviet espionage within a comparatively short time in Canada. During the war period, when Russia was a "noble ally" and when many comparatively sophisticated folk had no conception of long-range Russian aims, there was no reason why some United States scientists should not have been similarly affected. A series of postwar hearings by the House Un-American Activities Committee revealed that they were in fact affected.

Clarence Hiskey and Joseph Weinberg were native-born physicists implicated in shadowy operations at Chicago and at Berkeley, California, respectively. They had been campus Communists together at the University of Wisconsin, and it was through his former Wisconsin connections that Weinberg was eventually spotted on the West Coast.

Hiskey was approximately the same age as Fuchs, May, and Gold. Both of his parents were native born; his father, a machinist, came from Green Bay, Wisconsin, and his mother from New Denmark, Wisconsin. The family name, Szczechowski, was shortened to Hiskey for convenience. Clarence Francis Szczechowski was born in Milwaukee on July 5, 1912, which meant he reached maturity during the depths of economic depression. As a boy, he took eight years of religious instruction at the Holy Cross Parochial School at La Crosse, Wisconsin. Like Klaus Fuchs, the strictly raised Lutheran, Clarence Hiskey, the Roman Catholic, may have swung to Communism with a little extra vehemence because it provided a substitute for the lost religion of his youth.

Hoping to become a teacher, Hiskey studied at the La Crosse State Teachers College from 1929 to 1933, but he did not get a degree. He then switched to a career of political agitation in science. He attended the University of Wisconsin for six years, winning his B.S. in 1935, his M.S. in 1936, and his Ph.D. in 1939.

During his university days, Hiskey met and married Marcia Sand, a Communist student who after quite a few years left the Party, and Clarence. As undergraduates, the couple associated chiefly with other Communists, and for two years at the University of Wisconsin lived with an individual whose brother headed the Young Communist League. Hiskey followed each twist in the Party line, from the wild "Third Period" ending in 1935 into the reformist era ending with the Hitler pact of 1939. He did some teaching while pursuing his graduate studies, and earned a reputation for mixing instruction with Stalinist propaganda. In speeches and conversation, he praised Russia as a model country which revealed no defects and could do no wrong. The American form of government was "no good," he declared repeatedly; each political measure which fell short of what he considered necessary to help Russia, proved, so he stated, that America was cowering under a dictatorship.

Since the revolution would eventually need men trained to pull a trigger and explode a grenade, Hiskey urged Leftist students to flock into R.O.T.C. for military training. As a result of attending CMT camps and taking examinations, he himself obtained a reserve commission in 1937 or 1938, a step which contributed to his later undoing.

From 1939 to 1941, Hiskey lived in the Tennessee Valley region. For about a year and a half, he directed a University of Tennessee rhenium research project at Knoxville, financed by

133

WPA funds. For the next six months, he worked as an associate chemist at the TVA aluminum nitrate plant at Sheffield, Alabama.

In the fall of 1939, the Communist party branch at Knoxville went into a decline, as a result of mass resignations over the Hitler-Stalin pact. Hiskey co-operated with Francis Martin, the Communist party section organizer, in trying to revive Party spirit. One of his achievements was a front called the Knoxville Peace Council. This noisy outfit, which attracted only ten or fifteen members, denounced what it called the Downing Street-Wall Street axis somewhat more severely than it denounced the Nazi-Fascist axis. Right up to the minute Hitler invaded Russia in June, 1941, the Knoxville Peace Council wanted no part in a shoddy imperialistic conflict. After Russia was attacked, things were different. Some of Hiskey's students, who were swept into his activities, recall how in statements for the Knoxville Peace Council he would employ every Stalinist catchword of the day from "Fascist beasts" to "the Zaibatsu." Hiskey persuaded one student to send money to the International Publishers in New York for a dozen copies of Hewlitt (Red Dean of Canterbury) Johnson's book on Russia. The pretext was that he himself lacked cash at the moment. When the books arrived, the chemistry instructor paid the student in full, gave him a free copy and distributed the other copies to friends.

Clarence Francis Hiskey sought student subscriptions for the magazine *In Fact;* if a favorite pupil pleaded temporary poverty, Hiskey was likely to pay for a free trial subscription, and to inquire tactfully later whether the subscription had been renewed. He was generous in loaning out his own copies of the *New Masses,* to adolescents or to colleagues. Frequently he and Marcia Sand Hiskey would invite a student to their home for dinner and political discussion. Some students admired Dr. Hiskey, without necessarily sharing his views; they labeled him provocative. Others sneered at him as a Red-hot, a dyed-in-the-wool radical. A similar division prevailed in faculty circles. A few teachers at the University of Tennessee tried to maintain nonpolitical relations with Hiskey as a competent chemist who liked long walks and chess. Except for one or two fellow travelers, the rest considered him a troublemaker.

Still a rather obvious Communist, Clarence Hiskey came to New York in the fall of 1941 to accept a job as an instructor in chemistry at Columbia University. A year later, at the request of Dr. Harold Urey, the Nobel prize winner, he joined Columbia's SAM (Substitute Alloy Material) Laboratory, whose highly secret work ranged from heavy-water research to the gaseous diffusion method of separating out U 235. The gaseous diffusion process was only one out of a half-dozen processes then being tested to separate out U 235. Proving eventually to be the best of the lot, it was tested as the basis for the huge K-25 plant at Oak Ridge, Tennessee.

Clarence Hiskey had something to do with the gaseous diffusion process, though he was by no means an international expert on it, like Klaus Fuchs. Disregarding all the loose talk about one, all-important "secret" of the atom bomb, it is obvious that a comparatively backward country like Russia could save considerable laboratory effort, money, and time if it learned which one of half a dozen possible processes had been chosen as correct by a slightly more advanced country like the United States.

Americans who can never forgive the British for trusting Fuchs despite his earlier Communist record may not be happy to learn that a 1942 United States Army intelligence report listed Hiskey as an active Communist. By this time he was a division head or section chief in the SAM project, a leader of a team of technicians ranging in size up to forty men and women. Included in his team were more or less Leftist students from here and there, younger men from the University of Wisconsin for whom he had wangled jobs at Columbia. Hiskey was imbedded in an expanding and exciting national program of research. Digging him out would have affected not only members of his team, but also colleagues and superiors who vouched for him.

In May, 1943, most of the SAM laboratory staff shifted to

Chicago. Hiskey's group did not move until summer. In Chicago, Hiskey's salary was around $9,000 a year, or almost double the highest salary ever paid to Klaus Fuchs. He was a moderately important figure in the scientific hierarchy of the Manhattan District Project.

Marcia Sand Hiskey did not accompany her husband to Chicago. After Dr. Hiskey secured living quarters there, he was visited by a young technician named Miriam Sherwood who had worked with him at Columbia in New York. Her purpose was to locate a job with the Metallurgical Project, she said. Her efforts to find employment were not immediately successful, but she remained in Chicago anyway. After a while, Hiskey confided to colleagues that he intended to divorce Marcia and marry Miriam.

Politically, Hiskey seemed brasher than ever. He boasted about being friendly with an important South Chicago Communist leader. He told technicians working for him that it would be a "smart thing" to join the Federation of Architects, Engineers, Chemists and Technicians, which was conducting an organizing drive at the Argonne National Laboratory. The FAECT was an arm of the Communist party which played a large role on both the East and West coasts in lining up domestic auxiliaries for the Soviet atomic spy ring. Hiskey and another atomic scientist organized the Abraham Lincoln School in Chicago, a Party-line educational front. Hiskey persuaded a dozen or more academicians and technicians from the project, including friends and subordinates, to take courses in subjects like the Russian language.

By this time, everything that Clarence Francis Hiskey did was being scrutinized by the secret eyes of counterespionage. According to a high-ranking Army official connected with the Chicago project, who was allowed to testify anonymously before a Congressional committee several years later, Hiskey had progressed from a mere suspect to something more than a suspect.

"We were convinced he was a subversive agent," said this

military authority. "Yes, a subversive agent. Now the question was what to do with Hiskey. We had trouble with scientists when we had to move one. Someone, I think it was Colonel Lansdale [Col. John L. Lansdale, Jr.], found in Hiskey's record that he had a second lieutenancy in college in the R.O.T.C. Providentially, he had not given up his second lieutenancy, and we called the Adjutant General, and we had him call Hiskey to active duty amidst a great furor that we were doing it deliberately, and so on, and we transferred Hiskey, I think, to the Canol Project, I think, in Canada, where in the Quartermaster Corps, he counted underwear until that went out of business. . . ."

A curious aspect of this switch was that during an earlier period in 1943, when Hiskey classed merely as a suspect, a note had been clamped on his file that he should not be called for military duty. This had to be rescinded; it was, and on April 13, 1944, Dr. Hiskey was told to get ready to go into uniform. He and his friends protested. Here was a waste of scientific ability, they declared. Hiskey himself complained of a lack of confidence in his integrity, which came close to the mark.

According to a persistent report lacking official confirmation, two Army counterintelligence men, late in 1943, trailed Hiskey to a Chicago park. The University of Chicago is on the Midway between Jackson and Washington parks, on the south side of town, but this was Lincoln Park, on the north side. Here Hiskey handed a package to an infirm, rather foreign-looking man. One of the agents followed the new trail to a rooming house. Subsequently, when the elderly suspect left his room for a while, agents took a look at it. They discovered highly confidential atomic data, some of it bearing on the K-25 plant in Tennessee, some of it involving the Metallurgical Project in Chicago, some of it describing Anglo-Canadian research.

Intelligence authorities in Washington were asked to help identify the spy. Secret movies taken of the fragile-looking foreigner revealed him to be Arthur Alexandrovich Adams, peregrinating Stalinist functionary and NKVD hatchet man.

The Atom Spies

Adams' phone was tapped, his mail read, his footsteps dogged. It developed that he had a room at the Peter Cooper Hotel in New York. Searched discreetly, that also revealed atomic data. Bit by bit, a microscopic survey revealed that the veteran Soviet agent was using a Brooklyn mail drop to receive information on nuclear-fission research from all over the country. Among Adams' contacts were fully one hundred persons wearing the military uniform of the United States, many Communist officials of unions covering plants where secret work was being handled, and not a few fellow travelers with money and social position.

By ranging back to Adams' 1938 arrival from Canada, the counterespionage agents spotted some other, rather unusual acquaintances. One of these was Samuel Novick, a New York manufacturer of radio equipment, who on December 19, 1937, had written the United States immigration authorities that he had employed Arthur Adams as a skilled radio engineer for ten years in Canada. This was impossible; Adams had been traveling for the Soviet Union much of this time, and had lived at intervals in Russia. Questioned about his statement, Novick said he first met Adams in 1938. This also proved false; additional investigation revealed that Adams, acting for the Amtorg Trading Corp., had made extensive purchases from Novick in the middle thirties. Novick was hardly a flawless front for Adams, despite the fact that his Electronics Corp. of America filled some $6,000,000 worth of secret government contracts during the war, and for a while was the only producer of several classified items used in radar work. Novick kept notorious domestic Communists on his payroll, and had a finger in a score of Communist party propaganda pies.

The chameleon measures employed by Adams also involved Eric Bernay, a former advertising manager of the *New Masses* who had turned to making Russian victrola records in New York, and who kept Adams on his payroll for a while as a part-time engineer, at $75 a week; and Samuel J. Wegman, a Hollywood

138

machine designer, who also had Adams on the payroll at $75 a week, because Adams had handed him $1,875 in cash to be spent for that purpose in weekly checks mailed to the Peter Cooper Hotel in New York.

Business fronts in New York utilized by Adams included a jewelry store operated in the name of Victoria Stone, who came from Canada; and a steel-importing business run by Julius Heiman, who had financed Victoria Stone's swanky Madison Avenue shop and who made frequent trips to Stockholm, ostensibly in connection with his own business but presumably involving Communist matters of some importance. Victoria Stone and Julius Heiman were intimates of Earl Browder; in fact, Heiman was credited with having engineered Browder's elevation as head of the American Party. He remained Browder's chief adviser until Browder fell into disfavor with Moscow.

On October 25, 1944, counterintelligence agents were watching the home of a New York lawyer. First they saw Victoria Stone and Julius Heiman leave the house together. Then Arthur Adams came out, and began hobbling along the sidewalk with a carrying case which seemed cruelly beyond his strength. As he paused to rest, a car registered in the name of Pavel Mikhailov, Soviet Vice-Consul, slid to the curb, picked up Adams and his case, and drove to the Consulate. When Adams emerged from the Consulate, sometime later, he moved with comparative jauntiness, without his burdensome case.

Every once in a while, the mysteriously rheumatic Adams had a fall in public, or was unable to escape spontaneously from a hunched-up position in a chair in his hotel room. A Dr. Louis Miller then appeared to treat him. It was suggestive of the nexus among this group, that Miller appeared also as a physician and friend of Samuel Novick, Victoria Stone, and Julius Heiman, all of whom knew one another intimately.

Just as contact with Clarence Francis Hiskey in Chicago eventually exposed this whole closely knit New York group, so the discovered connection with Arthur Adams blew Hiskey sky high. Even if Hiskey's commissioning for limited military service were dismissed as a quirk of overburdened military minds, the chemist had to be replaced. The inevitable flurry surrounding such an espionage emergency began to be evident. Its first sign was Adams' hurried arrival in Chicago from New York, one day after Hiskey received his military notice.

Adams and Hiskey conferred at length. On April 15, the following day, Hiskey traveled to Cleveland to see John Hitchcock Chapin, a chemical engineer employed at the Metallurgical Project who had been temporarily detached for hush-hush work in Cleveland. Chapin was on approximately the same academic level as Hiskey, in charge of a team of scientists varying in number but ranging up to thirty. His work in Cleveland was so secret that nobody in the Manhattan District Project was supposed to know about it, but Hiskey went straight to Chapin's hotel. The two men engaged in intense discussion during a long walk through the streets. FBI agents watching them decided to shift some of their attention to Dr. Chapin.

Hiskey and Chapin had become acquainted at Columbia University but they did not achieve any real degree of friendship until they accompanied SAM to Chicago. Chapin was a native of Rutland, Vermont, a year older than Hiskey. He had studied at home up to the sixth grade. He attended Loomis Institute at Windsor, Connecticut, for several years, won a bachelor's degree in chemistry at Cornell, and a Ph.D. from University of Illinois. He worked in a DuPont factory in West Virginia before joining the Manhattan District Project.

Dr. Chapin testified he was never a Communist, though he read Communist publications like *Soviet Russia Today* and was keenly interested in Russia. Hiskey and he often spoke of going to Russia someday to teach and conduct research. By the fall of 1943, Chapin knew Hiskey was collecting information for an outside source, but the knowledge did not prevent him from discussing fully his own work with Hiskey. At this time, scientists generally were restive under the military conception of security;

they were reluctant to limit discussion with colleagues on the ground that the eventual result of their combined work might have military value. Chapin was a member of the more outspoken wing among United States scientists urging sharing of atomic secrets with the world.

Several weeks before he was called into the Army, Hiskey suggested Chapin ought to meet Arthur Adams, his friend, sometime, and Chapin said he'd be glad to, sometime. Though nothing was spelled out fully, Chapin knew by then that Adams was a Soviet agent, and that any meeting with him would involve more than casual conversation. The Cleveland conference brought things to a head. When would Chapin meet Adams? Chapin decided he did not wish to meet anybody in Cleveland. He would be willing, he said, to get together with Adams after he returned to Chicago. He had no idea how long his hush-hush Cleveland assignment would take. Since Hiskey was about to go into service, it was agreed Chapin would write a letter to Hiskey, care of Marcia Sand Hiskey in New York, just as he was leaving for Chicago. Mrs. Hiskey would forward the letter to her husband. The letter would be innocuous but it would serve as signal of Chapin's return. Hiskey would pass the signal in some clandestine fashion to Adams, and Adams would appear.

Acting under instructions from the Soviet agent, Hiskey asked Chapin for some small personal object which he would be certain to recognize. Chapin rummaged around in his pants pocket and came up with an odd-looking key to a basement locker in his apartment house in Chicago. Hiskey took the key; he would give it to Adams, he said. Any man coming to Chapin with the key would then be identified clearly as Adams.

Chapin did not return to Chicago until the fall of 1944. As agreed, he wrote a meaningless letter, which was forwarded by Marcia Sand Hiskey to Dr. Clarence Francis Hiskey, who by this time was counting heavy underwear at White Horse, Yukon Territory, some five hundred miles east of Alaska. On September 24, Chapin received a phone call from somebody who said he was the man Hiskey spoke about in Cleveland. The unidentified caller said he might drop around that evening for a visit. Adams rang the apartment bell that evening, but did not come upstairs. Chapin went down to the lobby to see him. "I have company," he said. "My father came for a visit." Adams suggested that the pair take a walk to the corner. When they were outside, on South Drexel Avenue, he slipped Chapin the odd-looking key to the basement locker, and asked Chapin to drop around to his room at the Stevens Hotel the following evening. Chapin agreed. He did go around to the hotel the next night, and talked for an hour and a half with Adams.

Chapin had already turned over in his mind the possibility of giving Adams confidential information, but he had not reached any decision. Adams stalked him warily; he discussed the industrial development of Russia, and Russia's need for the latest processes, in nuclear fission as in other fields. Most scientists understood the desirability of exchanging economic data, he said, but they were restrained by narrow military minds. Those enlightened Americans who helped Russia get the industrial information to which it really had a right, as an ally, would naturally be well rewarded for their help. Chapin looked startled at the hint of cash on the barrel. Adams asked quickly: wouldn't Chapin as a chemist with an interest in world progress like to visit Russia after the war as an honored guest, perhaps to teach or conduct research there? Chapin agreed amiably that he would like that. The conversation meandered on, with occasional references by Adams to Chapin's own work which showed far more understanding than any outsider could obtain legitimately. There was an implied questioning of Chapin which never sharpened to a point. The two men did not quite see eye to eye. Something about Adams' manner, and the whole conspiratorial procedure gave Chapin "cold feet," he told the FBI later. He made a note how to reach Adams in New York, and promised to "think things over," but he had inwardly decided to go no further. He continued with his secret group of government scientists at the Metallurgical

142

Project in Chicago until May, 1945, when he was released as a result of natural curtailment of the work, but at no time, he says now, did he give any illicit help to Adams.

At least one technician connected with the Metallurgical Project is known to have been approached as a possible substitute for Hiskey. This was Edward T. Manning, a student from the University of Tennessee who had followed Hiskey to New York and then to Chicago.

On three or four occasions before Hiskey acquired his military uniform on April 28, 1944, Manning dropped around to his superior's one-room apartment on Dorchester Street, near the University, and each time found Adams there. The Russian was introduced merely by name, as an engineer. Later Hiskey said Adams, as a very close friend, was the person to whom Manning should go for advice, if anything came up affecting Hiskey or his wife Marcia. Hiskey explained how to get in touch with Adams, as well as with Marcia in New York.

That summer, many of the scientists at the Metallurgical Project in Chicago, Manning among them, got permission to attend an American Chemical Society meeting in New York. By this time, the Tennesseean had heard reports that security reasons were behind Hiskey's exile to Alaska. On the day of the meeting, he had lunch with Adams, and asked the engineer if he had received any explanation from Hiskey by mail for his impressment into service. Adams had heard nothing; what had Manning heard? he asked. Manning said he had heard nothing, either. When he went around to see Marcia, she was more explicit. The Army, representing a powerful group in the government, was mad at Clarence because he was a "liberal," she said. She suspected that the Army had removed Clarence from his work because of his political leanings.

Before he returned to Chicago, Manning had a second, longer talk with Adams, at a quiet bar in the midtown section of New York, during which Adams stressed the employment possibilities for good American technicians after the war, in rebuilding

Russia, and implied that a record of helpfulness in providing needed information would be remembered.

Counterintelligence was still watching Adams. The growing friendliness between Manning and the Soviet agent seemed to present a hazard. As a result, when Manning returned to the Metallurgical Project, he was called in by his section chief, Dr. E. C. Creutz, and told he was being suspended. "You are being offered a chance to resign," Dr. Creutz added. Manning insisted he had done nothing wrong, demanded that he be dismissed. The personnel officer at the laboratories said he had no authority to issue a letter of dismissal, and why didn't Manning make things easy for everybody by resigning? Manning reiterated he would never resign. Thereupon he was handed a letter saying that they had been directed by the Army to suspend him.

The following January, Manning got into uniform. In July, 1945, after several months of service in the Army, the young chemist happened to be in New York. He decided to test his suspicion that Adams was the basis for his disgrace. When he and Adams met, Manning started out flatly and bitterly by announcing he knew who was to blame for all his troubles. He had been under surveillance, he said, and Adams had been under surveillance, and they both knew why.

Hunched over in a chair as though in pain, Adams said he had not been feeling too well. There had been some litigation over one of the companies he worked for as an engineering consultant, he declared, and the strain had bothered him. He was planning soon to make a trip back to his native country of Canada. It was silly to talk bitterly, like Manning, he said, since it was all for the good of the world. While the young American eyed him steadily, the elderly Bolshevik revolutionary spoke discursively of some work he had done in connection with a large hydro-testing tank, and from that swung into anecdotes of the days when he was traveling extensively through Europe, purchasing materials for the Soviet Union. Again and again he spoke of the Soviet Union, until Manning realized he was getting close to the specific revelation he sought.

This was the month of the Alamogordo blast in New Mexico. Abruptly Adams was suggesting to Manning that it might not be too late for him to furnish information on things like uranium and the atomic bomb with which he had some contact during his Metallurgical Project work. Didn't Manning agree, pressed Adams, that information about such scientific work should be made available to all mankind? Manning replied, so he told the FBI later, that he didn't think so. Perhaps the knowledge should be shared eventually with the world, he declared, but as for himself, he was committed to security and secrecy, and had no wish to discuss it further. That concluded the final meeting between the two men.

Neither John Hitchcock Chapin nor Edward T. Manning told their stories to the FBI before the war ended, but there was an earlier revelation of the attitude of Clarence Francis Hiskey.

Once in uniform, Hiskey was whisked out of Chicago in about three days. Because of the flurry surrounding his departure, James Sterling Murray, a wartime member of the Army Counter-Intelligence Corps (CIC), assigned to the Metallurgical Project, decided to take a little extra precaution. To Hiskey's outfit, unknown to Hiskey, Murray assigned a young CIC lad named Charles Clark, with instructions to watch the suspected chemist all the way to his destination, a remote Arctic base near a place called Mineral Wells. When the outfit reached Edmonton, Alberta, in Canada, still heading north, Clark became a little jittery and decided on drastic measures. He made arrangements to go through Hiskey's belongings at a time when the chemist was detained elsewhere. He said he found a notebook full of data on research in nuclear fission. Hiskey was not informed of the seizure. Security regulations of the Manhattan District Project required an immediate report of the loss of any material of a restricted nature, but Hiskey never did report his loss. According

145

to Manning, only after the war did he discover how accurate his suspicions had been: a rendezvous with an agent of some sort, acting for an allied but never friendly power, was reportedly arranged for a spot in Alaska. Except for the capture of the notebook, the rendezvous might have been kept.

As for Hiskey, when he finished counting all the heavy underwear required in Alaska, he was transferred to an Army laboratory in Hawaii to manufacture soap for the servicemen in the Pacific.

On the ground that his mother was seriously ill, Hiskey secured permission to return to Wisconsin for a visit early in 1946. He was discharged from the Army in May of that year. In the postwar period, he got divorced from Marcia Sand, married Miriam Rebecca Sherwood, and taught analytical chemistry to classes of young men at Brooklyn Polytechnic Institute, in Brooklyn, N. Y.

At Congressional hearings after the war, Hiskey refused to answer questions, lest they incriminate him, as to whether he was a Communist or had turned over secret information to an unauthorized person. On the same ground he refused to discuss his relationship with Arthur Adams or John Chapin. In a 1949 interview with Ed Reid, Pulitzer-prize-winning reporter on the *Brooklyn Eagle*, Hiskey declared he was not a Communist and had never engaged in espionage. He had ducked these questions under oath, he said, lest he get involved in a "perjury entanglement of a Hiss-Chambers nature." With no particular relevance, Hiskey added he was "just a small cog in the fight to blacken David E. Lilienthal and see that the Atomic Energy Commission gets into the hands of the military."

In 1950, Hiskey was indicted in the District of Columbia for contempt of Congress, because of his persistent refusal to talk to investigating committees. Brooklyn Polytechnic Institute thereupon suspended him as a teacher. On April 13, 1951, Federal Judge Matthews in Washington dismissed the indictment against Hiskey, ruling that he was within his rights in declining to answer questions on the grounds of possible self-incrimination. Brooklyn Poly reinstated him the following month, with full back pay.

2

A Stalinist drive to infiltrate atomic research at the University of California took shape during the summer of 1941. Spearheading this attempt, with more or less awareness of its implications, was Kenneth May, twenty-six, a mathematician who had lost his teaching job at the University the previous fall because of his Communist activities. May's suitability as a front depended partly on long residence in Berkeley, site of the ultra-secret Radiation Laboratory, and partly on the fact that his father, Prof. Samuel Chester May, was serving as dean. Professor May had disowned and disinherited his son publicly on September 26, 1940, for assuming the duties of Communist party campaign manager in Alameda County. On October 10, the University regents had fired Kenneth May. Though all Berkeley took sides in the father-son quarrel, Kenneth May managed largely to keep his social standing in academic circles, which was vital for his purpose.

Manipulating May from behind the scenes were Rudy Lambert, a middle-aged Soviet careerist with a heavily lined face, who directed underground work in California, and Marcel Scherer, a charter member of the United States Communist party, who had come from New York to lead personally an organizing campaign of his Federation of Architects, Engineers, Chemists and Technicians. Still further in the background, behind Lambert and Scherer, lurked Steve Nelson, the burly ex-commissar of the Abraham Lincoln Brigade in Spain, whose surface role as Party organizer in the nearby bay area concealed an NKVD assignment to handle atomic espionage.

Kenneth May was a brilliant youngster, who had graduated from the University of California in 1936 with a Phi Beta Kappa record and membership in the Golden Bear Honor Society. He

147

won a scholarship under the Institute of World Affairs, studied in Europe two and a half years, spent five months in Russia, and returned as an open and vehement Communist. He broke privately with his parents some time before his father denounced him in public.

"For twenty years," said Professor May, a descendant of West Coast pioneers, "I have been fighting Communism. I have students scattered all over the country who know how I stand. When I became convinced that my son had become an irreconcilable Communist I took the only honorable course consistent with my personal views and the position I hold as an executive of the Defense Council."

Kenneth May had added fuel to the controversy by persuading Ruth McGovney, the daughter of another professor at the University, to become a Communist and his wife. The Party decided to make the most of its advantages by holding a mammoth housewarming for young May and his bride in August, 1941. Like iron filings responding to a magnet, Party stalwarts from all over the United States converged quietly on the Radiation Laboratory, the Shell Oil Co., and the other private scientific installations centering around the campus. One of these arrivals was Clarence Francis Hiskey. Being between universities, so to speak, since he had already left Tennessee and did not have to report in New York at Columbia until the fall, Hiskey found time for the jaunt to the West Coast.

The housewarming for the Mays served not only as a show of strength behind two spectacular recruits, but also as a mobilization for future efforts of a less open kind. The visiting scientists, like Hiskey, did what they could to further both objectives. They buttonholed former students and quondam colleagues in the Party interest. Hiskey himself was seen in animated conversation with Steve Nelson, as well as May. Nelson (born Steve Mesarosh, in 1903, at Chaglich, Yugoslavia) mixed easily with the erudite and adolescent guests; though not precisely a youth, a scientist, or a scholar, he had been schooled during the late thirties at the

Lenin Institute of Moscow in all the social arts of subversion.

It is easy now to see why, of the three great university centers of research in nuclear fission—Columbia, Chicago, and California—California offered such a particularly tempting target for espionage in the summer of 1941. The previous spring—on March 6, 1941, to be precise—a group of young physicists and chemists, most of them in their twenties, working under Dr. Glenn T. Seaborg and Dr. Edward M. McMillan, had bombarded U 238 with neutrons of intermediate speeds and had discovered that these neutrons transformed U 238 into a new element, unknown in nature, called plutonium. (Drs. Seaborg and Mc-Millan received a Nobel prize in chemistry for this work in 1951.)

The Seaborg-McMillan discovery changed the whole prospect of nuclear-fission research. Each ton of natural uranium produced only fourteen pounds of U 235, but by a chain reaction it could be made to yield 1,986 pounds of plutonium, which was just as good for explosive purposes. Uranium was scarce. The tremendous multiplication of the total atomic energy which could be derived from the stuff gave some assurance, for the first time, that an atom bomb might explode before the war ended.

The entire atomic project slid into high gear following a report on July 11, 1941, by Dr. Ernest O. Lawrence about the Berkeley discovery to the National Academy of Science, which was studying the uranium problem. Contagious enthusiasm swept the scientists in Berkeley; new miracles seemed to be waiting in every test tube and retort. That fall Professor Lawrence converted his precious cyclotron into something called a calutron and by an electromagnetic method produced thousands of times more U 235 than had ever been produced before. Plans were drawn to place the new electromagnetic method in production at a huge plant in the Tennessee Valley. Within the next year, the electromagnetic work alone at Berkeley was to require a staff exceeding 1,200 persons. Figuring began on the final atomic research and bomb-assembly area at Los Alamos, New Mexico, where Dr. J. Robert Oppenheimer, one of the most brilliant improvisers at Berkeley, was to serve as scientific commander in chief.

Meanwhile the NKVD-MVD boys were taking advantage of every bit of misplaced idealism about Stalinism, every wisp of romantic misunderstanding of Russia, every practical consideration of personal advantage on the campus to bore deeply, and persistently, at Berkeley. Since Soviet spies were apparently in on things from the start, the question arises as to who told them. Actually, it could have been any one of a number of people. May, for example, knew just about everything, and everybody, in Berkeley. He had been living in the town for fifteen years. As a boy, he met all the important colleagues of his father at the dinner table. He knew neighbors like Haakon Chevalier, the professor of French, part of whose education had been acquired at the Leningrad Institute. During his days as a student and a part-time instructor at Berkeley, May had become acquainted with most of the young crop of academicians and technicians at the Radiation Laboratory. Except for two years of study in Europe and Russia, May had not been away from Berkeley since he outgrew knee pants. Incidentally, he was no kin of Britain's Allan Nunn May, though he had English relatives through his mother, who came from there. Besides their last name, the two Communist Mays were connected chiefly by a joint interest in atomic energy.

Soon after he was dropped from the University faculty, Kenneth May had attended a Party school for underground work held at the Berkeley Hills home of Wilhelmina Lowrey. William Schneiderman, state Party leader, served as teacher at the school.

Putting his new techniques to quick use, May soon organized a Marxist study group among the Berkeley scientists working in the campus area for the Shell Oil Co. and other companies. This study group resembled the Marxist study groups in which the Canadian scientists were conditioned for espionage. Asked about his group, almost a decade later, under oath, May could remember only that he taught it. At every name suggested as a possible pupil—Haakon Chevalier, George Charles Eltenton and his wife Dolly, and various university teachers—Kenneth May shook his head. He knew all these people, he said, but not one of them had been a Marxist pupil. He was unable to dredge up from memory the name or description of a single Marxist scholar. It was a long time ago, said May. His students, many of them older than himself and wiser in other matters, had been shy, not to say apprehensive, and they might have used false names, declared May, leaving unsolved the mystery as to how such students could have concealed their identities from the man who recruited them for the class.

George Charles Eltenton, a physicist at the Shell Development Corp., and his wife Dolly were being cultivated in those days by the Communist party for a role in a Communist atomic conspiracy of breath-taking boldness. They had made a trip to the Soviet Union in 1930. On the basis of this, they were sought out by young zealots like May, for confirmation of the rosy pictures of propaganda; they seem to have enjoyed the local status of Stalinist oracles. In July, 1940, Louise Bransten, one of the Party's West Coast sponsors, got Eltenton to send congratulations to a Soviet gathering of physicists headed by Peter Kapitza. In return Louise Bransten urged Gregory Kheifets, the Soviet Vice-Consul, to place Dolly Eltenton in a job with the American Russian Institute. The McCarran Committee hearings in 1951 revealed that Mrs. Eltenton also played a role in the early forties at conferences of the Institute of Pacific Relations.

Kenneth May was at his suave best with people like Haakon Chevalier, the Eltentons, and the Branstens. He pleased big-name dupes like Anita Whitney, who was used as a speaker at fund-raising drives. He got along magnificently with Wilhelmina Lowrey, a sort of intellectual bellwether for the Party on the West Coast; he helped her conduct two bookshops, one in Berkeley and one in Oakland, and he shared her interest in the Oakland Workers School, an educational front.

Like Hiskey in Chicago, May in Berkeley tried to enroll Leftist university intellectuals as instructors or students at the Party-line school. Like Hiskey, he did what he could in the laboratories for the Federation of Architects, Engineers, Chemists and Technicians; in this he worked closely with Marcel Scherer, and Scherer's wife, Lena Davis, one-time United States Politburo member. Subsequently May's wife Ruth, who had proved her proletarianism by becoming a machinist, followed up his work by becoming secretary of the San Francisco branch of the FAECT. Both husband and wife repeated the Party catchwords on all possible occasions and pushed the Party press.

Setting up a secret cell within the Radiation Laboratory proved a ticklish business. Converts were taken into a special section of the Party, details of which were known only to May, Lambert, Scherer, and Nelson. Even the county organizer was kept in the dark about the special section. Members of the cell took elaborate precautions against being followed to meetings, which were held generally in large, expensively furnished homes in Berkeley. Outside speakers were guided to the affair in a roundabout way to avoid surveillance. Names were taboo at meetings. The most frequent outside speaker turned out to be Steve Nelson.

By the fall of 1941, either because of excitement in Moscow over early tips about the importance of the Radiation Laboratory, or later reports on the development of an underground apparatus, a decision was reached to put May into closer contact with Nelson. May was then working as educational director and member of the county secretariat in Alameda County, where Berkeley is located, under the ostensible direction of Paul Crouch, county organizer.

Crouch, a native of North Carolina, had previously been in charge of United States Army indoctrination for the Party, and had held other important posts. He was restive over the way Berkeley matters were being handled; he spoke up at meetings in general terms about the need for democracy in the Party. Privately, he broached the idea of being relieved as county organizer, but the district bureau rejected that. Late in December,

1941, at a routine district bureau meeting, Crouch rendered a report. Kenneth May arose and furiously criticized Crouch as incompetent. Crouch was doing such a miserable job, he said, that he should be thrown out as organizer. Nobody defended Crouch. The dozen members of the county committee solemnly took under advisement this attack by a comparative upstart in the Party, who undoubtedly had been nudged from above. The issue was referred to William Schneiderman, who remarked that Steve Nelson would be glad to take the job. That was enough. Crouch was told to shift himself and his family to Los Angeles for reassignment. He refused, and was reduced to rank-and-file status. This rough treatment in the indirect interest of Stalinist atomic infiltration led Crouch to resign from the Party, after several years of vacillation, during which the Party alternately tried cajolery and persecution as ways of getting him back into harness.

With Crouch deposed, Steve Nelson, one-time intimate of Togliatti and Tito, and a former associate in Chinese underground work with Arthur Ewert, the Comintern agent who engineered the unsuccessful Brazilian revolution of 1935, moved in from the San Francisco Bay area to become Alameda County organizer. His office was in Oakland. There he brought young May as his assistant, with the title of organizational secretary.

May was becoming jittery and underweight. In the summer of 1941, he had been given an assistant by the Communist party county committee, a young married woman named Jackie who had just recovered from a nervous breakdown occasioned by spats with her husband, Steve, a giant of a fellow who was away most of the year organizing fishermen in Alaska. Even with her help, May was still overburdened with work, much of which he had taken on voluntarily. One of May's problems was a running quarrel with his wife Ruth, from whom he decided finally to separate. Nelson promptly took advantage of this domestic difficulty. He and his wife had acquired a home in Berkeley to be near the focus of their attention, the Radiation Laboratory. They invited Kenneth May to stay with them, indefinitely, as a guest. May ac-

The Atom Spies

cepted; he was inordinately grateful for this eminently practical step on Nelson's part. He told friends that the Nelsons were the only family he had left.

Nelson maneuvered carefully for the coup which he hoped would deliver into his hands, at one stroke, the entire Anglo-American atomic program.

The Soviet agent had one tremendous hidden advantage. Back in 1937, in Spain, he had encountered Katherine Puening Harrison, an American woman who had come there in search of news about her husband, a volunteer with the Loyalist army. Steve Nelson, as a lieutenant colonel in the International Brigade, with the tremendous resources of the NKVD at his command, was able to inform the woman that her husband was dead and to facilitate her return to the United States. He claimed to have known the man (though whether he did is uncertain) and to have been with him when he died. After her return to the United States, Mrs. Harrison took a graduate course in mycology (the science of fungi) at the University of California, and there in 1940, she met and married J. Robert Oppenheimer, who at the age of thirty-five was becoming recognized as one of the key figures in atomic research.

For extra leverage, Steve Nelson had a knowledge of the Communist record—then unsuspected at the Manhattan District Project—of Dr. Frank Oppenheimer, younger brother of J. Robert Oppenheimer, and Frank's wife Jacquenette. Dr. Frank Oppenheimer had come from Stanford University in 1941 to work as a research assistant at the Radiation Laboratory in Berkeley. He and his wife retained membership in the Communist Party branch at Palo Alto, but they lived in Berkeley and they saw the J. Robert Oppenheimers there fairly frequently.

How Steve Nelson set the stage for the final approach is not known. It seems reasonable to assume that he used every social and political advantage at his command, and every bit of campus knowledge he could extract from his house guest and executive assistant, Kenneth May.

154

Nelson managed several social meetings with the Frank Oppenheimers in Berkeley. He and Kenneth May became frequent visitors at the canyon-side home of the J. Robert Oppenheimers in Berkeley, where the guests frequently had varied interests and the talk might range from politics to Hindu philosophy.

When the atmosphere was as favorable as Nelson could make it, the approach was arranged from another direction. Late in 1942, Peter Ivanov, Soviet Vice-Consul in San Francisco, asked Eltenton, in the words of a Congressional committee report, "to secure information concerning some highly secret work pertaining to the atomic bomb which was being carried on at the Radiation Laboratory of the University of California. Ivanov . . . offered a sum of money in return for Eltenton's cooperation." Eltenton went to Prof. Haakon Chevalier, and Chevalier went to J. Robert Oppenheimer. "Eltenton told Chevalier that he had a line of communication with an official of the Soviet government who had advised him that since Russia and the United States were allies, Soviet Russia should be entitled to any technical data which might be of assistance to that nation." In a subsequent open hearing in California, Chevalier said he merely repeated to Dr. Oppenheimer a talk he had with Eltenton, at Eltenton's request.

Dr. Oppenheimer told Chevalier he considered efforts to secure secret information to be treasonable. He would have nothing to do with such a scheme, he said, showing his friend to the door. When he recovered from his feelings of astonishment and shock, the scientist went to General Groves and in guarded terms mentioned the approach which had been made.

In March, 1943, General Groves named Dr. Oppenheimer as scientific director of Los Alamos. Together they selected the site, and recruited the initial cadre of thirty scientific workers around whom in two years was built the biggest and most elaborate scientific establishment in history. Sometime during this period, J. Robert Oppenheimer had a frank talk with General Groves about the earlier acquaintance between his wife and Steve Nelson, and his own brother's Party record. The elder Oppenheimer is said to have given personal assurance of Frank Oppenheimer's loyalty. Frank and his wife had resigned from the Communist party, he revealed. Frank went to work at Los Alamos, under his brother's direction, and at the close of the war received special commendation from General Groves for patriotic and useful service.

Kenneth May had made periodic efforts to get into the Army during the early part of the war. After the collapse of the conspiracy to take over Dr. J. Robert Oppenheimer, he made another attempt; this time he was accepted. He served gallantly in the Aleutians, and later in Italy, where he grew a red beard and rose to the rank of a second lieutenant.

3

With his NKVD background, Steve Nelson should have realized that failure to corrupt Dr. J. Robert Oppenheimer was bound to kick back and disrupt his atomic net. Instead of decamping in the middle of the night, to save his young American contacts, the Soviet agent decided to stick things out in Berkeley. He did take certain precautions. At the next meeting of the secret Merriman branch of the Party, consisting of scientists working at the Radiation Laboratory, Nelson told members they must destroy their Party cards, to avoid accidental disclosure, and must swear off drinking, among other things, lest they slip while in their cups. The branch was dissolved, Nelson declared a couple of meetings later, though he implied there might still be some useful contact among specially trustworthy members.

Mail had been moving regularly from Steve Nelson on the West Coast to the wife of a Brooklyn employee of the Transformer Corp. of America, owned by the ubiquitous Samuel Novick. Nelson had also been in contact, by mail or courier, with somebody called Al, who was really Rudy Baker, alias Ralph Bowman, a native of Hungary who had served the Party previously as an organizer in Detroit and as a courier between the United States and Canadian parties. It was only revealed in 1950 that interception by counterespionage, in 1942, of a message from Steve Nelson to Al, saying that Dr. J. Robert Oppenheimer and his wife had been tested and had proved unsympathetic to Communism, was one factor in General Grove's decision to place complete trust in Oppenheimer.

One evening late in March, 1943, the phone rang at Steve Nelson's home in Berkeley. Somebody named Joe wanted to see Steve in a hurry. Mrs. Nelson said her husband would be home in a few hours. Around midnight, a small, thin, dark man with glasses slipped into the house. Nelson didn't arrive until 1:30 A.M. Joe said he had some information he thought Nelson could use. He read a complicated formula, which he asked Nelson to copy, since it was in the handwriting of another scientist, and had to be back on his desk that morning. Nelson obliged. Several days later, Nelson phoned Peter Ivanov, the Soviet Vice-Consul in San Francisco. "I'll meet you at the usual place," said Ivanov. The usual place proved to be an open park on the ground of St. Francis Hospital in San Francisco. San Francisco is only about ten miles from Berkeley. Nelson handed a package to Ivanov at this rendezvous. After another interval of several days, Vassili Zubilin, third secretary of the Russian Embassy in Washington, appeared in San Francisco on a visit to the Consulate. He phoned Nelson, then visited Nelson at his home. During their conversation, which was cordial, Zubilin handed Nelson ten bills of unknown denomination.

The security officer at the Manhattan District project in California, during the spring of 1943, was James Sterling Murray, the same man who a year later ordered surveillance on Clarence Hiskey from Chicago up into the Arctic. Murray suspected that Joe was Joseph Woodrow Weinberg. In addition to a sketchy physical description, he had several broad clues.

Joe's wife came from Wisconsin (Weinberg's wife Muriel had studied at the University of Wisconsin). Joe was comparatively young, and recently out of college (Weinberg was twenty-six, and had just finished work for his doctorate at the University of

California). Finally, Joe worked in a particular field of physics which turned out to be Weinberg's specialty. Weinberg had been a smart kid, almost a boy prodigy. Born in New York City on January 17, 1917, he finished De Witt Clinton High School at the age of fifteen and went through City College in the regulation four years. He belonged to the Young Communist League before he reached the West Coast, and he seems to have held some sort of official Young Communist League position for a while in Oakland.

Surveillance of Joseph Weinberg revealed that he associated with a fairly tight little circle of young scientists at the Radiation Laboratory. One of these was Irving D. Fox, a physicist with a similar American Student Union, Young Communist League background. Fox was born in Brooklyn in 1920. At Los Angeles Junior College, which he attended from 1936 to 1938, Fox was rebuked by the dean for littering the campus with Communist leaflets. Later he became an organizer with the Cannery Workers Union along the West Coast and in Alaska. The wives of Weinberg and Fox were as active as their husbands; Murray's security officers soon found the two women sending out free copies of Earl Browder's latest book, and other Stalinist literature, to selected scientists at the Radiation Laboratory. The security officers also noted carefully that Bernadette Doyle, Steve Nelson's secretary, made occasional visits to Weinberg's home.

Giovanni Rossi Lomanitz, a physicist from Bryan, Texas, born in 1921, was a conspicuously unconcealed Communist in the Weinberg circle. He was organizing vigorously for the Federation of Architects, Engineers, Chemists and Technicians, and he saw to it that every FAECT convert landed also in the Communist party. Robert R. Davis, a Radiation Laboratory scientist from Idaho, and his wife Charlotte, a native of California, learned to their sorrow how close scrutiny was being kept by CIC, though at first they did not know what hit them. The Davises were recruited by Lomanitz into the Merriman branch of the Party just before Steve Nelson dissolved it. Davis got an offer of a job at the newly established atom-bomb center of Los Alamos and promptly accepted. His Communist record reached Los Alamos before he did, and he was dismissed on the ground of questionable character and associations. After the war, Mr. and Mrs. Davis told the FBI fully about their brief career in Communism, which they said was undertaken chiefly out of curiosity.

In addition to keeping a close watch on the Lomanitz-Fox-Weinberg clique, CIC naturally kept an eye on the Soviet Consulate in San Francisco after Nelson's contacts with Zubilin and Ivanov. Late in June, 1943, the security officials got a shock; Gregory Kheifets, the Soviet Vice-Consul who had been ordered home to Russia, and Gregory Kasperov, who was to succeed him, had planned a dinner with Martin Kamen, one of the top United States chemists in nuclear-fission research.

Dr. Kamen, a native of Canada, had been brought to the United States as a child, and reared in Chicago. Having worked at the Radiation Laboratory in Berkeley since 1936, he was an obvious choice for group leader when the Manhattan District Project developed.

As a codiscoverer of carbon 14, and of an improved method of making iron 55 in the cyclotron, as well as being a specialist in biological tracer-research, Dr. Kamen stood solidly in science. In politics, on the basis of attendance at a William Z. Foster defense meeting, a brief membership in the American League against War and Fascism, and some activity with a Joint Anti-Fascist Refugee Committee branch which had met in the Berkeley home of Dr. Frank Oppenheimer, Dr. Kamen classed vaguely as a fellow traveler. He had showed some interest in Russian War Relief (his parents came from Russia) and some in the American-Soviet Science Society headed by Dr. Edward U. Condon, director of the National Bureau of Standards. Along with many other American scientists, he had turned over stacks of old scientific journals to replenish destroyed Soviet libraries in Kharkov and Kiev.

It seems Dr. Kamen had met Kheifets only once before. It was at a cocktail party at the San Francisco home of Louise Bransten, and Kheifets mentioned a request from the Soviet Surgeon General Burdenko for some radioactive phosphorus to treat a Soviet consular official in Seattle who was critically ill with leukemia. This was no secret; Dr. John Lawrence, head of the Radiation Laboratory clinic and brother of Ernest Lawrence, had published papers on the subject. It happened to be Kamen's specialty; he prepared these materials. Kheifets said he had been unable to reach John Lawrence by phone, so Kamen offered to speak to his colleague. The purpose of the dinner, set for July 2, was ostensibly to thank Kamen for his courtesy in the matter of the radioactive phosphorus, and to introduce Kamen to Kasperov "in case you ever have any business you want to transact in the Russian Consulate."

The dinner took place in a booth at Bernstein's Fish Grotto in San Francisco. It lasted two hours and forty minutes, which for a formal Russian dinner, with drinks, was not excessive. Two FBI men with a sound-amplifying device sat in the next booth. Unfortunately, the Fish Grotto was extremely noisy, and reception was poor. Phrases and occasional sentences came through: a reference to Dr. Niels Bohr, the Danish nuclear physicist hired as a consultant by the British and dispatched under an assumed name, for reasons of secrecy, to Los Alamos; some talk of the dangers of radioactivity in handling an atomic pile; a mention of Santa Fe. A scientist with the Manhattan District Project puzzled for hours over the record, and concluded finally that the American chemist had been less than cautious. Ten days after the dinner, on July 12, 1943, Dr. Kamen was suspended for indiscretion, without a hearing or any chance to put in a defense. He took his suspension, not stoically, but not hysterically, either, and went to work in a shipyard. Some important scientists connected with the nuclear-fission research felt sure of Kamen's loyalty, though they made no issue of it at the time. After the war, the chemist got a chance to talk back to parts of the FBI record, and he made quite a convincing case for himself. No doubt the two

Russians were skittering on thin security ice throughout the dinner. Quite clearly, they were sounding out the American as to willingness to share secrets in the atomic field. When they pressed him, Kamen argued that sharing should be a two-way street. He pointed out that when the Americans landed in Normandy they had a terrible time with Nazi antitank guns which had been stolen from the Russians, but which the Russians had never shared with their allies. He was able to isolate parts of this argument in the FBI record.

Though he seemed to have cleared up, finally, any doubt remaining as to his loyalty, Dr. Kamen was unable, on three occasions in the postwar period, to obtain a passport to travel abroad. He was not too upset by this; he realized he had been caught, partly because of his own carelessness, in the middle of a spy situation, and was now paying the penalty.

On the afternoon of August 12, 1943, CIC Operative Murray got a tip that there would be an important meeting that night in Weinberg's home. Murray stationed himself in the house next door to Weinberg's apartment house on Black Street, in Berkeley, and watched Steve Nelson and Bernadette Doyle arrive around 9 P.M. Two other agents, Harold Zindle and George Rathman, climbed up on the roof of the house next door and looked down into the second-story apartment of the Weinbergs. It was a hot and sticky night. At 9:20 they saw Weinberg come to the window to get some more air. The window stuck; Nelson came over to help open it. The agents got a good look at the pair at the window and several others seated around a table in the room, including Irving Fox and Giovanni Lomanitz. The meeting broke up at 10:15. When Steve Nelson and Bernadette Doyle emerged together, one of the CIC men deliberately jostled Nelson on the sidewalk, said, "Excuse me, sir," a few inches from his nose, to be certain of the identification. As Nelson and Miss Doyle proceeded down the street, the CIC men noticed FBI shadows picking up their trail.

That meeting about ended the activities of the secret remnant of the Merriman branch of the Communist party. Lomanitz was drafted in a couple of weeks, despite his protest, and the others were scattered one way or another.

Appearing at postwar hearings of the House Un-American Activities Committee, Dr. Weinberg denied that he knew Steve Nelson or that he had given unauthorized scientific information to anybody. Steve Nelson had previously refused to say whether he knew Weinberg lest he incriminate himself. The House committee urged prosecution of Weinberg on charges of perjury. Hailed before a Federal Grand Jury Weinberg refused repeatedly to answer questions on the ground that they might incriminate him. He was indicted on four charges of contempt of court, but these charges were dismissed in May, 1951, by Federal Judge Holtzoff on the ground that the scientist had a right to avail himself of his constitutional protections. However, Weinberg was discharged a month later from the faculty of the University of Minnesota for failure to co-operate with the Grand Jury investigation of subversion. He had been an assistant professor of physics at the University, and among other things, had been responsible for supervising the work of an Atomic Energy Commission fellowship student.

Any possible counterespionage complacency over the outcome of affairs at the Radiation Laboratory was shattered by the postwar revelation of the role played by David Hawkins—there and at Los Alamos. Hawkins, who was born at El Paso, Texas, on February 23, 1913, was recruited into the Communist party in 1938 at Berkeley, when Kenneth May was the campus organizer. Moving on to Stanford University, Hawkins enrolled in the secret cell headed by Dr. Frank Oppenheimer. In 1941, Hawkins returned to teach philosophy at Berkeley. Two years later he accepted an offer to go to Los Alamos as an administrative aide, charged with drawing up personal regulations, making out draft deferment forms, and acting as liaison between the atom plant, the Army engineers, and the town. As the historian of the project, directly responsible to Dr. J. Robert Oppenheimer, though not hired by Oppenheimer, Hawkins had access to the most secret data.

On July 8, 1946, David Hawkins made a curious speech at the Episcopal Church in Albuquerque, New Mexico, defending Allan Nunn May, the British physicist who had just issued a propaganda sort of confession to sweeten up the revelation that he had been a Soviet spy. Dr. Hawkins, who had developed a close friendship with some of the British scientists at Los Alamos, declared from the pulpit that Dr. May was really just a romantic person, acting from altruistic motives.

In 1951, Dr. Hawkins made no bones about having a prewar Communist record. He and his wife, Frances Pockman Hawkins, had dropped out of the Party, he said, when he began to do war work, and they had never picked up the threads. One trouble with this confession was that investigation disclosed active and continuing Party work by other members of the Hawkins family, and the Pockman family. Another was the strangely Stalinist fashion in which Hawkins had been acting at the University of Colorado, where he had become a professor of philosophy. In 1948, David Hawkins sponsored a conference of the National Council of the Arts, Sciences and Professions, which was an obvious front, already cited as subversive. In 1949, he sponsored a Civil Rights Congress conference in New York, an even more obvious front. In 1950, he sponsored the Communist Cultural and Scientific Conference for World Peace which pushed the pseudo-pacific program of Stalinism. Moreover, Dr. Hawkins had been quite busy on the campus out in Colorado, acting as faculty sponsor for a student Marxist study group. He had contributed a talk on biology before this group, as had Art Barry, the Colorado regional director of the Communist party, on another subject at another meeting. Dr. Hawkins had joined the Colorado Committee for the First Amendment and the American Association of Scientific Workers, both of which joined with the Young Progressives in sponsoring a meeting at which Hawkins himself denounced legislation designed to curb the Communist party.

This Party-line philosopher, who had obtained a key post in the most secret of the American atomic installations, was willing to reminisce, in a limited way, about Joseph Weinberg, Steve Nelson and other figures in the duel at Berkeley between espionage and counterespionage. Dr. Hawkins did not recall anything unfavorable about any of these old colleagues. He did not recall anything which would reflect unfavorably on the political party he had served. In fact, he demonstrated a memory about past events and people so faulty and vague as to suggest that of Kenneth May himself.

7. Escape and Confession

W HEN a spy faces exposure, he may choose one of several alternative courses of action. He may make a dash for safety or he may stand his ground with a determined pretense of innocence. He may also confess, though that cancels his status as a spy. Soviet spies sometimes follow another, confusing tactic, of confessing under instructions, so as to deflect public indignation and minimize the degree of counterespionage activity. A fake confession may usually be detected by the extent to which it protects the rest of the net, and serves Soviet political interests.

Since flight is a form of confession, it is important to note that the standard escape route for suspected Soviet agents in the United States is to Mexico to Switzerland to Czechoslovakia to Russia. For Soviet agents in the British Isles, the standard escape route is to Italy to Sweden to Finland to Russia. Morton Sobell, the neurotic radar expert who became involved in the first atomic espionage trial in the United States, got as far as Mexico City before he was nailed by extremely efficient, but tough, Mexican undercover men. David Greenglass made plans for going to Mexico, only to be delayed by various personal misadventures until it was too late to go anywhere. Bruno Pontecorvo, a cosmic ray specialist imperiled by impending revelations about his colleague and friend, Klaus Fuchs, slipped off to Italy on a supposed vacation from the British atomic center at Harwell, flew to Copen-

165

hagen, went from there to Stockholm, flew to Helsinki, and then went by Soviet ship to Leningrad.

Pontecorvo made an extra stop in Denmark; there is nothing inflexible about these escape routes. Though they have been fairly well fixed for years, they can be modified overnight. Obviously, they serve best where the suspect is not too hot. Once the noose of counterespionage actually settles around the neck of a Soviet spy, he may try almost anything to get away.

Arthur Alexandrovich Adams, the rheumatic cripple at the center of the most extensive known Soviet atomic web in the United States during the war, sensed surveillance long before Edward T. Manning prodded him with the fact at their New York meeting in July, 1945. Despite what he told Manning, he had no intention of trying to get out of the United States the way he came in, via Canada. He realized that for him the borders to the north and south were likely to be sealed.

After some preliminary sleight of hand, including smuggling of clothes from his hotel room to the home of a friend, Adams made an abortive rush toward safety as early as February, 1945. From the New York home of Victoria Stone, the jewelry-store operator, he sped across country under arrangements and with funds provided by Eric Bernay, the New York manufacturer of Russian victrola records. Adams reached a pier in Portland, Oregon, where a Russian ship was berthed. FBI agents materialized at the gangplank, and prevented him from going on a sea trip for his health. Adams had nothing to do but return to New York; which he did. For another year, the Soviet agent remained in New York, almost a recluse in his hotel room, seeing few persons and doing little of an ostensibly subversive nature. He may even have placed his net in other hands in hope of wearing out surveillance.

The FBI submitted the Adam dossier, along with those of his associates, Rudy Baker and Steve Nelson, to President Roosevelt, and later, after FDR's death, to President Truman, with a request for an order of arrest. In each instance, the President reportedly left the decision up to the State Department, which avoided action on the ground that working up a national spy fever would not contribute to pending efforts on the part of the United States to reach a decent postwar understanding with the Russians.

Early in 1945, when the Gouzenko revelations had made his position more precarious than ever, Adams disappeared. Rudy Baker also managed to elude observation. This pair may have sailed on the Polish liner, *Batory;* certainly they were not reported subsequently in the United States. Steve Nelson, technically an American citizen, gambling on the tolerance or softness of his fellow citizens, switched to other matters than atomic espionage, and remained in the country. He was kept under investigation, and early in 1952, he was tried in western Pennsylvania on a charge of sedition, found guilty, and sentenced to jail.

To Russia, the escape of an important agent was always important enough to justify changing the route, or time of sailing, of a Soviet ship. Adams and Baker were important enough, in this sense, though neither amounted to what the public terms a spy chief. A Resident Director in Canada presumably guided each atomic net in the United States. Adams and Baker and Nelson were cut-outs, that is, liaison men or go-betweens, operating under instructions from a Resident Director. On occasion they acted as couriers, talent spotters or recruiters, duties below the dignity of a Resident Director.

In utilizing standard escape routes, there may be an escalator arrangement, whereby an exposed spy is shifted automatically from country to country, or, more likely, an approach may be required to the Soviet Embassy in each country. Greenglass was told to go to Mexico City and write a letter to the Russian Ambassador there, praising Soviet policy on atomic energy before the United Nations, and signing it, "I. Jackson." Three days later, he was to visit the Plaza de Colón, taking a stance before the statue of Christopher Columbus. Greenglass was required to keep a middle finger of his right hand placed in a guidebook. A man would approach and share Greenglass' admiration for the statue.

The Atom Spies

Greenglass was to say, "Isn't this a magnificent statue? I come from Oklahoma and we had no such statues there." The man would reply, "There are more beautiful statues in Paris." That would be the start of a satisfactory, if brief, acquaintanceship, during which the man would produce a passport and money, so Greenglass could proceed to Switzerland, and later to Czechoslovakia, to repeat the same performance.

Greenglass never did get a look at any of those statues. Morton Sobell, more or less fortunate, managed to reach Mexico City, only to encounter delay, confusion, and violence. A great deal is known about Sobell's attempt to escape, almost enough to make it a case history in espionage failure, though some details are lacking because he refused to take the stand in his own defense at his trial, which resulted in conviction and a thirty-year jail sentence.

Sobell had been working as an electrical engineer in New York at the Reeves Instrument Co., on extremely secret experiments in the use of rockets and guided missiles, called Project Cyclone, including just about everything needed for atom-bomb and H-bomb warfare. On June 16, 1950, Sobell secured a vacation on the ground that he was run down and needed a rest. On June 20, he left his home in Flushing with his wife, Helen Gurewitz Sobell, their 15-month-old son Mark, and Mrs. Sobell's 12-year-old daughter Sydney by a previous marriage. Neighbors who saw them leave in the family car and who had heard they were driving down to Washington for a few days were mildly puzzled when Mrs. Sobell's sister, Edith Levitov, drove the car back into the garage on June 21, locked up, and left.

A week later, William Danziger, a New Yorker who had been with Sobell at City College (class of '38), received a note from Mexico City reading: "Dear Bill: Had a nice trip, held the kid in my lap all the way, and located a place to stay." A postscript said: "Please forward the enclosures and I will explain to you when I get back."

The enclosures were for Sobell's father Louis, a Bronx pharma-

168

cist; a relative in Long Island City named Max Pasternak; and Edith Levitov, who lived in Arlington, Virginia. These letters were all presumably from a Morty Sowell of Mexico City. In another week, Danziger received another note: "Dear Bill: I am having a nice time. I have moved from one place to another." This time the enclosures came from a Morty Levitov at a new Mexico City address. During a seven week summer period, Sobell used seven different aliases, including M. Sand, Morris Sand, Marvin Salt, N. Sand, and Morton Solt, and seven different addresses. One week he was in Vera Cruz, the next in Tampico. Mexicans with whom he tried to get on a friendly footing testified at his trial that he was jittery in the extreme. He was trying to get out of Mexico without papers, he explained, to avoid being taken back into the United States Army as a result of what was happening in Korea. "I already had one horrible war experience," he told Manuel Giner de los Rios, an interior decorator in Mexico City. Actually, Morton Sobell never served in the United States armed forces, having secured a 4F classification during World War II on the basis of his own claim of neurosis.

Every Soviet agent of any consequence has certain control data—a series of questions and answers known only to him and to the Spy Center in Moscow and the Resident Director. His photograph is on file in Moscow. If he is stranded in a country other than the one where he has been working, he can go to the Soviet military attaché, hand in a message in his own cipher and wait for verification of his identity at a specified time and place, by means of the picture and control questions.

Sobell must have suspected he was being closely pursued or he would not have been so shifty, or utilized his friend as a mail drop in such a callous way. On July 20, about a month after his departure, FBI agents came to his house in search of him. On August 3, a sealed warrant for his arrest was issued by United States Commissioner McDonald in New York. The chase ended on August 16. The Sobell baby was in bed, and its parents were lingering over their after-dinner coffee in their Mexico City apartment.

My older daughter opened the door and three men burst into the room with drawn guns and bodies poised for shooting [Sobell declared in a sworn statement for later court use].

These men did not ask my name, did not say what they wanted. I demanded to see a warrant, or some other legal process. No reply, except some vague charge that I was one "Johnny Jones" and that I robbed a bank in Acapulco in the sum of $15,000. Of course I vehemently denied the charge and tried to show them my papers, visas, etc., to prove that I was no bank robber. One of the men showed a piece of metal in his hand and said they were police. They were dressed in civilian clothes. A fourth man came later. He also was in civilian clothes. Only about ten minutes elapsed from the time that they came until they hustled me out and that was after I insisted on calling the American Embassy, without being permitted to do so.

They picked me up bodily and carried me down from the fourth floor to the ground floor. In the street I kept shouting for the police. A taxi was hailed and they opened the door, tried to force me into the taxi. Then two more men came in and beat me over the head with blackjacks until I lost consciousness.

I woke up in the taxi and I was stretched horizontally at the feet of the three men. When the car stopped in front of a building they ordered me to get up; they told me to get into the building but not to make a scene or they would plug me. We walked to the elevator, we went upstairs and we went into an office. I might say that those men spoke English. They sat me down and a slim, tall, dark man came over. He looked at me. I asked him what it was all about. He slapped me in the face and told me that they were the ones that were asking questions. At that point I discovered that my head was bloody and my shirt bespattered with blood.

However, they asked me no questions but they photographed me in several poses. We stayed in that building from approximately 8:30 P.M. until 4 A.M. At 12 midnight they offered me something to eat but I had no appetite for food. During all this time no one questioned me. Some persons who identified themselves as officers to guard me chatted with me but expressed ignorance of the reason I was there. At 4 A.M. I was moved into a large four-door Packard and seated in the rear with two armed men, one on each side of me. At that moment, the same tall, thin man came to the door and spoke to my guards in English, saying to them, "If he makes any trouble, shoot him."

The driver of the car, who apparently was the leader of the expedition, and who answered to the name of Julio, told me that they were taking me to the chief of the Mexican police for further action. With a number of stops for one reason or another, we drove on until about 6 P.M. At that time Julio tried to make a phone call, or he did make one, and he told me that he was trying to get the Chief of Police. The same thing happened at about 10 P.M. and at midnight on August 17, telling me that he was trying to make sure the Chief of Police would be available.

At about 1:30 A.M. we arrived at Nuevo Laredo. We stopped in front of a building and Julio went into the building and returned in about ten minutes, and told me that he had spoken to the Chief, and that the Chief told him to take me across the border, and let me go. . . .

When the Mexicans, in a motorcade which had swelled to twelve cars, reached the center of the international bridge leading to Laredo, Texas, they informed Morton Sobell, riding in the front car, that he was free to get out and go about his business. It so happened that four FBI agents—John Lewis and Rex Schroeder from New York, L. G. Taylor of Laredo, and Jack Peden of San Francisco—were waiting on the bridge to receive him. They popped Sobell into a Texas jail, and after he waived extradition they flew him to New York for a trial.

Sobell did not tell the story of his ride through Mexico until after a jury found him guilty of conspiracy to give Russia documents affecting the national defense. Then he produced his affidavit to support a motion for a new trial, on the ground that he, an American citizen, had been "brutally assaulted" and "abducted" in a foreign country. Government counsel, opposing the motion, pointed out that Sobell had been trying to escape from his American status, and that his affidavit itself made a false claim to visas, when he had no visas, that he had cashed in the return half of his airplane tickets after reaching Mexico City and that he had put down fake Philadelphia addresses in registering at Mexican hotels. The United States lawyer said further that the emphasis on American citizenship came with rather poor grace immediately after conviction for treason. The Judge after hearing the arguments denied the motion for a new trial.

2

When suspicion fell upon him after seven successful years of espionage, Klaus Fuchs made no attempt to escape. Why not? Unlike David Greenglass, he was not immobilized by illness or family trouble; he was a bachelor, in fair health, without relatives in England. Didn't he realize what he had done, or what the penalty might be? Did he want to be punished, the way bad children, according to psychologists, subconsciously want to be spanked? Harry Gold had three months' leeway, between the Fuchs arrest in February, 1950, and the FBI knock on his door in May, 1950, yet he did not try actively to escape, either. Why not? In 1947, Gold had talked his way to freedom. This time he lied halfheartedly for a while, then confessed. After fifteen years of double and triple dealing, was Gold overcome by the desire to cleanse himself by full confession? Was there any chance that his confession, or that of Fuchs, really constituted a subtle final service to the Soviet Union?

The best approach to Fuchs is through his operations in America, since his movements can be verified by Gold's statements. From the time the British theoretical physicist first met the American biochemist on a teeming East Side New York street one windy Saturday afternoon in January, 1944, they both conducted themselves, so far as espionage was concerned, in a highly responsible manner. Fuchs carried an unseasonal tennis ball in his left hand, and Gold held a pair of kid gloves and a book with a green binding. After exchanging recognition phrases, they went by cab to a Third Avenue restaurant for a discussion of what Fuchs had to offer and what the Russians wanted.

One thing Gold requested immediately was the organizational setup of the British atomic mission, the Manhattan District Project and the co-operating U. S. firms, like Kellex Corp. and Carbide & Carbon Chemicals Corp. Fuchs rattled off names and titles as fast as Gold could write them down. He had already met General Groves, and had discussed scientific problems with such United States authorities as Dean Richard C. Tolman of the California Institute of Technology, President Conant of Harvard, and Professor Urey of Columbia. Though he had only arrived in New York on December 7, 1943, he had quickly absorbed just about everything there was to learn about nuclear-fission research in the New York and Tennessee areas. The extent of his penetration was revealed in 1951 by Senator McMahon (D-Conn.) of the Joint Congressional Committee, in the form of a statement by Dr. Karl Cohen, one of the wartime leaders of the project.

"Work on the control problem [of the gaseous diffusion method of producing U 235] was being carried out by the SAM theoretical division [at Columbia University] under my direction," wrote Dr. Cohen, "and by a section of the Kellex Corp. under Manson Benedict. The future operating company [in Tennessee], the Carbide & Carbon Chemicals Corp., was also interested. Fuchs arrived in New York . . . and a series of meetings were set up, to be held alternately at the Kellex Corp. and at the SAM laboratories wherein the two American groups and the British [Peierls and Fuchs] could compare results. After several meetings in December, a division of work was adopted, Fuchs' part of which was to calculate numerically for the plant being actually designed [for construction in Tennessee] the effects of fluctuations on production rate.

"All phases of the control problem depend on the intimate details of plant construction, and in the course of his assigned task, Fuchs obtained from the Kellex Corp. complete knowledge of the process design of the K-25 plant [the one built at Oak Ridge]."

Another 1951 statement released by Senator McMahon, from Dr. Benedict, stressed the fact that research reports of Fuchs from England had been outstanding for originality and usefulness. Furthermore, though Professor Peierls was chief of the British contingent in New York at first, he soon left, delegating authority to Klaus Fuchs.

Semen Markovich Semenov of the Amtorg Trading Corp., who had taken Gold off other contacts to concentrate on Fuchs, was delighted to open up such a rich vein of information. He insisted on scheduling with great care meetings between Gold and Fuchs, alternative meetings (at the same place but at a different hour and different day of the week), and emergency meetings (in case both a regular and an alternative meeting had been missed). Particular precautions were taken to detect and offset any possible surveillance. It was agreed that Fuchs would give advance notice of intention to pass information, so it could be relayed with split-second precision by Raymond (Gold) to Sam (Semenov). One afternoon in March, 1944, Fuchs and Gold approached each other on Madison Avenue in New York. They took a few steps together, turned west onto a side street. There Fuchs handed over papers and left. Gold went down Fifth Avenue and ten minutes later met Semenov, in the same manner, and handed on the papers to him. On one occasion, when no documents were involved, Gold and Fuchs strolled for an hour and a half along the winding paths of Central Park; on another they tramped for miles down the Grand Concourse in the Bronx.

One important transfer of SAM and Oak Ridge material occurred late in June, 1944, at Borough Hall, Brooklyn, after John (Anatoli Antonovich Yakovlev, the Soviet Vice-Consul) had succeeded Sam as Gold's boss. Klaus Fuchs sat down in the sun on a bench facing the statue of Henry Ward Beecher in Borough Hall Park. Harry Gold found a vacant seat alongside him on the bench. Both had newspapers. After a while, they exchanged papers, wordlessly, as friends might do. Fuchs got up and strolled away. Gold arose and crossed the park, to exchange newspapers again, this time with Yakovlev. The information was in an envelope concealed in the folded paper. Twice more, in July, this procedure was followed, once at 96 Street in Manhattan and once in Woodside, Queens. Then an alarming break occurred.

Harry Gold knew Yakovlev only as John and had no idea where to reach him. Klaus Fuchs knew Gold only as Raymond and had no idea where to reach him. This "cut the chain in two places," Yakovlev explained to Gold. It was a routine precaution against somebody from outside climbing up the chain, link by link. That summer the chain snapped of its own accord. Fuchs did not appear for a scheduled meeting with Gold. He did not appear for the alternative meeting in August. He did not appear for the emergency meeting.

Yakovlev knew Fuchs's address, though he had not revealed it to Gold. In desperation, he sent Gold up there: 128 West 77 Street. Fuchs had gone. The janitor, whom Gold consulted, knew nothing except that his tenant had left. Yakovlev and Gold knew that Fuchs had a sister, Mrs. Robert B. Heineman, living in Cambridge, Massachusetts, because Fuchs had told Gold he was considering asking her and her two children to come to visit him in New York, if the apparatus had no objections.

Under peremptory instructions from Yakovlev, Gold arranged for time off from his laboratory job in Philadelphia, and traveled up to Cambridge. Mrs. Heineman knew nothing of her brother's espionage role. Klaus was working somewhere in the Southwest, she said vaguely; he would probably visit her around New Year's Day on a short vacation. If Klaus appeared before then, she agreed, she would ask him to call the number which Gold left, not his own number in Philadelphia, but the number of somebody in New York trusted by Yakovlev. Gold tarried to talk with the Heineman youngsters, whose hearts he had won with gifts of candy. He told them and their mother amusing and affectionate stories of his own imaginary twins, David and Essie. He spoke so much of his son David that Mrs. Heineman, under questioning by the FBI six years later, remembered the talk and said she thought her mysterious visitor might have been named Davidson.

Because the interruption of contact seemed ominous to him, Yakovlev applied to Fuchs the usual test for possible ideological waverers. Early in January, when Gold went up to Cambridge again, he carried $1,500 in cash for Fuchs. The scientist, whose aloof profundity in physics had already led Gold to consider him a "genius," waved aside the money. He was not working for money, he said. Gold was then earning $50 a week as a chemist and receiving only the barest expenses for his courier duty. Something in Fuchs's attitude stirred his imagination; from then on, even after he confessed, he always referred to the physicist as "noble."

Klaus Fuchs had his Los Alamos information all typed out. Before he turned it over to Gold, at the conclusion of a bedroom conference, the physicist went into some detail as to the principle used in bringing together in a bomb two noncritical masses of uranium so as to form a mass large enough to explode. He and Gold also arranged to meet in Santa Fe, at the Castillo Street Bridge, at four o'clock on the first Saturday in June. That rendezvous, of course, was kept, as well as a second one in September.

Though he was refused permission to visit Hanford, there is no evidence that anybody at Los Alamos questioned the loyalty of Klaus Fuchs. Many top-flight physicists there and at other atomic installations, entirely loyal scientists like Enrico Fermi, Edward Teller, George Gamow, and Hans Bethe, were accompanied everywhere they went by a personal security officer, but Klaus Fuchs did not quite rate such attention. If he wore what later seemed to have been a special cloak of invisibility, it was partly, in the words of Dr. Bethe, head of the theoretical physics division at Los Alamos, because he made "a great contribution," and partly because of his manner. "He was one of the most valuable men in my division," Dr. Bethe said, after Fuchs's exposure as a spy. "He knew everything we did. Everybody liked him. He was neither aggressively social nor a hermit. A bachelor, he would visit at the homes of his fellow scientists once or twice a week. When the others talked about international exchange of scientific information, Fuchs was not prominent in urging it, or reluctant. He was like the rest of us. He didn't attract any attention."

In a word, Klaus Fuchs was an excellent spy. It is impossible to avoid the conclusion that he constantly evaluated the effect of his behavior and the possible consequences of his acts. This conclusion is strengthened by the fact that, when he returned to England in June, 1946, he accepted his first substantial payment from the apparatus. When he gave a receipt for the money, he must have realized it would be available for use as blackmail, if he ever became restive.

In the fall of 1947, Fuchs revisited America. He was not included on a list of British scientists originally scheduled to make the trip, but his name was added at the last minute, it is said, on the recommendation of some American scientists. Fuchs participated in New York discussions about the wartime weapons work, dropped in one afternoon at the Argonne National Laboratory in Chicago for seventy minutes, and made informal contact with a variety of important and unsuspecting nuclear physicists. Because of his high theoretical point of advantage, and the freemasonry prevailing among scientists who had shared in a world-shaking achievement, it is reasonable to suppose that Fuchs was able to bring the Russians up to date on anything in the way of basic theory that they required. Certainly he knew about hydrogen-bomb speculation from his Los Alamos experience. Whether he got any inkling of the fact that President Truman had decided in 1945 to defer any active effort to produce a hydrogen bomb is debatable; many important United States scientists were unaware of this for years.

Back at Harwell again, Fuchs lived for almost two years at Lacie's Court, a boardinghouse for scientists near Abingdon. He drove the nine miles to the installation and back again daily in an old car which gave him constant trouble, his landlady recalled. He seemed to have no political opinions and no particular friends. Though absent-minded, so absent-minded that he might have to be summoned several times for dinner on a Sunday before responding, he could talk when he wished on a wide variety of subjects, from *Alice in Wonderland* to relativity. He rarely left Lacie's Court for visits to local pubs, tearooms, or restaurants. When he did leave, nobody noticed.

Not until the late summer of 1949 did Klaus Fuchs come under suspicion, as a result of a tip from the FBI that there had been a definite, serious, and continual leak of atomic information from the British delegation of scientists in America during the war, and after the war. The basis for the tip was never revealed, except possibly by Fuchs, who said later that he had "made a mistake in New York" during his 1947 visit to America. There was no certainty at first as to which member of the British contingent was involved, but British counterintelligence concluded Fuchs was a logical suspect because of his earlier, almost forgotten Stalinist record.

To put Fuchs at ease, British counterintelligence under Sir Percy Sillitoe arranged a promotion. The suspected spy was duly raised from deputy senior scientific officer at $4,480 a year to one of the twenty-five senior officers, at $5,040 a year. He was also given a prefabricated house on the Harwell site as a home.

The $10-a-week raise and a home of his own made no particular change in Fuchs's mode of living. When surveillance and investigation over a period of weeks brought up no clues, William J. Skardon, the Harwell security officer, approached Fuchs personally. During a friendly visit, he mentioned that Fuchs was under suspicion of having turned over confidential information.

"I don't think so," said Fuchs.

"I have in my possession precise information in this matter," said Skardon.

"I don't think so," repeated Fuchs.

"That's an ambiguous reply," noted the security officer.

The tall, broad-shouldered, balding scientist decided to meet bluff with bluff. "I don't understand," he said, with a thickening of accent which betrayed strain. "Perhaps you will tell me what the evidence is. I have not done any such thing."

Since Skardon had no evidence at this point, he did not produce it, but the color of suspicion in his mind darkened. At a subsequent meeting, the security officer brought up the solemn oath of allegiance to Britain which Dr. Fuchs had taken when he became a citizen in 1942. "Doesn't that oath mean anything to you?" demanded Skardon.

Fuchs said it was a serious matter, "but if circumstances should arise comparable to those existing in Germany in 1933," he would feel free to act according to his conscience. This conveyed to Skardon an unmistakable intimation that if Fuchs had served the Soviet underground in Germany he might still be serving the Soviet underground in England. The security officer's visits increased in frequency. The next break came when Fuchs announced that his father, that 76-year-old religious crusader, Dr. Emil Fuchs, who had been living in Frankfurt, Germany, had decided to accept a job as professor of theology at Leipzig in the Soviet zone of Germany. "Because of my father, I cannot talk to you any further," said Fuchs, repudiating the unspoken assumption which had grown up between them that he would eventually reveal what was in his mind.

"You want to protect your father, is that it?" said Skardon. Klaus Fuchs nodded. "I couldn't bring myself not to ask him to go," he said, "but I did feel I should tell you about it." The subject of his father seemed to have stirred thoughts in his mind of the forces, personal and political, which had shaped his early life. Fuchs went into great detail about his boyhood and early manhood, including his revolt against his father's pacifism which led him into violent anti-Nazi activity at the University of Kiel. Skardon, who had a gift of silence, listened intently.

179

When Fuchs had finished, the security officer said good day and left.

On January 24, 1950, Fuchs invited Skardon to lunch at his house. Upon arrival, the security officer said, "Well, you asked to see me, and here I am." Fuchs replied, "Yes, it is rather up to me now."

With some evidence of mental stress, Fuchs began talking again of the psychological background of his life. "You've given me motives for your acts," said Skardon, "but you haven't mentioned the acts themselves. Why don't you unburden your mind and clear your conscience and tell the whole story?"

Dr. Fuchs peered intently through his heavy glasses. "I will never be persuaded by you to talk," he said. "Let's have some lunch." After lunch, Fuchs decided to answer questions after all. It was not, he insisted, because anything weighed on his conscience; his conscience was clear, he said. What bothered him was the effect his story might have on close friends at Harwell.

In response to a question as to when he began spying, Fuchs said it was in the middle of 1942. His first contact had been of his own seeking, with a foreign Communist, at a house in London. He confined his tale-bearing at first to his own work; later he turned over anything he could find of value. Those he met were occasionally Russians, more often persons of unknown nationality.

"I realized I was carrying my life in my hands," he told Skardon, "but I had done this from the time of my underground days in Germany." (The penalty for wartime treason in the United States was death, but Fuchs was not an American. The punishment in England for what Fuchs had done did not exceed fourteen years.)

"Since I am under suspicion," he told Skardon, just as though the point of suspicion had not passed into certainty, "I may, upon reflection, find it impossible to continue at Harwell. If I come to that conclusion, I will offer my resignation."

Did Klaus Fuchs, in his agitation, really believe that a traitor could continue working at the empire's chief atomic center? He told Skardon that in the last two years, the flow of his information had gradually lessened, as he entertained doubts about the propriety of his actions. He had decided fairly recently that he could only settle in England, that he did not want to go anywhere else. Was this formal notification that he had disposed of suggestions of flight to Russia? He still believed in Communism, said Fuchs, but not as it was presently practiced in the Soviet Union.

That ended the January 24 colloquy. Two days later, Skardon made another visit, at Fuchs's request. "I want to resolve my situation as quickly as possible," the scientist said. Skardon suggested they go together from Harwell, which is near Oxford, to London on the following day, to produce a formal statement in writing. This was done. Fuchs was still, as the British say, a free man; he was not yet under arrest. His formal statement included a claim that his first espionage contact in America was with a Russian in Boston in February, 1945, a claim which under a cloak of frankness completely covered up his relationship with Harry Gold. He spoke of meetings in London with a Soviet agent, before and after his visits to America. These meetings took place about once every two months, he said.

On January 30, Fuchs went to the War Office with the ever-obliging, ever-tactful Skardon and specified, for the benefit of atomic scientist Michael Perrin, all the technical information he had turned over to his Soviet contacts.

News of Dr. Fuchs's arrest went out to the world on February 3, 1950. He was said to have confessed. On February 10, at a preliminary hearing in Bow Street Court, London, Fuchs's lawyer, Thompson Halsall, asked only one question of William J. Skardon, the chief government witness, "Would it be fair to say that since lunchtime on January 24 he has helped you and been completely co-operative in every way?" Skardon replied yes; that was the way it seemed at the time.

Fuchs's halting conversation with Skardon had a peculiarly bumbling quality. Here apparently was a professor whose traditional absent-mindedness extended to politics. Fuchs encouraged this impression with his claim about being able to separate his normal and his secret life by means of "controlled schizophrenia."

If British counterintelligence, known as M.I.5, was ever confident it had gotten to the bottom of the Fuchs case, several things began to shake its confidence. One was the effect on delicate negotiations in Washington between the British, Canadians, and Americans for interchange of atomic information along the broader lines which had prevailed during the war. Chairman David E. Lilienthal of the United States Atomic Energy Commission, Secretary of Defense Louis Johnson, and Under-Secretary of State James E. Webb were not entirely agreed among themselves, it was reported, but there was a chance of agreement on a new exchange-of-information deal until word came about Fuchs. When the American public learned that its confidence in a single atomic secret which would give immunity from war for years was misplaced, it reacted so violently that the British and Canadian representatives, Sir Oliver Franks and Hume Wrong, conceded nothing further could be done at the moment. As late as 1952, Winston Churchill was still trying to bring negotiations in this field back to where they were before Fuchs's espionage activities came to light. Even then, Americans, British, and Canadians generally did not appreciate the extent to which thousands of Communists in each country had been scouring laboratory corners for odds and ends of stray techniques and theories in nuclear-fission research. They did not know that counterespionage in all three countries revealed a similar record of success and failure in meeting this new sort of mass ideological espionage, and that the remedy was not increased suspicion among the three countries, but wider co-operation.

If the Fuchs confession had been timed to split the Anglo-American atomic co-operation, it could not have met with greater success. The first question was: could the fencing with Skardon have been an act? In view of the equally, if not more deceptive act staged at Harwell and Los Alamos, the answer had to be maybe. As a matter of fact, the approach to Skardon could have been sincere, and still have culminated in a calculated statement, issued under orders.

The full Fuchs confession was shipped across the Atlantic and read at a secret session of the Joint Congressional Committee on Atomic Energy, Senator McMahon's committee. It was not released to the public, on the ground that Fuchs might have "over-confessed," that is, listed technical details which he had not found an opportunity to pass on to his Soviet contact before he fell under suspicion. Reports spread that the statement contained psychological time bombs on the order of the divisive propaganda released by Allan Nunn May in his fake confession.

To judge from the excerpts from his confession which were released to the public, Klaus Fuchs felt no compunction over what he had done to his country. His only concern was the attitude of his friends, including scientists generally, which might have been a matter of sentiment, or of calculation.

In describing the agents with whom he had worked, Klaus Fuchs was not too specific. His verbal picture of Harry Gold as a man of about forty, five feet eight inches tall, 180 pounds, stocky build, Slavic appearance, receding forehead, and a round face was descriptive enough but it could have fit thousands of people. When Mrs. Heineman gave her confused account of the courier with a name somewhat like Davidson, the FBI fixed tentatively on a New York engineer named Davidson and flew his picture over to Klaus Fuchs for identification. Fuchs looked at it and said, "Yes, I believe that is the man." Mrs. Heineman looked at another copy of the photograph, and said immediately it was not the man. The FBI did a tremendous job of narrowing down the field of suspects. They concentrated on New York because most of the contacts with Fuchs had been in New York, but by this time Harry Gold was back in Philadelphia. Starting with a list of 1,200, the FBI narrowed the suspects down to several hundred, to scores, then to a dozen, finally to three. Gold was one of them, and particularly vulnerable because of his earlier work in New

York and his admitted (though false) relationship with Golos. Two FBI men showed Fuchs a photo of Gold. Fuchs shook his head; this was not the man, he said. Not until Gold confessed, did Fuchs glance at some moving pictures of the Philadelphia chemist and concede at last that this was the courier known to him as Raymond.

Why did Gold confess? His own statement was that he decided to tell the truth, in a limited way, as soon as he read newspaper stories about Fuchs's arrest on February 3, 1950. Before then, he had flirted with the idea of escape. After three years of separation from the apparatus, he was contacted in Philadelphia in December, 1949, and asked to keep a February rendezvous in New York, at which he was to receive $2,000 for the purpose of leaving by the standard escape route to Mexico, to Switzerland, to Czechoslovakia, to Russia.

The rendezvous in New York fell, by a curious coincidence, on the day that the newspapers told of the Fuchs arrest. Harry Gold put in an appearance, but he did not reveal himself to the go-between who was scheduled to hand over the money. According to a report from FBI circles, but which has not been officially confirmed by the FBI, the paymaster in the case resembled Julius Rosenberg. As for Gold, he decided then to tell everything that had to do with Fuchs, but to conceal his other activities, making no mention of his various Soviet superiors, or of his other informants. Next the thought came that perhaps any confession was unnecessary.

"I wanted to spend as long as possible with my family, and to keep them in ignorance of what I had done," he testified at a trial in 1951. "I wanted to get my work in as good a shape as possible. I decided I would fight for time. That was my course of action and I stuck to it." If he eventually abandoned this course of action, it was partly because of an emotional impulse too strong to resist, and partly because of the logic of events.

Back in 1947, Harry Gold had lied when he ran into the FBI,

and he had implemented his lying with a majestic performance before the Grand Jury. What made the difference between 1947 and 1950? For one thing, Gold had quarreled with Abe Brothman, the friend and associate in espionage he had saved by his inspired mendacity. The friendship between the two could not survive the death of Harry Gold's mother in the fall of 1947. Gold blamed himself for her death, but the fact remained that he would have been at home, and not in New York, except for Brothman. Brothman in turn was fed up with Gold. The fact that Abe Brothman Associates ran into financial difficulties precipitated trouble. Salaries were not being paid, and when Gold complained, more for other employes than himself, Brothman asked him, as the chief chemist of the company, and a partner to stand firm. "When there is no money, I'm a partner," said Gold. "When there's money, I'm an employee." Miriam Moskowitz, Brothman's business associate, told Gold to keep his mouth shut. "Go to the laboratory where you belong, you worm," she shrilled, and Harry did go to the laboratory. He was afraid of her temper.

Conditions worsened steadily in the company, and when Brothman and Miss Moskowitz went to Switzerland on business in June, 1948, Gold presided over an indignation meeting of employees. The employees wired Brothman to return and pay some attention to the contracts already in the house instead of gallivanting around Europe on obscure errands of his own. Brothman and Miss Moskowitz came back in a rage. Brothman accused Gold of trying to steal the business while he was away. Miss Moskowitz was equally angry. Harry Gold walked out finally after presenting a formal demand for $4,000 in back pay. "Don't pull a Budenz on me now," was Brothman's final insult. Later Gold returned to the laboratory for some clothes, and was accused by Brothman of stealing a $600 refractometer and a couple of lesser pieces of equipment.

Back in Philadelphia, resuming once again the comfortable old routine with his father Samuel and his younger brother Joseph in their stone and brick row house up near Oxford Circle, Harry

Gold located a $4,340-a-year job at the Philadelphia General Hospital, doing experiments in heart research.

The FBI caught up with him on May 15, 1950. Gold agreed to come with them to the FBI office in the Widener Building in Philadelphia, and to return there every evening after work, for as long as they wanted him, provided they would stay away from the hospital and his home. The setting was different, but there were some of the elements here, once again, of the Skardon-Fuchs meeting at Harwell. The FBI asked Harry Gold to explain his activities over the years, where he had been, what he had done, and Harry Gold obliged, on the assumption that his life was an open book.

Cross-checking of Gold's answers, however, revealed discrepancies. He denied, for example, having been west of the Mississippi, yet he admitted marking the Castillo Street Bridge on a map of Santa Fe found in his living room. Journalists dedicated to a cult of romantic exaggeration about the FBI claimed later that this "broke" Gold. According to the spy's own sworn statement in one of the trials where he later appeared, he did not break for another seven days. His asserted real reason for breaking was chiefly his feeling of guilt toward his family.

"I realized that I couldn't possibly fight this thing," said Gold. "I knew if I did that my father and brother, all of my boyhood friends, would rally around me, all of the people at the Heart Station, Dr. McMillan, Dr. Bellet, and Dr. Steiger, who trusted me and who had faith in me, would rally around me, but I knew that once the FBI began to probe into the hideous snarl that was my life, once they pulled one thread, the whole horrible skein would become untangled and inevitably I would be exposed. I made my choice because I didn't want these people who would rally around to be so terribly disillusioned. I said, 'Yes, I am the man to whom Klaus Fuchs gave the information on atomic energy.' And I sat down in a chair, and the FBI man gave me a cigarette and I asked for one minute—and they gave it to me—during which a thousand things went through my mind, and I didn't even need that minute to come to the decision."

That didn't end it. Harry Gold had decided to confess, but there were varieties of confession.

"I wasn't going to squeal," said Gold, later. "I was simply going to admit what had happened with Fuchs. I was going to cover everything up, Sam's identity, everything. There was this mountain in front of me. When I saw my brother, part of the mountain came down. I told him what I had done. He went white. Two of the FBI men jumped up. They thought he was going to collapse. But he didn't. He said, 'You jerk, how could you have done it?' Then he says, "You couldn't have done it. You are trying to cover somebody else up.' I told him I wasn't, that I had actually passed on information which I had gotten from Klaus Fuchs and had given it to a Soviet agent. The following night my father was brought down. I told him. He said, 'Was it the Russians?' I said yes. When I saw my father, the rest of the mountain came down. Later they visited me at Holmesburg Prison and they said they were going to mortgage the house. This I did not want."

It was at this point that Gold appealed to Federal Judge McGranery for appointment of a widely respected lawyer who would allow him to co-operate with the FBI and tell his whole story, without reservation. He gave names and dates and places. On June 3, 1950, FBI agent Fred G. Birkby went to Harry Gold's home, with special agent Forrest Burgess, and in the cellar they found a corner closet and a large wooden box, three feet square and thirty inches deep, full of papers, blueprints, and records of espionage instructions, data on rendezvous after rendezvous, in short, full documentary confirmation of the story Gold had been telling. This was not a Fuchs confession; this was the real thing.

There was, incidentally, a curious postscript to the Fuchs confession. Documents were supposedly found during a tardy search of his house at Harwell.

These documents went far beyond the meager details of Fuchs' own confession, according to gossip stories in the Parisian papers. On March 8, 1950, the Soviet government issued a statement denying it had ever received any information from Klaus Fuchs, or had ever, in fact, heard of anybody named Klaus Fuchs. This repudiation, supposedly in punishment for Fuchs' indiscretion in keeping incriminating material, contrary to all the rules of espionage, was rumored to have broken the scientist's spirit in prison. According to rumors which have received not the slightest official confirmation, and are not likely to be confirmed if they are true, Klaus Fuchs invited his old friend, William J. Skardon, to come to Brixton Prison, near London, and listen to a confession that was really a confession.

Bruno Pontecorvo, a more brilliant nuclear physicist than Klaus Fuchs, and one with wider access to Anglo-American research—he was actually coholder of a 1940 United States patent on which the atom bomb itself allegedly infringed—had a mysterious conference with two visitors in mid-August, 1950, at Lake Como, Italy. The visitors, one an Italian and the other a Czech, were seen in agitated discussion with him. After they left, as abruptly as they came, Pontecorvo seemed depressed. In the presence of strangers, he told his wife, "I can't go back to England. They'll put me in jail if I do."

The Lake Como conference followed publication of gossip stories in Parisian newspapers to the effect that Sir Percy Sillitoe of British counterintelligence had finally broken Fuchs, and in a second confession had obtained a solution of the long-standing puzzle embodied in a spy chart removed by Igor Gouzenko in 1945 from the Soviet Embassy in Ottawa. Particularly mysterious was this reference:

GINI—Jew   Auxiliary Group.
   Owner of a drug store. He provided a place for photography. He has a photo-laboratory. There are working at his place:
   (a) Golia, a young artist . . .

Back of the espionage double talk, according to the stories, Golia was Fuchs, and Gini was an associate of Fuchs at Harwell. Speculation about the "four Gs" in the Canadian spy report has never drawn any comment from the FBI. It could be fantastic nonsense; on the other hand, the whole Pontecorvo story had a fantastic quality.

Bruno Pontecorvo had left Harwell July 25, 1950, on a leave of absence expiring August 31. Already the leave was half gone; only a week or two remained for a decision. There is a convention that the lives of condemned prisoners pass in review before their eyes—a convention which lacks documentation, perhaps, because the prisoners rarely survive for questioning—and Bruno Pontecorvo might have been pardoned a backward glance at the events which led him to irresolution on the shores of Lake Como.

In a general sense, he had been shaped by the same anti-Fascist pressures as Klaus Fuchs. He came from a family of intellectual stature and more than moderate means. His father Massimo owned textile mills in and around Pisa until the Italian depression swept away his holdings. The fourth of eight children feeling the pinch of comparative poverty, Bruno struggled for a scientific education, with considerable help from his oldest brother Guido, who became a biologist of note. Bruno studied at the University of Rome, as an undergraduate for two years, and as a graduate student for three more years. His physics teacher was Enrico Fermi, the Nobel-prize winner who later contributed so greatly to the Manhattan District Project.

In the April, 1935, *Proceedings* of the Society of London an article appeared entitled, "Artificial Radioactivity Produced by Neutron Bombardment," which became famous in later years because of what it foreshadowed in atomic development. Its six authors, all connected with the University of Rome, included Pontecorvo's physics professor, Enrico Fermi; Pontecorvo himself; Emilio Segre, later with the University of California Radiation Laboratory; and Franco Rasetti, subsequently with Johns Hopkins University.

The Atom Spies

Just as Pontecorvo took his first step upward on the ladder of scientific achievement, Mussolini began grinding the Jews, to please his fellow dictator, Adolf Hitler. As a Jew, Pontecorvo saw his future foreclosed in his native country. Through friends, he wrangled a government fellowship in 1936 for study with Prof. Frédéric Joliot-Curie, the Communist physicist in Paris. The fellowship was renewed for a second year, and a third, with financial help from French sources. During this period, Pontecorvo ran with a mixed international set of Leftists and anti-Fascists who vied to see who could hurl the worst insults at Hitler and Mussolini. When hostilities began, the Communists in this group turned lukewarm to the war effort, or actually sabotaged French defense. Those young scientists who had firmly replaced the paternal picture in their minds with Stalin, and had substituted Stalinism for their original religion, found at hand plausible explanations for the deceptive tactics of the Party. They were instructed to continue their scientific education elsewhere, in whatever way they or the Party could arrange, in preparation for the day when they would assume Soviet scientific leadership in their native country.

While in Paris, Pontecorvo met and married a Swedish girl named Mariana Nordblom, and had a boy named Gil by her. When the Nazi troops neared Paris, in June, 1940, the Pontecorvos left by bicycle for Bordeaux, taking turns carrying their two-year-old son in baskets attached to their machines. Early the next year, the family moved to the United States. The Italian scientist's first job in America was radiographic oil well logging for the Wells Survey Inc., in Tulsa, Oklahoma. It was characteristic of the man's technical competence that he soon developed an improved method of doing the work.

Pontecorvo decided to become an American citizen. He took out first papers, and to protect his standing, continued to pay taxes to the United States Internal Revenue Bureau after moving to Canada.

In the fall of 1942, Pontecorvo received an offer, which he promptly accepted, to join the contingent of British nuclear physicists heading for the United States to take part in a tremendous allied research problem of military significance. According to Canadian sources, he was recommended initially by American scientists for a role in this joint effort. He worked briefly in New York, then shifted to Montreal, as part of the Anglo-American-British atomic team being formed under Dr. H. H. Halban.

Allan Nunn May arrived in Canada early in 1943, and became friendly, though not ostentatiously so, with Pontecorvo. They were both members of the British group of scientists which visited the Metallurgical Project in Chicago for secret talks with United States physicists in January, 1944. Subsequently Pontecorvo concentrated on experiments for setting up the Canadian heavy-water atomic pile at the Chalk River plant near Petawawa, Ontario.

This Chalk River plant was the one which aroused such intense interest in Colonel Zabotin and the other spies operating out of the Soviet embassy in Ottawa during the war. It still houses the reactor of most advanced design and performance in North America. The Pontecorvos moved to Chalk River in 1944 to be close to the work, and he made important nuclear contributions there.

From 1943 to 1949, Pontecorvo traveled regularly to scientific gatherings in Canada and the United States. In addition to his secret work at Chalk River, which could not be discussed, he made a specialty of cosmic rays, the great Russian wartime field of exploration. Since cosmic rays—particles which bomb the earth from somewhere in outer space with energy factors thousands of times greater than man has been able to produce artificially—were unclassified, Pontecorvo could, and would, if encouraged, talk about them at length. In this field alone, he could certainly have been of great help to Russia. More importantly, his latest studies at Chalk River involved ultra-secret work on tritium, a substance intimately related to the hydrogen bomb.

The Atom Spies

Despite his earlier European record, and some hints of Communist party agitation in Oklahoma, no substantial suspicion seems to have caught up with Pontecorvo during the war. He didn't look like a spy, any more than Selzinger, who furnished the Russians with a daily, up-to-date report on the line-up of the Nazi armies in the East during World War II, or Judy Coplon, the little Brooklyn girl who provided the Soviet with tips on the United States exposure of Russian spies in the postwar period so they could be replaced with minimum damage to the apparatus. What successful spy ever did look like a spy, for that matter?

Pontecorvo did not act secretively. He and his wife (who seems to have been nonpolitical) acquired two more sons during this period: Tito (named after the Yugoslav partisan leader) in 1944, and Antonio, in 1945. Unlike May and Fuchs, those gentle bachelors, Pontecorvo was a good family man and a fond father. Unlike May and Fuchs, who were socially reserved and shy, Pontecorvo reveled in social affairs, hearty laughter, and outdoor exercise. Acquaintances from this period recall no hint of Communism in his reading, talk, or behavior.

Bruno Pontecorvo may have still hoped to become an American citizen. Early in 1946, he visited the General Electric plant in Schenectady, looking for a job, without success. He returned to Canada to his old job at Chalk River, which had been taken over by the British Ministry of Supply, Atomic Energy Division. In 1948, Pontecorvo visited the University of California Radiation Laboratory, which still maintained a key atomic role, as may be judged from a significant paragraph in a publicity release that year from England on the building of a cyclotron at Harwell:

> The machine will permit the breaking-up of the nuclei of most atoms, and will also provide new types of nuclei which even the piles cannot produce. It will also make possible experiments in nuclear physics which can only be carried out at present in one place in the world—in the Radiation Laboratory of the University of California.

Pontecorvo's ostensible purpose for visiting the Radiation Laboratory was to look for a job. If that was his real purpose, he failed to connect.

Later in 1948, the Italian refugee scientist received British citizenship in absentia for his valuable war work. Early the following year he crossed to England to take a $5,500-a-year job as a senior principal scientific officer in the nuclear physics division at Harwell, a notch higher in rank and pay than Fuchs ever achieved. He and Fuchs became acquainted, inevitably, but they were not particularly close friends.

In June, 1950, Pontecorvo agreed to accept a professorship of experimental physics at Liverpool University starting January, 1951. Deputy Director Skinner of the Harwell installation was going to Liverpool to expand its scientific program, and he was looking for brilliant assistants. Pontecorvo's professional qualifications, particularly in cosmic rays, could not be denied. He declared, and nobody then doubted his sincerity, that he was accepting the job because it promised a wider research opportunity, rather than because of the improved status, and salary.

If Pontecorvo had any dream of eventual wealth at this time it was probably anchored to America, where a patent had been applied for in 1935 on behalf of the six University of Rome scientists, including Fermi and himself, who had written the famous paper on neutron-bombardment. In 1940, United States Patent No. 2,206,634 was granted to the scientific sextet. A later suit in their names for $10,000,000 against the United States government for infringing on the patent during and after the war—which if successful would have netted Pontecorvo at least $1,500,000— was pending when he disappeared behind the Iron Curtain.

Many aspects of the Pontecorvo disappearance were puzzling. If he were under any suspicion at all, why was he allowed out of the country? Apparently the answer was that, short of arrest, the British did not then restrict the international movement of their citizens. Supply Minister Strauss, during a House of Commons debate in October, 1950, hinted that a tightening-up of security rules at Harwell had played a role in Pontecorvo's decision to go to Liverpool. "As he was the holder of a British passport," added Strauss, in relation to Pontecorvo's Continental trip, "there was no means of retaining him in this country."

Were the Pontecorvos under surveillance by the British in Europe? The delay in learning what happened to him suggested the contrary. Certainly there was nothing harried, or hurried, about the way the Pontecorvos took their own car from England to France, and drove south through France to Italy for a visit, as it turned out, to one of Bruno's sisters, who had married an important Communist official in Italy. Emilio Sereni, a member of the Italian Politburo, was a cousin of Bruno Pontecorvo, it developed later. At least one of Bruno's brothers was said to be an Italian Communist of some standing. Friends of the family insisted that the parents, Bruno's brother Guido, a professor in eugenics at Edinburgh University in Scotland, and another brother, unnamed, doing radar work in the United States, were not associated with the Party.

After he reached his decision at Lake Como, Bruno Pontecorvo began accumulating luggage. He had been traveling light, but by the time he started north he had twelve suitcases. Did these contain scientific material accumulated with an eye toward a possible, eventual migration?

To cover his escape, Pontecorvo wrote a letter to Harwell on August 31, the last day of his leave, explaining that he had trouble with his car, which was true enough, but that he hoped to be back in time, which was apparently untrue, for an important mid-September scientific conference in England. Simultaneously a letter went to him from Harwell suggesting that he attend an important European conference on cosmic rays in Switzerland, on the way home. If this were designed to suggest continued confidence, to put him off his guard, like the promotion of Klaus Fuchs after he fell under suspicion, it failed in its purpose. That same day, the Pontecorvos started on the road to Russia. Because of uncertainty about the scientist's plans, embodied in these cross-communications, no inquiries about his movements were initiated by the Harwell authorities until September 21. By then, the Pontecorvo family had been in Russia at least two weeks.

Abandoning his ailing auto, Pontecorvo took his wife and three boys, on the regular passenger plane from Rome to Copenhagen, on August 31. They left the plane there, "for fear of being followed," and traveled by express train to Stockholm. The night of September 1 they stayed at the Soviet Embassy in Stockholm. Next morning, they did not visit, or even phone, Mr. and Mrs. Hans Nordblom, Mrs. Pontecorvo's parents, living nearby in Stockholm. At 11 A.M., they arrived in a Soviet Embassy car at the Bromma Airport, Stockholm, with all their bulging suitcases. During the plane trip to Helsinki, their youngest boy, Antonio, told one of the other passengers, "We are going to Russia." Later the boy noticed land under the plane, and asked, "Is that Russia?"

Bruno Pontecorvo chatted with Finland's Interior Minister, Johannes Virulainen, during the plane trip to Helsinki, and upon arrival, handed Virulainen his British passport, saying he had no further use for it. Mrs. Virulainen noticed Mrs. Pontecorvo because the latter was "conspicuously nervous, pale, and haggard," she said. Mrs. Virulainen's recollection was that the Pontecorvos traveled to Helsinki with the other passengers in an air-lines bus. Enrico Altavilla, the Stockholm correspondent of *Il Tempo*, a Rome newspaper who happened also to make the trip, declared that the Pontecorvos did not travel in the air-lines bus, but waited at the airport for a car from the Soviet Legation, which took them and their precious suitcases to the harbor. The Soviet ship *Byelostrov*, scheduled to sail at 10:40 that morning, was waiting with steam up. When the scientist and his family came on board at 5 P.M., the gangplank was immediately raised, lines cast off, and the voyage to Leningrad begun. The *Byelostrov* reached Russia September 5.

When the Pontecorvo story broke in Rome on October 20, a wild orgy of speculation developed. Some experts contended that the scientist had been kidnaped by the Russians. Others asserted he was insane. A few analytical minds deduced that the scientist had been lured to the Soviet by some fake offer, under the illusion that he could serve as an intermediary between the scientists of the West and the scientists of the East. There did not seem to be any supporting evidence for these assorted assertions and beliefs. The stark fact remained that Pontecorvo had followed the standard escape route for British agents of the U.S.S.R., after the circulation of reports that another important atomic spy at Harwell was in jeopardy.

Ostensibly on the basis of Swedish intelligence reports, Victor Riesel, an American labor columnist, declared on April 16, 1951, that Pontecorvo's assignment in Russia was to develop, by June, 1952, an air-defense system based on cosmic rays which would destroy America's ability to deliver atomic or hydrogen bombs. Riesel said Pontecorvo was expected to help in the accelerated production of A-bombs, and to work on a rocket capable of accurate guidance between distant continents.

On September 24, Kenneth de Courcy, editor of the *Intelligence Digest* in London, said the Russians expected to explode an H-bomb under the guidance of Pontecorvo by June, 1952. An earlier deadline of October, 1952, said De Courcy, had been moved up to June by Stalin personally. De Courcy, who did not reveal any particular understanding of atomic energy, said his tips came from anti-Soviet persons behind the Iron Curtain who had access to classified material. He declared Pontecorvo was working at a main Soviet H-bomb research center in the extreme south of Asiatic Russia.

Issa Yusuf Bey Aliptekin, former Secretary General of Sinkiang province in China, declared in Cairo on November 11, 1951, that Pontecorvo was working in a huge atomic stronghold in Sinkiang centering around a new octopus-shaped city at Kualja, not far from Urumchi, the capital. Issa Bey traced his information to refugees from Sinkiang as well as to Soviet broadcasts over Radio Turkestan. Two or three days later, the *China Union Press,* from Taihoku, reported that Wang Wen-Hao, a famed geologist and former National Premier, had joined Pontecorvo in Sinkiang on H-bomb work.

United States scientists were inclined to dismiss the Sinkiang rumors, on two grounds: (1) that the sources did not seem reliable enough, and (2) that atomic energy plants needed connections with sources of supplies and machinery, and well-developed communications, which would not be available in Sinkiang. Riesel's tip was considered more to the point, though no verification of a June, 1952, deadline, or any Soviet deadline, had reached United States atomic leaders.

Toward the end of November, 1951, two newspapers in Rome, *Il Tempo* and *Momento Sera,* quoted unidentified Russian sources in Stockholm to the effect that Bruno Pontecorvo had been jailed in Russia on suspicion of being an American atomic spy. These sensational yarns asserted that Stalin had come to the conclusion that Pontecorvo had been slipping data about the Russian atomic explosions to President Truman. The British did not seem impressed. "It is intriguing," said one Ministry of Supply official in London, "that such news, if true, should have percolated through the Iron Curtain." Reliable Western listening posts in Finland and elsewhere did not seem to have picked up any reports of Pontecorvo's arrest. Furthermore, President Truman's first announcement about a Soviet atomic blast came on September 23, 1949, a full year before Pontecorvo left England. The second and third White House announcements on the subject were dated October 3 and October 29, 1950, which did not allow Pontecorvo much more than a month, after his arrival, to start spying, which seemed silly on the face of it. Toward the end of December, 1951, some slight evidence developed that could be interpreted as suggesting an improved scientific status for Pontecorvo in the Soviet Union, rather than arrest. The Alichanian brothers, who had received a Stalin prize three years previously for discovering varitrons, were repudiated by the leading Soviet scientific journals, according to a dispatch in the *New York Times.* Since Pontecorvo was one of the foreign physicists who had doubted the existence of varitrons, this could have meant a victory for him of a personal sort.

Nothing surpasses spy fiction, of course, and occasionally spy fact. All sorts of elaborations were possible on the basis of the Pontecorvo rumors. In a country like Russia, where officially sponsored suspicion of anybody who had ever been abroad had sharpened almost into mania, and where the ordinary intellectual impatience over restraint was not given any leeway, it was conceivable that Bruno Pontecorvo, despite his past services, could have been arrested on some pretext or other. It was conceivable that Mrs. Pontecorvo had gotten fed up with life in Russia, and wished she were back in England again, only to find, as thousands of others had found before her, that it was easier to get in than to get out of Russia.

All these suppositions did not actually add up to much in the way of fact. Why should the Soviets antagonize Pontecorvo, his wife, or any of the little Pontecorvos? What greater appeal could there be to any scientist than responsibility for a research program as broad as some of the reports suggested? Some American students of espionage wondered whether the stories could involve an effort to force disclosure of Bruno Pontecorvo's whereabouts and activities. If so, they did not succeed. No flaw appeared in the monolithic secrecy imposed by the Kremlin in scientific matters.

8. Ruth and David Greenglass

DAVID GREENGLASS, who usually slept late because he worked nights, was awakened by screams at 11 A.M. on February 14, 1950; his wife Ruth's flannel nightgown had caught fire from the gas heater which furnished the only warmth for their $20-a-month flat. David jumped out of bed and extinguished the flames with his bare hands. His fingers were so deeply burned that they required attention later at the hospital, but he disregarded the pain in his frenzy of concern for his wife, who was six months' pregnant at the time. Ruth was rushed in an ambulance to Gouverneur Hospital. Her critical condition required transfusions, but her blood proved to be a rare type difficult to secure. The Red Cross broadcast an immediate emergency appeal for O-negative plasma. The boldface front-page box carried that day by the *New York Post* read: "Donors should call Red Cross at Murray Hill 9-1000. Blood may be given at 70 W. 50th St. and 57 Willoughby St., Brooklyn." It never fails in a big city; any cry for help that is sufficiently publicized arouses a response. Volunteers provided the necessary O-negative plasma to give Mrs. Greenglass the strength to survive.

David Greenglass told reporters excitedly that he had been trying for years to escape from the lower East Side of New York, to get away from just such fire hazards. Whenever he located a centrally heated apartment within his means in another section of town, he said, some emergency would wipe out his slender cash reserve, and whenever he had cash, apartments became elusive. Once he appealed to a public-housing development, he said, only to be turned down because he already had housing, of a sort.

As soon as her name was removed from the critical list, Ruth Greenglass expressed a wild desire to leave the hospital. She worried constantly over her three-year-old son Stephen at home, she said. In a high fever, she cried out to a nurse that David might not wait. Doctors explained that her sister, Mrs. Dorothy Abel, was already taking care of the boy, as well as David, but only a personal visit from her husband quieted her down.

Neither of the Greenglasses revealed the core of their restlessness, or hinted at the kind of escape which was churning in their minds. Things had been happening too quickly for them. Within four days, they had learned of the Klaus Fuchs arraignment in London, they had been visited by the FBI, and they had received Stalinist instructions for flight via Mexico and Switzerland to Russia.

The newspaper stories about Fuchs on November 10 had listed only four overt acts of treason, in New York, Boston, Berkshire, and Birmingham (the latter two locations in England), although speculation focused naturally on Los Alamos, where the scientist had worked for two years during the war.

Greenglass, though he was not one of his contacts, could tell from the newspaper stories that Fuchs had been in the same net which had involved him as a wartime sergeant machinist at one of the three technical area shops in Los Alamos where the atom bomb was finally fashioned.

The FBI agent phoned at eleven in the morning. He wanted to talk to David Greenglass. Ruth took the call, but David caught the sharp edge of concern in her voice through his sleep, woke up, and insisted on inviting the man around. They were finishing breakfast when the agent arrived. He was a very polite man who apologized for bothering them and found some kind words to say about little Stephen. Eventually he got around to Los Alamos.

With a steady hand, David offered the visitor a cup of coffee. The Fuchs case, he suggested. The FBI man congratulated Mrs. Greenglass on her coffee. Sergeant Greenglass must have known Dr. Fuchs out there, he said. Greenglass replied that he had known Fuchs as the name of one of the British scientists, that was about all. He had no idea, he said, who were Fuchs's associates. He remembered nobody taking samples of uranium as curios, or for any other purpose. After some polite questions about scientists whom Greenglass did remember, and some oblique talk about security rules, the agent took his leave; the entire visit had lasted less than an hour.

"I was pretty well on the verge of telling him something," said David Greenglass, abruptly, to his wife, as they talked it over.

"I wish you had," she replied.

David Greenglass had poor luck sleeping that week. Then one morning, he was waked up peremptorily, and without apology, by Julius Rosenberg, who insisted that David dress and go for a walk with him in nearby Hamilton Fish Park. Ruth was furious at the implication that she could not be trusted with Julius' secret, and she insisted on breakfast for David before letting him out of the house. Rosenberg had been immediately informed of the FBI visit, and he had consulted his local Soviet superiors. As Greenglass' superior in espionage, as well as the husband of David's older sister, Ethel, who had led David around by the nose since he was a boy, Rosenberg thought he had the right to speak with the voice of family and Party authority.

"You remember that man who came to see you in Albuquerque," he said, as soon as they reached the little park. "Well, Fuchs was also one of his contacts. Now Fuchs is talking. He will lead to the man you know. That man will be arrested soon, and he will lead to you. The FBI visit doesn't mean anything, but this other business means you will have to leave the country. There's no other way. Think it over, and we will make plans."

Greenglass grumbled about installments coming due on furniture and other things. "I wouldn't want to leave without a clear head," he said. "I would need money to pay those debts."

Rosenberg brushed the objection aside. "You don't have to worry what will happen after you leave," he said. "The main thing is to get going."

"I will worry about it," insisted Greenglass. Finally Rosenberg gave in; he would secure money for the debts from the Russians, he said.

"I wouldn't be able to go," said Greenglass. "I wouldn't dare go to the Consulate and ask for a passport."

"Oh, they let people out more important than you. They let Joel Barr out in 1947, and he was a member of our group."

Joel Barr had been a classmate of Rosenberg at City College. For years he and his roommate, Alfred Saurent, had used their Greenwich Village quarters as a sort of social center for a loosely defined Communist group, with guitar playing, folk singing, dancing, drinking, and some love-making.

"Barr had an excuse for going," noted Greenglass. "He was going to study music in Belgium."

"He's in Sweden now," said Rosenberg. "You argue too much, Dave. You'll just have to leave."

Greenglass got an inspiration. "Why doesn't this other guy, the one that came to me in Albuquerque, why doesn't he leave?"

Rosenberg replied, "Well, that's something else again," implying, perhaps, that Harry Gold had already been requested to leave, but had refused. On that note, Rosenberg and Greenglass parted.

As her husband expected, Ruth Greenglass was upset over the news. She had never liked the excessive, domineering role played by Julius Rosenberg in their affairs. She was about to have another child. Traveling furtively to an unannounced destination, probably Russia, in a pregnant condition, did not appeal to her.

As a result of her wartime taste of sunshine in Albuquerque, Ruth Greenglass knew precisely where she wanted to live: anywhere in the Southwest that David could secure a decent job. She did not want to go to Russia. Nevertheless, David was the boss, and David seemed reluctantly reconciled to the idea that if Julius Rosenberg said it was necessary for them to leave, it was necessary. Out of Ruth's partly suppressed mental turmoil came her careless movement near the gas heater the following morning which nearly caused her death.

Ruth Greenglass remained in Gouverneur Hospital until mid-April. She lost fifteen pounds, and her burns healed slowly. David Greenglass kept assuring her that under no circumstances, no matter how slowly she recovered, would he go anywhere without her. Underground reports meanwhile were filtering in from England, to the effect that Klaus Fuchs had been vague in identifying his contacts. This eased up the pressure; by mutual consent, talk about escape was dropped.

Shortly after Ruth returned to the Rivington Street apartment, Julius Rosenberg visited the Greenglasses again, more tense and businesslike than ever. They must leave the country as soon as possible, he said. They would go to Mexico, and from Mexico to Czechoslovakia by way of Switzerland or Sweden, and from Czechoslovakia to Russia. Ruth Greenglass, by then eight months' pregnant, had made up her mind to one thing in the hospital. She was not going to run away until her child was born. She told Rosenberg so flatly. He shrugged his shoulders. He would get the necessary information for departure. They might have to leave any day, he said coldly.

On May 16, Ruth Greenglass gave birth at Beth Israel Hospital to a daughter whom they named Barbara. After six days, she brought the baby home. Two days afterward, Julius Rosenberg burst into the apartment clutching a copy of the *Herald Tribune*. "This is the man who came to you in Albuquerque," he said, showing a large front-page photo of Harry Gold.

Ruth and David were doubtful of the identification. "You can take my word for it," said Rosenberg. "This is the man. You will be picked up next. The next arrest will take place between June 12 and June 16, so you have to get out of the country before then."

"We can't go anywhere," said Ruth. "We have an eight-day-old infant."

"Your baby won't die," said Julius Rosenberg, scornfully. "Babies are born on the ocean and on trains every day. My doctor says if you take enough canned milk and boil the water, the baby will be all right." He handed David $1,000 in bills of small denomination. "Buy everything you need," he said, "but don't be too obvious in your spending. You have a month to spend it in, and I will bring you more. Leave all your household effects. Just take your clothing and what you need for the children, and leave."

Rosenberg then turned to Ruth Greenglass. "Can you get a certificate from your doctor stating that you have been inoculated against smallpox?"

"I wouldn't think of asking the doctor for a false statement," she replied, stoutly.

"That is all right. I will take care of it." Rosenberg was being understanding. "My doctor will give it to me. You and I better take a walk, David. We have to go over the escape plan."

They walked down Delancey Street, then along the East River Drive. "First you go to the border," said Rosenberg. "You don't bother with the Consulate here. You wait until you reach the Mexican border to ask for a tourist card. To get it, you need a letter from your doctor saying you have been inoculated for smallpox or you will have to be inoculated there. I've been to see a doctor and he told me all about it. Next, you need passport pictures of the family, five sets of them, for use by the apparatus during the trip to Russia. You will give me the pictures. Now listen carefully. . . ."

When he reached Mexico City, and found quarters in some place away from the center of town, Greenglass was to write his letter to the Secretary of the Russian Ambassador there. Three days later he was to go at 5 P.M. to the Plaza de Colón, with his fingers stuck into a guidebook, take a stance in front of a statue of Christopher Columbus, and meet a contact who would produce a passport and money for the next stage of the trip.

"I have to leave the country, too," said Rosenberg, after Greenglass memorized the instructions. "I knew Jacob Golos, this man Golos you read about, and Elizabeth Bentley." He seemed depressed at the prospect of exile. Pulling himself together, he stressed that the passport photos must show David alone, Ruth alone, David with the children, Ruth with the children, and David with Ruth, in other words, five copies of each of five poses. He had gotten a lawyer, Rosenberg added, just in case the FBI pounced before he could get away, and he suggested Greenglass do the same.

David Greenglass turned over the $1,000, as he turned over all his money, to his wife. She paid off all the installments on the furniture, all the installments on a typewriter, and a National City Bank loan. She returned some money to a neighbor and cleaned up some small household bills. The remaining $500 was put in an account at the Manhattan Trust Co. Mrs. Greenglass wanted to use the money as a down payment on a cottage in the Catskills for the summer, so they could have one final vacation together before anything drastic happened. David Greenglass bit his lips to keep from crying. He was afraid they would have to go to Mexico, he said.

The following Sunday was a beautiful day. For the first time, baby Barbara left the apartment and learned about the street. The whole family, dressed in their best, went to a photographic shop at the corner of Clinton and Delancey Streets, near the Apollo Theatre, for the passport pictures. David had six sets of five poses taken, since he decided to save one set for himself. On Memorial Day Julius Rosenberg came around to collect the pictures. The Greenglasses had visitors, so he refused to come in. He took the photos in the hallway, whispered that more money would be available soon.

Early in the morning of June 4, Julius Rosenberg arrived at the

The Atom Spies

Greenglass apartment, before David was awake, and put a manila paper package of $10 and $20 bills, totaling $4,000, on the mantelpiece in the bedroom. He told David to get dressed for a walk so they could run through a final rehearsal of escape instructions. Sleepy and truculent, David did as he was told, and left the apartment without waiting for coffee.

On the way down Columbia Street to Delancey, David Greenglass saw Herman and Diane Einsohn approaching. Julius wanted to ignore them, but David shook off his hand, saying, "I can't do that. They're friends of mine. They would wonder why I walked by without saying anything." Diane and Herman were friendly. "I owe you $40," she said and insisted on making out the check on the spot. That raised the total of money being carried by Greenglass to $4,040.

Julius Rosenberg had slipped across the street to avoid the encounter, and he was frowning and jittery when David caught up with him. He kept glancing over his shoulder as if he were trying to establish whether he was being followed. On the way home, after leaving Rosenberg, Greenglass also acquired a sense of being watched.

By the time he reached the top of the five flights of stairs leading to his apartment, the feeling of panic was strong in David Greenglass. He rushed to the bathroom to flush the package of money from Rosenberg down the toilet. "It's dirty money," he said. "It's dirty!" Ruth cried and held on to his arm. "It isn't the money, it's us," she said. "You can't destroy value like that. It would be sacrilegious." David quieted down and agreed to put the package of money, for the time being, in the fireplace chimney. Later Ruth persuaded him to carry it to the home of Louis Abel, her sister's husband, with instructions that Louis keep it for their use, or use as much as he needed for himself, in an emergency. Louis hid the money in a hollow hassock in his living room, pasting up the opening after the insertion.

Julius made one final visit. He was pale and trembling. His

first question was: had they been followed? By this time, David Greenglass was convinced he was under surveillance. "I knew it, I knew it!" said Rosenberg. He himself had been on a visit to upstate New York, and he had intended to see somebody in Cleveland until he decided it was too risky.

"We'll all have to leave sooner than expected," said Rosenberg, in a shaky voice. "They're closing in on us."

Ruth stared at him. "Are you going?" she said.

"I'm going, but not at the same time as you," Rosenberg replied. "I'll meet you in Mexico."

"What does Ethel think of that idea?"

"She doesn't like the idea," Rosenberg said in a more normal tone, "but she realizes it is necessary. I was going to bring you an additional $2,000, but I was being followed and I didn't want to take a chance."

Ruth exchanged a look with her husband. "We're not going," she said, quietly.

David, just as quietly, backed her up. "We're staying here," he said.

At first Julius Rosenberg refused to believe that he had heard correctly. Then he lashed out in all directions. After enduring the insults for a while, David made for his brother-in-law, who dodged into the hallway.

"You're agitated," shouted Rosenberg from the stairs. "You're not yourself, David. I'm going now, I have some work to do. Take a cold shower, David, and think it over. We'll talk about it later."

They didn't talk about it later. They didn't meet again until they faced each other in court. Ruth developed a high fever from an infection in tissues which had been horribly burned; once again she had to be rushed to a hospital. David got time off from his job in order to care for the children. When four FBI men walked into the flat on June 15, the chunky young machinist smiled at them and asked them to sit down. "I'll talk to you just as soon as I finish the baby's formula," he said.

2

The original espionage lure held out to David Greenglass was the privilege of sleeping with his wife in wartime. This puts it rather crudely, since David and Ruth were as close psychologically as physically, but it states the basic fact. These two were lovers, and companions; they had known each other since they were kids of ten or eleven playing on the same city block, and they had rarely quarreled. David never actually proposed; it was taken for granted between them that they would get married as soon as it proved feasible. He was twenty, and she eighteen, when they slipped off to City Hall for the ceremony on November 29, 1942. David's mother went with them to get the license, since he was still under age.

Even before his marriage, David had been trying to get into uniform. He took tests for the Navy four or five times, unsuccessfully, because he was color-blind. Four months after the marriage, he was drafted. The Army gave him basic training at the Aberdeen ordnance school, and then for a year shifted him about from one Army post to another inside the United States. In July, 1944, Greenglass reached Oak Ridge. After a Manhattan District Project orientation course, including security lectures, he was sent in August to Los Alamos, New Mexico, and assigned as a shop machinist to Dr. George Kistiakowsky, a thermodynamics expert from Harvard University. For the next year and a half, Greenglass worked on the atom bomb.

Ruth Greenglass had been trying to keep in personal touch with her husband, so far as it was possible. In the late fall of 1943, she followed him out to the West Coast, to celebrate their first wedding anniversary, at the Pomona Air Base in California. Instead of returning immediately to New York, she visited the State Unemployment Commission on an impulse, and managed to secure a job as a file clerk with the nearby Joshua Handy Hemp Works. Ruth Greenglass rented an apartment near the air base, and David secured permission to live with her there for a couple of months, until he was transferred to Mississippi. Mississippi sounded rather formidable for a working wife, so Mrs. Greenglass went back to New York for a while.

During the first period of David's employment at Los Alamos, wives were not permitted visits. They were not told the nature of the work, or the site. Mail had to be addressed to P.O. Box 1663, Santa Fe, New Mexico. Incoming and outgoing letters were censored. Regulations relaxed somewhat after a while, so that wives could live in nearby towns like Santa Fe and Albuquerque, if they could arrange it, which was not always easy, because of the scarcity of adequately paid jobs for women.

In the fall of 1944, Ruth Greenglass began saving her pennies for a second wedding-anniversary trip. David confidently applied for time off to meet her in Albuquerque. Then one of the family emergencies which seem periodically to hit lower East Side families with a narrow economic margin wiped out the nest-egg. Ruth refused to acknowledge defeat but she was in an unhappy frame of mind when she accepted a dinner invitation from Julius and Ethel Rosenberg one evening in mid-November.

After the meal was over, Ethel Rosenberg led indirectly into the reason for the dinner invitation by calling attention to the fact that she and her husband had not been involved in Communist activities for some time. "You may have noticed, Ruthie," she said, "that we don't buy the *Daily Worker* at the usual newsstands, or attend meetings. The reason is that Julius has succeeded in doing what he wanted to do all along."

Julius cleared his throat. "For two years," he said, "I tried to get in touch with the people who would assist me to be able to help more directly than as a Party member."

While Ruth Greenglass wondered where all this was leading, Julius Rosenberg sprang his revelation. "My friends tell me," he said, "that David is working on an atom bomb."

"I didn't know that," said Ruth. "All I know is it's a top secret." Ethel joined her husband in a smile over Ruth's ignorance.

"It's an atom bomb," repeated Julius, "the most destructive weapon so far. It has dangerous radiation effects. The United States and Britain are working on this jointly, and refusing to share the information which should go to Russia as an ally. If all the nations have the information, then one nation can't use the bomb as a threat against another. I know David will help get me the information I need, if you tell him about it."

Ruth Greenglass had doubts. The people in charge of the bomb, she argued, ought to know best about sharing information. "I don't think it is a good idea," she said.

With an expression combining positiveness and patience, Ethel Rosenberg took charge of the argument. "I'm his older sister," she said, "and I think it's right for David. He'll want to help. The least you can do is give him a chance to make up his mind. You're going out there anyway, and Julius has put aside $150 for your trip. Just give David the message from Julius and let him decide for himself. You don't have to worry about the money. We both want you to have it. No matter how David decides, he'll have the pleasure of seeing you, and you'll have the pleasure of seeing him."

Before she left by train, Ruth Greenglass received final instructions from Julius Rosenberg as to the things to ask David: a physical description of the project, approximate number of employees, names of some of the scientists, camouflage of the site, security measures, and the distances and routes from Los Alamos to Santa Fe and Albuquerque.

"David must be very circumspect," warned Julius. "Tell him not to carry on any political conversations, not to take any papers or sketches or blueprints, not to be obvious in seeking information. It will be enough if he tells you what he keeps in his mind."

Ruth Greenglass reached Albuquerque one day before the wedding anniversary. She registered at the Hotel Franciscan. That evening David arrived by bus from Los Alamos, on a three-day pass plus a two-day week end. They enjoyed ideal weather.

Ruth and David Greenglass

They were so happy together that Ruth did not bring up Julius' message until the fourth day, when they had walked out beyond the city on Route 66, almost to the Rio Grande.

Until his wife told him, Greenglass had not realized he was working on an atom bomb. The relayed revelation carried conviction, because it fitted the stray facts and hints already in his possession. Rosenberg's proposition frightened him. "I don't like it," he said. "I won't do it."

She said, "I didn't want even to tell you about it, but Ethel kept saying Russia was our ally and was not getting the information due her, and you would want to help."

Greenglass reassured her. "It's all right, Ruth," he said. "It's all right. Don't worry about it."

During the walk back to town, they tried to avoid the subject, to recover if possible the magic of the anniversary celebration, but Ruth burst into tears in the midst of a song, after David remarked fondly that she sang "like a dead cat." When he apologized abjectly for the familiar comment, to which she had never previously objected, she said she wasn't thinking of her singing at all. "I was thinking of the dangerous radiation effects Julius was telling me about," she cried. "I don't want you to be hurt." When he figured out what she meant, David assured her that he worked in complete safety.

That evening David asked his wife abruptly whether the Rosenbergs had given her anything. Ruth told about the $150.

"Why did you take all that money?" he demanded.

Ruth tried to keep herself under control. "Julius is my relative," she said. "He said, 'Go to Albuquerque, and I am giving you this to meet your expenses,' and I accepted in the same light."

David shook his head. "But you had money of your own?"

Ruth explained the family emergency which had wiped out her savings.

"But this money from Julie, this $150, is it a loan or a gift, that's what I want to know," David said.

Ruth burst into tears. "I don't know," she cried. "I don't know!

211

He didn't say. I took it because there was no other way to come out and see you."

Ruth became so upset that David finally had to take her in his arms to soothe her. Next morning, he announced he had changed his mind. He had been thinking over what Julius and Ethel said about Russia being an ally, he said, and he was going to help them after all. "Are you going to write this down?" Ruth replied that Julius had told her to memorize it. "All right," said David, "now listen carefully. I'll repeat anything you don't get. Los Alamos was formerly a riding academy. It is 110 miles from here, and about 40 miles from Santa Fe by a very winding road. By airplane it would be 25 miles from Santa Fe, but no airplanes are allowed to fly near Los Alamos. Because of a hill, you can hardly see the project until you are on top of it. There is barbed wire, and guards at the entrance at all times, and everybody is checked going in and out. Badges come in three colors. . . ."

David Greenglass went from question to question, winding up with the names of scientists. He mentioned Dr. Oppenheimer, Dr. Urey, Dr. Kistiakowsky. Niels Bohr—N-i-e-l-s B-o-h-r—the Danish scientist, was there. He was called Nicholas Baker to keep his presence secret. Other famous scientists used fake names. In each case, they kept the same initials for the fake name as for their real name.

Before parting with his wife, David Greenglass mentioned that he expected a fifteen-day furlough, plus travel time of six or seven days, around Christmas. He told Ruth to pass along the news to Julius. Actually, Greenglass did not reach New York until New Year's Day. Two or three days later, Rosenberg came around to the Greenglass apartment on Stanton Street, avid for information about the atom bomb. Greenglass said he was working as a machinist on various high explosive lens molds. He agreed to make some sketches of the lens molds, and describe how they were used in experiments. He had a few more names of scientists, he said, including Dr. Hans Bethe, head of the theoretical physics division. Rosenberg asked for a list of "possible recruits for Soviet espionage." Greenglass said he would have to think that over, but he would include such a list with the rest of the material. He finished his report that evening and brought it around to Rosenberg in the morning. He and Ruth were thereupon invited to dinner at the Rosenbergs several days later. The Rosenbergs lived in a comparatively modern, $47-a-month apartment on the eleventh floor at Knickerbocker Village, a private housing development of the sort that had begun to replace some of the decayed areas in the lower East Side. Dinner there classed as a social occasion, because Ethel was a shrewd hostess, with a good sense of timing, though things usually revolved around some more or less veiled bit of political business.

When the Greenglasses arrived on this occasion, they were introduced with a little flurry to a woman named Ann Sidorovich. Ann and her husband Mike had known Julius Rosenberg since high-school days, and had been active with him and Ethel in the Federation of Artists, Engineers, Chemists and Technicians. For a year, the Sidoroviches had lived in the Knickerbocker Village apartment directly below the Rosenbergs. Then they had moved to Chappaqua for a year, and on one occasion the Rosenbergs had visited them for a month or so in Chappaqua. The Sidoroviches had recently moved to Cleveland.

All this personal history emerged rather clumsily from conversation. Mrs. Sidorovich said little, and she didn't stay for dinner. "I just wanted you to meet Ann, and know about her," whispered Ethel to Ruth after the mysterious guest left. "You'll see her again in New Mexico."

Julius Rosenberg came over in an expansive mood. "How would you like to go to Albuquerque, not for another visit, but to live there?" he asked.

"I would be happy to be near David," said Ruth.

Julius beamed. "You are going to go there," he announced. Ruth Greenglass mentioned that she had just lost her job in New York. How was she going to manage to live until David found a place for her in Albuquerque?

"Don't worry about that," said Julius. "I'll take care of expenses. Money is no object. The important thing is for you to go to Albuquerque where David can visit you week ends. Any money I give you is a gift. I'm getting it from my—er—friends, so there is no question of returning it."

During the meal, David Greenglass repeated an early, and generally ignored remark to the effect that he had never met Mrs. Sidorovich before, but he did have some acquaintance with Mike Sidorovich, and considered him a nice fellow. Julius said Mrs. Sidorovich would probably be the one to contact them for information. Did Mike know what Ann was doing, asked Ruth.

Ethel replied quickly, "No, no, he has no idea. He wouldn't approve. If Dave meets Mike again, he must be careful not to mention Ann in any way."

The actual rendezvous would be handled through Ruth, Rosenberg explained. She would travel to Denver from Albuquerque, and meet Mrs. Sidorovich or somebody else. The two women would go to a movie together, and in the darkness of the theater would exchange purses, so Mrs. Sidorovich, or whoever else it was, could acquire the Greenglass purse with its atomic information. Rosenberg asked Ruth how she liked the plan? "Isn't it a little complicated?" she replied, doubtfully. Rosenberg said it was complicated, but it would work.

In case Mrs. Sidorovich did not come, Rosenberg said after the meal, they needed an alternative plan to identify her substitute. He drew Ruth into the kitchen, with Ethel tagging along. Relaxed and well-fed in an overstuffed chair, Technical Corporal Greenglass, a military man on leave, stayed put in the living room. A few minutes later, Julius emerged triumphantly from the kitchen. He was holding up a jaggedly-cut side of a box of Jello (raspberry flavor). Ruth held up the other half to show how it matched.

"Oh, that is very clever," said Greenglass, nodding approvingly.

Rosenberg acknowledged the compliment. "The simplest things

are the cleverest," he said. After a pause, he suggested that the rendezvous might be arranged for Albuquerque itself.

As a meeting place, Greenglass suggested the Safeway store in Albuquerque, not inside the store, which might be too crowded, but just outside, on the sidewalk. Rosenberg said that was a clever idea. The two amateur spies smiled at each other in mutual appreciation of their common cleverness.

Ruth moaned. She was afraid she was going to be lonely in Albuquerque, she said. "You will make friends," Ethel assured her. Julius noted she would probably take a job to earn money, and get acquainted with people. Not that she had to work, he added hastily. She would be able to go out there, and live out there. If for any reason she was unable to work, the money would be forthcoming, he repeated, from his friends.

Ruth said Ethel looked a little tired, and Ethel replied gaily that if she did, it was from typing out those notes in Dave's awful handwriting. She typed all Julius' espionage reports, she said. "Julius is tired, too," she said. "He runs around a good deal. He has to spend time with his friends. Sometimes it costs him as much as $50 to $75 a night to entertain his friends."

One of Greenglass' sketches had showed a four-leaf clover mold, with a hollow center. The high explosive was poured in, and took the shape of the mold. When the mold was removed, a high explosive lens remained. Rosenberg had apparently studied the sketch carefully because he discussed it, and the general principles of detonating an atom bomb, in considerable detail. He volunteered his own general conception of the bomb, and wound up by arranging a meeting between Greenglass and a Soviet expert in this field.

The meeting, which took place several days later, contained a measure of humiliation for Greenglass. He took his father-in-law's car around 11:30 in the evening and drove up First Avenue to a block somewhere north of Forty-second Street where a corner saloon provided the only light in the darkness. He parked the car up the block and waited. In a few minutes, Julius rounded the corner, looked into the car and said, "Wait, I'll be right back." He returned with a stocky man whom he introduced by a common first name. The man got in alongside Greenglass, who drove off, leaving Rosenberg at the curb. "Just keep driving around," said the Russian, "while we talk." Immediately he began with a barrage of questions about the type of high explosive used in the lenses, the formula of the curve of the lens, and the means of detonation. David Greenglass was a machinist who did quite competently what he was told to do in a shop, but he was not a theoretical physicist. Having no direct knowledge of the matters involved, he could not produce positive answers. In less than twenty minutes, the ride was over. Greenglass delivered his passenger at the same place they had left. Rosenberg was still waiting on the sidewalk. The Russian got out of the car. He said something in a low voice to Rosenberg. "We're going to have a bite together," said Rosenberg to his brother-in-law. "Good night." The pair walked down the sidewalk without any further remarks.

After sitting there a minute, David Greenglass drove home and told his wife about his adventure. Ruth was disturbed. "Aren't we mixing in things that are too big for us, that are beyond our reach?" she said. Greenglass shook his head. "I've gone so far," he said, "and I will go on with it." He left New York for Los Alamos on January 20, and late the next month, his wife came out to establish a home for him in Albuquerque.

Before she left New York, Ruth had a final talk with Julius Rosenberg. She was to expect somebody to meet her outside the Safeway store in Albuquerque at 1:30 P.M. on the last Saturday of April, he said. If nobody appeared then, she was to return the following Saturday. Rosenberg instructed her to keep her torn half of the Jello box in her wallet at all times, in case an emergency should arise.

Finding adequate living quarters in wartime Albuquerque was not easy. Ruth Greenglass stayed at the Hotel El Fedel for five days and at another hotel for several days more. She and

David secured the use briefly of an apartment rented by a GI named Delman who had gone east with his wife on a furlough. Next they stayed for a while at another apartment rented by another GI named William Spindel. Finally they located their own place at 209 North High Street. Ruth worried steadily over her impending espionage rendezvous, and to get the feeling of what she must do, she stood outside the Safeway store for a couple of hours one Saturday afternoon. She returned to the apartment and had a miscarriage.

She was quite ill. From the home of a friend, where she was convalescing, she explained to Ethel Rosenberg by mail what had happened. Ethel's bland reply, arriving the first week of May, expressed sympathy over her sickness and promised that a member of the family would be out to visit her late that month, arriving probably on the third or fourth Saturday. In other words, it was the same play, though there had been a change in signals. On the third Saturday, Ruth Greenglass marched up and down like a sentinel outside the Safeway store virtually all afternoon. Several people regarded her with curiosity, but nobody approached with a torn half of a raspberry Jello box.

Disappointment left Ruth in a fearful state of despair. She wasn't ever going to do a thing like that again, she cried, not ever. The following Saturday she agreed to try once more, if David would only come along to give her courage. He agreed; the pair shifted from foot to foot outside the store for a reasonable interval before deciding to leave.

During his week ends in Albuquerque, David Greenglass tried to pattern his behavior on that of his wife, and as a rule, she did not feel conspiratorial. She wanted her husband to relax and laugh and feel that he was loved. None of this program displeased David. At Los Alamos, however, he worked quite consciously to acquire information of the kind that was wanted. Because his curiosity had been stimulated, during the humiliating interview with the Russian, he found he was picking up things which might normally have passed over his head. Taking an opportunity to talk with a mathematician in the theoretical physics department, he managed by sheer interest to capture a pretty general idea of what the lenses were about. On one occasion, the man came to Greenglass with a sketch and a piece of material, and said, "Machine it up, will you, so I will have square corners to lay out a lens?" Greenglass nodded. "What's the idea?" he said, and the man explained the idea, which was his own, willingly and with no intention of fracturing secrecy rules.

By the time Harry Gold appeared at the North High Street apartment early in the morning of the third Sunday in June, David Greenglass had a mind packed with facts about the atom bomb. Since several hours would be required to write up a report, the elusive Gold decided to disappear for a few hours and come back later. The most important part, perhaps, of the material he picked up that afternoon was a series of sketches of a flat-type lens mold, with the detonator on, and the steel tube in the middle which would be exploded by the lens mold. These represented a considerable advance over earlier sketches Greenglass had made.

In September, the Greenglasses took advantage of another furlough to visit New York at a time when the war was ending in an atomic climax. Since they no longer had the Stanton Street apartment they found room in the apartment house of David's mother on Sheriff Street, not far away. Julius Rosenberg came around early on the morning after they arrived. He handed $200 to David, who passed it on to Ruth without comment.

"You remember last January," said David, with more excitement than was usual with him, "you remember how you described an atom bomb with the fissionable material at one end of a tube and at the other end of the tube a sliding member that was also of fissionable material, and how when these two came together under pressure, a nuclear reaction would follow?"

Julius Rosenberg remembered. "What about it?" he said.

"What about it! When I got back there to Los Alamos, and

looked around, I learned you were describing the very bomb we dropped on Hiroshima. How in the world did you know that so soon?"

Rosenberg smoothed his mustache. "I have friends, Davy, I have friends," he said. "You know about my friends. Did you bring me anything?"

It was David's turn to conceal pride. "I think I have a pretty good description of the atom bomb, Julius. Not the Hiroshima bomb, you know about that, but a new type of bomb that works on an implosion effect. I mean the bomb dropped on Nagasaki."

Rosenberg whistled. "Come to the house this afternoon and we'll put it down on paper," he said. "When we get finished, I want to take you over to Sammy's to shoot a little pool. You probably got rusty down there in the Southwest."

The two men were probably more amiable at this moment than they had been for years, or would be again, but Ruth was deeply dissatisfied. When Julius had left, she argued at length with her husband. The papers had come out, she said, and now they knew just how big the thing was. It was too big for them to understand, or handle, alone. She begged David to take the money back to Julius and tell him there would be no more information.

David Greenglass put on his stubborn look. "We're late for breakfast," he said, and they went down to his mother's apartment in the same house. That afternoon, they visited the Rosenberg apartment at Knickerbocker Village. David wrote out his report in longhand, and Ethel copied it, page by page, on her portable typewriter set on a bridge table. Ruth and Julius helped correct David's grammar as they went along. Greenglass also did a few new sketches. "This is very good, Davy," said Julius Rosenberg, in one of the great understatements of history.

3

Indoctrination of David Greenglass began at the age of thirteen, when he was still shooting marbles. His political intensity communicated itself gradually to Ruth Lee Printz, a red-cheeked, blue-eyed girl of eleven who considered him the smartest boy on the block, and one of the smartest at old P.S. 4. The precocious development of these youngsters fed on the weakness of authority which exists in the homes of many immigrants, where parents have difficulty with the language and customs of their adopted country. Even so, others in the Greenglass and Rosenberg families escaped the cramping effects of Communism.

Barnet Greenglass, a machinist from Russia, and his wife Tessie, who was from Austria, reared four children in a small coldwater flat at 64 Sheriff Street, near the geographic center of New York's lower East Side. The children were born in this order: Samuel, 1907; Ethel, 1915; Bernard, 1917; and David, 1922. Samuel became a successful jewelry salesman, though he never finished high school. He moved away from the East Side, and separated himself somewhat from the problems of the others. Ethel and David ensnarled themselves in a ruinous personal, political, and business relationship.

Ethel was an active Stalinist before she reached her twentieth birthday. She was a Third Period zealot who, according to David, held forth about twice a week on the workers' paradise in Russia and the defects of capitalism.

By-passing Bernie, Ethel concentrated on the political development of her thirteen-year-old brother David. Though initially uninterested, he was always courteous. He had an inquiring mind. Noticing his father using black paint on Singer sewing machines being repaired in the Greenglass machine shop, David tried the paint on several electric light bulbs. He was trying to produce "black light," he said, which was not as silly as it sounded to some of his elders. Before he reached high school, David was devising chemistry experiments. One unexpectedly explosive success ruined a fur coat belonging to a visiting cousin. It wasn't such a valuable fur coat, but David never heard the end of it.

David Greenglass was a husky, hard-working, uncomplaining youngster. By the time he reached the Haaren Aviation High School, he was spending week ends regularly as an electrician's helper. He reacted nicely to responsibility; on one occasion, when he was only fifteen, he handled the wiring of an entire house. All his earnings went as a matter of course to his mother. He did not begrudge them. When Mother's Day neared, and he had no cash for a present, he pinch-hit evenings as a soda jerk to raise the money. He and his mother were always very close.

Beginning in 1937, when David was fifteen, Julius Rosenberg became a regular visitor to the Greenglass apartment. Julius was a City College student in science who, among other things, shared Ethel's Communist sympathies.

Young David Greenglass had hazel eyes, wavy hair, an easy smile, and a pleasant disposition. Most people liked him, and Julius Rosenberg proved no exception. To show his liking, Julius used to bring little presents of fruit for David when he visited Ethel. He also left behind him scientific magazines and political pamphlets. David ate up the scientific stuff as avidly, and absent-mindedly, as he munched apples. The political pamphlets he burned in the large stove used for heating the apartment. Ethel caught him at it one evening, and raised an unholy row. David said he had a right to burn his own property, Ethel denied he had any such right, and both appealed to their mother, who made the decisions in the household. Mrs. Tessie Greenglass could not write or read English but she possessed a veneration for the written word. Destruction of printed material seemed immoral to her, so long as one person wanted access to it. As a result, the propaganda piled up around the apartment with an apparent parental imprimatur which it did not really possess. At the age of sixteen, when he was just acquiring some local reputation as a handball player, David Greenglass joined the Young Communist League.

221

Party agitation definitely affected David; for one thing, it diverted his energies into new channels at a critical time. Entering Brooklyn Polytechnic Institute, David cut classes so extensively that he flunked every subject. Later he tried evening courses at Pratt Institute, but union-organizing efforts in the shops where he worked led to frequent changes in jobs. Eventually he landed a night job, which ended the evening courses at Pratt. He secured a comparatively promising job at the age of eighteen with the International Telephone & Telegraph Co., only to lose it during efforts to organize the plant for the United Electrical, Radio and Machine Workers, the largest union ever captured by the Communists in America.

For reasons connected perhaps with the mildness of his nature, David Greenglass showed no particular aptitude as an agitator. By the time he got married, he had given up all but routine Party duties and was working quietly as a machinist at the Peerless Laboratories, Twenty-third Street and Madison Avenue, New York, which were under United Electrical, Radio and Machine Workers of America contract. Right up to the day of his marriage, David's salary went untouched to his mother, who returned $8 a week for his expenses. After marriage he turned over part of his pay to Ruth's family, since her weekly check, as the eldest of four children, was indispensable. When he entered the Army, David made allotments both to his own mother and to Ruth's.

Ruth Printz Greenglass, an intelligent girl who looked sturdier and more sure of herself than she really was, came out of the same milieu as David. Her mother had emigrated from Russia, and her father from Hungary. They were an uncomplaining, nonpolitical hard-working couple. As a little girl, Ruth developed a bad sinus condition, which resulted in violent headaches and frequent nosebleeds. Her parents made efforts to place her, each summer, in one of the camps maintained by settlement houses and other benevolent groups organized to help poor people on the lower East Side. These outdoor vacations in the country only accentuated the contrast between Ruth's apparent robust health and her recurring periods of misery. Ruth finished high school at the early age of sixteen, with a gold-seal or high-average diploma. She paid down the entrance fee at Brooklyn College before she realized she would have to go to work. Her father, who had been a coal miner, a grease monkey, and other things, was working currently in a New York slaughterhouse, at $20 a week, because that was the best job he could find. The family income had to be supplemented somehow.

Ruth's first job, with a small East Side insurance company, paid $8 a week, for some typing, some bookkeeping, and some floor sweeping. Subsequent secretarial positions paid from $20 to $30 a week. After a while Ruth plunged into the same Party whirlpool as David, with the endless round in which employment swirled into agitation and agitation into new employment. She worked for various Communist unions, including Local 65, United Retail and Wholesale Workers, a turbulent catchall outfit whose membership ranged from waterfront warehouse workers to department store sales persons, and the United Office and Professional Workers. During 1943 and 1944, Ruth served as a functionary of the Sperry local of the United Electrical, Radio and Machine Workers of America, whose members were handling defense contracts. All three of these unions—Local 65, the UOPW and the UERMA—were later expelled from the CIO.

Despite their Communist background, David and Ruth seem to have maintained a vestigial political innocence. They were open-Party people by instinct, not conspirators. They didn't look behind the Party slogans at the real Party purposes. They didn't regard Russia with any critical sense. They didn't perceive the total lack of democracy in their movement, but then many fellow travelers took no cognizance of these matters, either. When touched by inner Party activity—through indirect contact with the Russians who operate behind the scenes in the American and every other national Party—David and Ruth got balky. If they stayed so long in harness, it may have been due partly to the difficulty of breaking loose, not only from the Party, but also from David's older sister Ethel and her husband Julius, after accepting orders and favors from them over a period of years.

David's concealed purpose at Los Alamos actually contributed to his advancement. He showed more interest in his work than the half dozen or so loyal machinists in his small shop, and he was punctilious about security rules. When he was required on one occasion to make a complete lens mold, he copied a blueprint for his shop use, but he was careful not to run the gauntlet of the guards at the gate with any such incriminating data. All he removed from Los Alamos was a radio he had made, and a phonograph attachment for it; this was perfectly permissible, and the guards waved him on when he showed the set and attachment. No secrecy rules could prevent a man from taking away details of his work in his mind. While David Greenglass did just that, his supposed faithfulness and reliability resulted in promotion first to assistant foreman and later to foreman. He was honorably discharged from the Army February 28, 1946, at El Paso, Texas, as a technical sergeant. Among the various curios of his military service was a good-conduct medal.

When he first began furnishing information to the Russians, David Greenglass had doubts about it. These doubts increased. During his September, 1945, furlough in New York he mentioned that he could continue at Los Alamos after the war in a civilian capacity if he wished. Ethel had finished typing out David's notes and Julius had burned the original notes in a frying pan and flushed the ashes down the toilet. Everybody was relaxing, but the effect of this announcement was electric. Julius implored David to take the civilian job, since it would provide him a continuing source of information. David had been in doubt until then, but he decided at that moment, privately, to decline the Los Alamos offer. He wanted no further role in espionage. Later, when he had a chance to go to Eniwetok, he declined, for the same reason. He was afraid he would be unable to resist Rosenberg's importunities.

Ruth and David Greenglass

Because of their diverging points of view, the postwar years resulted in a strange duel between the Greenglasses and the Rosenbergs. They were entangled in business through the well-intentioned connivance of Mrs. Tessie Greenglass. That indefatigable old lady engineered the collection of $4,000 from various relatives to establish the G & R Engineering Co. Bernard Greenglass, David's older brother, was to run this business with Julius Rosenberg, who took Ethel's share of the investment. While still out in Los Alamos, David acquired a silent partnership through a family contribution in his name.

Somehow G & R failed to make a fortune. To salvage the family funds, it was suggested, about the time of David's discharge from the Army, that machines already secured from surplus war goods sales be used as a backbone of an East Side machine shop. Since David returned from Los Alamos with prestige as the head of the machine shop which, loosely speaking, made the atom bomb, it was decided that he should boss the machine shop. Older brother Bernie would learn a trade in the shop and several other ex-GIs would take on-the-job training there, which would among other things produce a cheap labor force. Julius would be the salesman and idea man. On paper the organization looked flawless, particularly since Rosenberg implied that he could get unlimited orders through his Russian friends. So it was arranged: G & R dissolved and after some reshuffling of partners outside the family circle was replaced by the Pitt Machine Products Co.

David started work in the shop in May, 1946, but there was no income until October or November of that year. The financial arrangement between the four partners—the Greenglass brothers, Julius Rosenberg, and an East Side matzoh manufacturer named David Schein whom Rosenberg had talked into putting up $15,000—was that all would receive an equal return, varying with the profits, but that if the business did not yield enough for all four, nobody would get anything. This was easier on the matzoh manufacturer and on Rosenberg, who had outside in-

225

terests and outside incomes, than it was on the Greenglass boys, David and Bernie, who had all their money tied up in the shop.

Julius Rosenberg and Ethel were kind to David and Ruth, in a condescending fashion. They let the Greenglasses use their Knickerbocker Village apartment once or twice when they were off on vacation. Periodically, they invited the Greenglasses in for dinner parties at which Julius managed to describe how useful his Russian contacts had been. He exhibited a fancy wrist watch with a sweep second hand which he said had been awarded him with a Soviet citation carrying certain privileges in the event he ever went to the U.S.S.R. Ethel had a similar watch. They also bragged about a console table with photographic attachments which the Russians had given them to aid in the work. The implication was that the Greenglasses also might receive such rewards, if they managed to overcome their tardy scruples and get back into espionage.

At one time in 1946, Ruth Greenglass experienced such a revulsion against what she and David had done during the war that she urged her husband to go to the FBI and tell them all about it. It was difficult for David to turn informer on his own sister and on his own business partner. He postponed taking any action. As time passed, with no particular flurries in the press over the theft of atomic secrets, Ruth relaxed her pressure. She reasoned that it might be best to let the memory die away. She did possess an unalterable determination not to slide back into that same groove, and she did talk, from time to time, to David about escaping from the Street, which for her personified the dirt and noise, crowding and roughness, temptations and frustrations of East Side life. As a girl of ten, Ruth had been called upon to identify a girl friend who had been smashed so badly by a truck that identification was possible only by means of her shoes. The shock of that experience crystallized in Ruth's mind a determination to get away from the Street as soon as she grew up. What she saw of the Southwest during the war intensified that resolve. David said he was willing to leave the city, but he couldn't just take off with a baby (Stephen was born in 1946) and no job at the end of the road. Just as soon as he pulled his economic stake out of the machine shop, he would go, job or no job, he promised Ruth.

During 1947, the shop did produce some revenue, but a family emergency always seemed to arise to swallow up the profits. David's father, for example, who was in his seventies, broke his leg that year, and had to be supported until he was able to resume work.

As the shop picked up, Julius Rosenberg urged David to return to school. He suggested the University of Chicago, for a full four-year course, because of its exceptional record in nuclear physics and the presence there of many scientists from Los Alamos whose friendship could be cultivated by somebody like David Greenglass. The GI Bill of Rights would take care of basic expenses, said Rosenberg, and his friends the Russians would provide an allowance up to $100 a month for more comfortable living, since Greenglass would be preparing himself for greater usefulness.

Greenglass said he would think it over, but he and Ruth were determined to accept no more Soviet money. Julius returned to his idea from time to time. He suggested Massachusetts Institute of Technology as a good place for atomic study, and even New York University, when that institution offered a nuclear engineering course. Rosenberg remarked that he "had people going to school in various places," under conditions such as he outlined. Some months later, David Greenglass began attending night school in New York under his own steam, in subjects having nothing to do with atomic energy. Rosenberg was furious. Instead of fitting his schedule to David's he raged that David was disrupting production by leaving the shop in mid-afternoon for classes two or three days a week. He created such a fuss that David quit school.

Julius Rosenberg made a casual remark at this time which infuriated Ruth Greenglass. He said he didn't care too much whether the machine shop was a success since he could always obtain $10,000 or $15,000 from his friends as a business front for his other activities.

"It may not mean much to you," raged Ruth, "but it means a living to David and Bernie. They have all their money in the business. What's more, they do the bulk of the work on the machines, while you walk around and give orders!"

Throughout 1948, the family feud festered, because the Pitt Machine Products Co. didn't make a dime that whole year. David and Bernie simply couldn't understand it; here they were running what seemed to be a thriving business, yet they and their families led a hand-to-mouth existence, owing everybody and with no hope or relief. Bernie's lot was particularly tough, since his baby Sharon was quite small, and his wife Gladys had the dreaded Hodgkins disease. The two brothers decided on one occasion to ask their elder sister Ethel for advice. She pounded their ears with her wrath; they were completely to blame, she asserted, for coming in late at the shop and loafing on the job. David and Bernie did not know how to talk back to Ethel, so they left quietly. Later they and their wives agreed that they worked hard enough, and long enough hours, when there was business in the shop. Either the terms on which they did business were wrong—and this was up to Julius—or the amount of business was too low for cheap production—and again this was up to Julius. David and Bernie contended that they knew their jobs, whereas Julie was a novice as a business executive, and as a salesman. Continuing to run the shop as a personal enterprise, instead of as a partnership, Julius Rosenberg blamed everybody but himself for lack of profits. He never mentioned the lucrative Russian contracts he was supposed to get. When he did land a contract, he said, the Greenglass brothers fumbled it so badly they lost business. He blamed David for technical inadequacy; at one point he promoted a shop workman to foreman.

Greenglass felt too humiliated to protest in public. He waited until he and Rosenberg were alone to make his case. "How do you think I feel, Julie," he said, "when I have to work for my own worker?"

Rosenberg was obdurate. "If you keep on producing rejects and losing money in the business, and you don't know how to handle the men, we will never make a living," he said, sternly. After a few days, he restored David to his former job as foreman.

The break between Julius Rosenberg and David Greenglass occurred over a comparatively minor matter. Julius accused David of "sneaking off in the middle of the day to do housework for Ruth." The shop was only a few blocks away from his apartment and David did return for lunch, and he did occasionally handle some domestic chore or other for Ruth, when business was not too pressing. He was a bigger man than Rosenberg, with fully 190 pounds on a five-foot-ten frame, and a furious one at that moment. "I'll knock your head off for that," he told Julius Rosenberg, and if Julius hadn't run off down the street, he would have fulfilled his threat.

After getting a $300 bank loan in the spring of 1949, to cover immediate expenses, David Greenglass trained a successor to run the machine shop, and walked out. Three months later, Bernie also walked out of the shop. The brothers had stock to show their interest in the company, but in January, 1950, they turned the stock over to Julius Rosenberg, without compensation or even a promissory note, to enable him to make a deal with Schein, who wanted to retire from the business.

Julius Rosenberg obtained sole control over a business which he estimated to be worth $20,000, only a short time before the FBI knocked on his door to ask if it were true that he had instructed his brother-in-law to obtain atomic information for Russia.

9. The Conspirators

THE Marxist study groups which operated during the war in Montreal and Knoxville, Chicago and Quebec and Berkeley, among scientists engaged in secret research, had their counterparts in Washington, D. C., among government employees. The purpose was always and inevitably the same: converting idealists into Communists, and properly responsive Communists into spies. The District of Columbia civil-service groups of Communists were organized horizontally at first, regardless of departmental lines. At a later period, they were split up into small vertical groups in each government agency or bureau, for greater efficiency and furtiveness. An outline of the way the members were indoctrinated gradually with an ethic and a code of conspiracy has been provided by Max Elitcher, a rather disturbed young electrical engineer whose psychological problems kept him on the fringes of subversion. As a Communist and a close friend of two Communists who had slid into espionage, Elitcher was wooed at times—as his own lawyer said at his trial—like a desirable woman. The strange thing was that when the apparatus became most ardent in its pursuit of Elitcher as a possible spy, he became most coy; when he turned willing, the spy to whom he virtually offered himself was in trouble and necessarily unreceptive.

Elitcher was a native of New York, born September 1, 1918. He received his Bachelor of Science degree at City College in

230

June, 1938. After graduation he took a civil-service exam for junior engineer, and did postgraduate work until his appointment came through that fall. He worked almost a full decade for the Navy Bureau of Ordnance.

Elitcher felt tense and lost at first in Washington. He found quarters at 1466 Columbia Road, N.W., not too far by trolley from his desk in the Navy Department building at Seventeenth Street and Constitution Avenue, but he had no friends. He relaxed somewhat after switching to a large rooming house at 1316 Delafield Place, where a number of other young government employees resided. Then in December, 1938, Morton Sobell appeared on the scene. He and Elitcher had known each other in New York since high-school days, without becoming close friends; in Washington, among strangers, they soon became almost inseparable.

Sobell, who had graduated from City College at the same time and with the same degree as Elitcher, needed a job and a place to live. Elitcher helped him to land with the Navy Bureau of Ordnance, and in a boardinghouse next door to the Delafield Place establishment. In the spring of 1939, Elitcher and Sobell secured a top-floor apartment for themselves at 4925 Seventh Street; this brought about a curious twist to their intimacy. Elitcher had flirted with the Young Communist League at City College, but had resisted efforts to recruit him as a formal Party member. Under similar pressure from Sobell as his roommate in Washington, Elitcher joined the Party. The pair attended Marxist study meetings together. There were about fifteen members in their cell, and meetings were held in rotation at the homes of the members. Sobell served as chairman, and in that capacity collected dues and provided inspirational guidance. World events, as interpreted by the *Daily Worker* and the *Communist* (now defunct) were discussed at these meetings, as well as fine points of Marxist, Leninist, and Stalinist theory. The energies of some members were focused on open-Party work like the American

Youth Congress and the American Peace Mobilization. Others were groomed quietly for more sinister duties.

Max Elitcher liked open-Party work. He was a tall, dark sliver of a man who always wore heavy horn-rimmed glasses. Because of his self-consciousness, a political meeting in which he managed to fulfill some small predetermined role gave him tremendous relief and satisfaction. He found a special field for his talents in a union of federal workers over which the Communists exercised a hidden control. Quiet organizational activity provided a ready-made approach to other employees during which he could shrug off, for a time, the embarrassment which seemed always to overcome him in his social or personal relationships.

One humid afternoon in midsummer, 1940, Sobell, Elitcher, and Elitcher's brother, who was visiting Washington, went to the Wardman Park Hotel swimming pool to cool off. This was one of those open-air pools in Washington which resemble the Café de la Paix in Paris; almost anybody can, and does, turn up there. Max Elitcher and Morton Sobell were therefore not too surprised to run into another alumnus from the class of '38, City College— Julius Rosenberg. Julius explained that his wife Ethel was working in the Census Bureau in Washington. He had come down to see if he also could snare a job, from one of the various government lists for junior engineer. He had been down more than a month, he said, but the best offering was a United States Signal Corps job which would take him back to New York. He was inclined to accept, he said, since Ethel was willing to leave Washington in a few months and rejoin him in New York. Rosenberg had been one of those at City College who tried to lure Elitcher into the Young Communist League. Now he winked at Sobell and said he had heard favorable reports about Elitcher. In farewell, he expressed a hope that they would see more of each other in the future.

Though Sobell may have been already engaged in espionage, Rosenberg did not canvass Elitcher as a prospect until 1944. Meanwhile Sobell shifted to the University of Michigan for his master's degree, presumably with financial help from the apparatus, and then moved up to the crucial General Electric plant in Schenectady, where the Communist party had a tremendous advantage in the existence of a union membership under its control. Whenever he was in Washington, roughly once a year, Sobell took care to visit his roommate and Communist protégé. The cells among government employees in Washington were realigned in 1942 according to agencies, so that Elitcher found himself in a new group of eight in the Navy Communist-party branch. His continued union activity led meanwhile to marriage with an almost equally zealous union member.

On June 6, 1944, when Elitcher and his wife were living in a small apartment on Delaware Avenue in the southwest section of town, Julius Rosenberg phoned around dinner time to reveal that he had come to Washington, on a brief Signal Corps assignment to the National Bureau of Standards, and wondered whether he could renew their old friendship. Elitcher said he'd be glad to see Rosenberg, and had dessert and coffee for the guest when he appeared. After a quarter of an hour of general talk about work, marriage, and children, Rosenberg mentioned enjoying a drink with some friends to celebrate D day. Considering this a hint, Mrs. Elitcher dug out a bottle of wine, and the three drank ceremonially to the Allied invasion of Western Europe, and the relief it would bring to the hard-pressed fighters of the Soviet Union.

Rosenberg turned to Elitcher. "I would like to see you alone," he said.

Uncomfortably, Elitcher relayed the message, "Helene, would you step out a minute or two? We want to talk privately."

Mrs. Elitcher thereupon went into the bedroom, and carefully closed the door.

Rosenberg talked circuitously for quite a while. The Russians were doing a great job in the war. Military information had been denied them by Fascist groups in America. Because this was impeding the Soviet effort, many persons who knew the actual

situation were implementing aid to the Soviet by providing classified information about military equipment. All these things he
said, and more in the same vein. He had reached the point personally, he declared with an air of frankness, where he was
looking for persons to help the Russians get the assistance they
needed and deserved. In an offhand way, he flashed the ace in
his hand. One of those already helping, he revealed, was Elitcher's
old friend and former roommate, Morton Sobell. Following up
his advantage quickly, Rosenberg asked what Elitcher's work
consisted of and whether he would be able to turn over information. Elitcher said he was working on fire-control equipment for
directing missiles automatically against targets. Anybody leaving
his Ordnance Bureau building with a package, however, had to
disclose it to security guards at the gate, he pointed out.

Somewhat scornfully, Rosenberg said security rules could be
evaded. In his own part of the arrangements, he declared, utmost
secrecy and speed were observed. Documents intended for him
were taken immediately to New York, processed photographically
that evening, and returned before they could be missed. The
material moved in the form of film in containers which afforded
special protection, since any tampering by an outsider would
destroy the evidence. These precautions meant that anybody
co-operating with him need have no fear for his personal safety.

Elitcher did not commit himself one way or another to the
proposal, which carried no cash or other material inducement.
It was presented on strictly ideological grounds. Elitcher agreed
to look up Rosenberg, when he and his wife visited New York
that summer, and he took down Rosenberg's address and phone
number. Meanwhile he would think things over, he said. Elitcher
retrieved his wife Helene from the bedroom, and the three had
some inconsequential talk before the farewells. Elitcher owned a
car, and he was willing to give Rosenberg a lift, but the espionage
scout preferred to pick up a cab. Rosenberg's entire visit had
lasted less than an hour and a half.

When the Elitchers did appear in New York that summer,

they received the grade-A social treatment reserved for one of the lesser underground arms of the Communist party. Several former City College classmates materialized for an elaborate restaurant dinner which seemed vaguely in honor of a visiting government engineer named Elitcher. There was a jovial exodus to an establishment in Greenwich Village, where victrola playing and dancing and guitar strumming whiled away the hours in more or less nonpolitical camaraderie.

That fall, the Elitchers spent a week's vacation at the Kumbabrow State Park in West Virginia, with Morton Sobell and Helen Gurewitz. Elitcher made the mistake of mentioning that Rosenberg had disclosed Sobell's espionage efforts. "He shouldn't have told you that," Sobell said angrily.

Elitcher tried to smooth him down. "Julius knew of our close relationship, and that anything he said to me about you would be completely confidential. Besides, you must have known he was going to visit me," he said shrewdly. "That's probably why he felt safe about it."

"It makes no difference," Sobell growled. "He shouldn't have done it."

Though he continued to grumble about Rosenberg's amateurish indiscretion, Sobell seemed more fond of Elitcher than ever. When he and Mrs. Gurewitz decided to get married in March, 1945, Sobell insisted that the Elitchers come to the wedding in Virginia, or it would not be held.

Julius Rosenberg's past, though not his present, caught up with him on May 28, 1945. The Signal Corps dropped him for Communist activity, mentioning among other things that he had transferred in February, 1944, from Branch 16B of the industrial division of the Party to the Eastern Club of the 1st A.D., under Communist Transfer No. 1217. The evidence was solid and irrefutable, but Rosenberg fought the case, because that was the Communist tactic at the moment. When the Elitchers came to New York that summer for a visit, and made use of the Rosenberg apartment, since Ethel was living in the country, Julius read part

235

of his brief to Elitcher, commenting as he read, that the situation could have been worse, since the charge might have referred to espionage.

Rosenberg's difficulties had the effect of making him more direct, in some respects, and Elitcher more cautious. One day in September, Rosenberg phoned around 10 A.M. from Union Station and asked if he could visit the Elitchers. Within a few minutes after his arrival, he came bluntly to the point. "The war is over," he said, "but there is a continuing need for new military information for the Soviet Union. What are you working on now, and what are you willing to contribute?"

Elitcher, who was then working on sonar or antisubmarine fire-control devices, replied ambiguously, "I'll see, and if I have anything and I want to give it to you, I'll let you know."

Mrs. Elitcher broke in to remind her husband that they were due at the CIO Federal employees union headquarters for a picture of a committee on which she was working. Rosenberg protested that they had not finished their talk. Elitcher said he had promised to drive his wife to the union hall; Rosenberg could come along, if he wished.

"I wouldn't be seen at a place like that with you," Rosenberg declared. When neither of the Elitchers showed any sign of yielding, he decided to go along. The union hall was located on Eighteenth Street just off Connecticut Avenue. Mrs. Elitcher went upstairs, while her husband and Rosenberg stayed downstairs for a while. Elitcher announced he would have to rejoin his wife upstairs for the picture. Unexpectedly, Rosenberg said he would come up, too, since he had some time to spare. After the picture-taking, during which Elitcher was careful not to introduce his guest, the three of them went downstairs together.

Rosenberg decided to take the trolley which passed the union hall and went directly to Union Station, but he didn't seem in a hurry. He had been planning to visit the office of Representative Dickstein (D-New York) to see if he could secure some support for a campaign to reopen his discharge from the Signal Corps, he said, but after an earlier runaround from the Congressman, he wasn't sure whether the trip would be worth making. The Elitchers proffered no advice, nor did they suggest a ride in their car to the Hill or the station. After a while, Rosenberg said good-by and took the trolley.

A series of minor events at the office, in his union and at home conspired during 1946 to increase the always considerable turbulence in Max Elitcher's mind. Out of a growing annoyance at his marriage, his job, and the world in general came an increased receptivity to Rosenberg's shadowy plans. During an official visit to the General Electric plant in Schenectady, during which he stayed overnight at Sobell's home, Elitcher mentioned that he had become a project engineer on a fire-control system. What about reports on the equipment, demanded Sobell. Elitcher said there were some. "Can't you get them for me?" pressed Sobell. Elitcher hesitated. The reports were unimportant, that is, isolated; they dealt with specific problems, he said. There should be an ordnance pamphlet on the subject, Sobell pointed out. Elitcher said none had been written yet but one was due for completion around the end of the year. Sobell said he'd like to see it, if possible. Later that same year, Elitcher visited Sobell's home in Schenectady, and was reminded of the net's interest in the fire-control report.

While in New York shortly before Christmas, Elitcher phoned Julius Rosenberg and said he would like to see him. "Come over," said Rosenberg. Elitcher was hardly inside the door of the Knickerbocker Village apartment before he began talking, with unusual freedom, about some new work he had undertaken for the Navy. Rosenberg interrupted in an agitated fashion. "We've been having difficulty," he said. "There's been a leak in this espionage business. I have to take precautions. It would be best if you stayed away from me entirely, don't visit me at all unless I tell you, or somebody else informs you. You'll have to give up the Party, and quit your union activities."

Elitcher was appalled. "I couldn't do that," he protested.

"That's my life down there in Washington. I couldn't withdraw. Helen wouldn't let me."

"You'll have to," insisted Rosenberg, but they could reach no agreement that day.

Elitcher's difficulties with his wife rose gradually to a climax. He mentioned his problems one day in 1947 when he met Sobell for lunch at the Sugar Bowl in New York. Sobell had shifted from General Electric to the Reeves Instrument Corp., 215 East 91st Street, New York, the same place which had been Julius Rosenberg's headquarters during the war as a Signal Corps inspector.

"Does your wife know about this espionage business?" Sobell demanded after he listened to his friend's marital woes.

"She might know," confessed Elitcher. "I'm not sure."

"Well, that is not good," said Sobell. "That is not good."

Elitcher shrugged. "It is just too bad," he said. "If she knows, she knows, and I can't do anything about it."

Though he questioned Elitcher's reliability, Sobell asked him, almost in the same breath, for names and details about engineering students who were "progressive," and who "would be safe to approach on the question of getting classified material." Arrangements might be made to work out educational help for those needing degrees which would increase their usefulness, he suggested. Elitcher replied that he could not think, offhand, of anybody that was suitable.

Since they already had a child, a daughter, born in 1946, the Elitchers decided to make every effort to save their marriage. Starting in June, 1946, they both went to a psychiatrist twice a week, for a whole year. They gained some new feeling of self-respect and confidence in themselves as a result. To ease part of their remaining problems, Elitcher decided to leave government service. During a business trip to New York in June, 1947, he mentioned to Sobell his intention of resigning.

"Don't do anything rash," said Sobell, excitedly. "I want to talk to you about it at length, and Rosenberg will want to talk to you about it, too."

238

An appointment was made for 6:30 in the evening at Forty-second Street and Third Avenue, the same meeting place used by Yakovlev and Harry Gold. Rosenberg, Sobell, and Elitcher arrived separately for the rendezvous. They walked up Third Avenue and then up and down side streets as they talked.

"I want you to stay at the Bureau of Ordnance," Rosenberg told Elitcher. "I need somebody there for espionage purposes. You will have to change your mind. I have plans in my pocket for you to meet somebody in Washington, to establish contact."

Elitcher said his intentions were fixed. "My wife and I want to leave Washington. There are investigations all over the place. The political atmosphere is terrible. We want to get away and we're going to get away."

"Rosenberg is right," interjected Sobell. "Julie is right, you should do what he says."

"I can't," said Elitcher. "It's all decided."

Sobell left them after a while, and Elitcher and Rosenberg walked into a restaurant on Third Avenue for dinner. Rosenberg requested the names of some civilian places where important military work was being carried out. Elitcher suggested the Bell Telephone Laboratories at Whippany, New Jersey, as one place. "All right, get a job there," said Rosenberg. "Maybe I can," said Elitcher. "I don't know. We'll see."

Rosenberg had an alternative idea: if Elitcher wanted to take courses which would improve his technical status, and his eventual usefulness, that could be arranged through his friends, he promised. Taking advantage of the cordial atmosphere, Elitcher asked how Rosenberg got started in his venture. "I decided a long time ago, this was what I wanted to do," said Rosenberg, "and I made a point of getting close to one person after another until I reached a Russian who would listen to my proposition about getting information to the Soviet Union."

Though he did not agree to remain in Washington, seek employment at the Bell Laboratories in Whippany or return to some college on a Russian scholarship, Elitcher remained under espionage cultivation. Sobell set the stage for a job like his own at Reeves, and invited the Elitchers to live with him in Flushing until they found a place to live in New York.

Toward the end of July, 1947, the Elitchers drove north from Washington in their car. They stopped briefly outside Baltimore at a store off the main road in order to buy some dishes. Returning to the main road, Elitcher found a suspicion taking shape in his mind that two cars behind them had been on their trail steadily. By one device or another, he verified his suspicion. When he reached Sobell's house at 164-17 73 Avenue, Flushing, Elitcher did not mention the motor surveillance until his baby daughter had been put safely to bed.

Sobell shook his mop of heavy black hair in rage over the news. "You should never have come to my house under the circumstances," he cried.

"What could I do?" pleaded Elitcher. "I intended staying at your house. The fact that I was followed couldn't change anything. Whoever was following me would probably know about it. In any case, it was my only destination."

Sobell told Elitcher to pack up and go to the Catskill Mountains, some other mountains—any place, in fact, except where he was.

Finally Sobell agreed to let his guest remain. He was deeply upset, however, and his restlessness erupted in a rather strange manner a half-hour later. He had some valuable information in the house, he announced, which should have gone to Julius Rosenberg long ago. "It's too valuable to destroy," he said, "and too dangerous to keep around the house. I'm going to deliver it to Julie tonight, and you're going with me."

If Sobell had produced a pistol and pointed it at his head, Elitcher could not have been more amazed. This was a foolish thing, a silly, dangerous thing to do, under the circumstances, he said. Sobell looked wild. He was tired, he declared, and he might not be able to drive both ways. Elitcher had to come along to help with the driving, he insisted. Eventually Elitcher gave way. When they got into the car, he noticed Sobell place a 35-millimeter film can into the glove compartment. They drove over to Manhattan down the East River Drive to a spot outside the New York Journal-American building. They noticed no sign of surveillance.

Taking the can from the glove compartment, Sobell stepped out of the car. "You might drive around the corner and park on Catherine Slip," he suggested, and left. Elitcher drove up Catherine Slip and then down so that the car, when parked, faced the Drive. In about twenty minutes, Sobell returned and took the wheel for the drive back to Queens. Elitcher asked him what Rosenberg's reaction had been to the news that he had been followed.

"He told me to tell you, 'It's all right, don't be concerned about it,'" Sobell said, in a self-satisfied way. "I'm certainly glad I got that stuff off my chest," he declared.

During a leisurely drive home, a grinning, relaxed Sobell confided that Julius Rosenberg had talked repeatedly over the phone to Elizabeth Bentley, and that she might have seen him on one occasion. Nevertheless, she did not remember him well enough to lead the FBI to his door. "This will probably blow over, too," said Sobell.

It is difficult to refrain from speculation about that strange drive of Sobell. Did he plan to involve on-again, off-again Elitcher in a specific treasonable enterprise, so that the other would hesitate to talk if approached directly by the FBI men who seemed to be hovering offstage? Had Rosenberg approved the strategy as excellent? These are purely conjectures. Some facts are clear. The Elitchers soon moved into a house at 164-18 72 Avenue, Flushing, whose rear yard abutted on the rear yard of the Sobell property. In October, 1947, Max Elitcher began working at Reeves, where Sobell worked; he remained employed there until March, 1951, when he was dropped in the wake of revelations of new FBI interest in his career. Sobell and Elitcher remained close, apparently friendly neighbors until Sobell fled to Mexico in the summer of 1950.

Elitcher asserted that he and his wife had dropped out of the Communist party in 1948 and stayed away from Party affairs since then. His story revealed a great deal about the amateurish espionage conduct of Sobell and Rosenberg. Assuming always that he did not suppress anything of the full story, he certainly emerges as the most unprofitable spy prospect in all history.

2

Julius Rosenberg was a man who gravitated naturally toward the sources of power. Being a Communist did not suffice for him; he had to become a radical ward heeler, a bureaucrat, advising and manipulating others. When he discovered that the open Party in the United States served merely as a cloak for international conspiracy, he felt impelled to seek out the Russians who ran things. Common sense, as well as the conspiratorial nature of the Stalinist apparatus, dictated that he should abandon some of his outer functions as he acquired inner ones, but Julius Rosenberg yielded no title or privilege. Among City College classmates, he remained a campus radical. Among technological workers, he paraded his status as chairman of the civil service committee of the Party-line Federation of Architects, Engineers, Chemists and Technicians. Among Communist careerists, he flashed his badges as a talent spotter, recruiter, and courier for an espionage ring. No man could wear all those uniforms properly at once. As a spy, Julius Rosenberg was an inept flop. Yet he channeled a vast amount of military information into Soviet hands, including (with the help of David Greenglass) the trigger heart of the third, or Nagasaki, atom bomb.

Repudiation of religion seems to have played a role in increasing the vehemence with which Julius Rosenberg embraced Communism, as it did with Clarence Francis Hiskey, the Catholic, and Klaus Emil Julius Fuchs, the Lutheran.

Harry Rosenberg, Julius' father, dominated his family and

exercised considerable influence in the community where he lived. A union operator in women's clothing, he brought home a comparatively good salary, by East Side standards, to his wife and four children. He paid his debts and he trained the children to be neat and mannerly. He was a good neighbor, a civic leader, and a man of deep religious learning. As an immigrant among immigrants, he felt more patriotic perhaps than the descendants of some earlier arrivals. Yiddish was still spoken at his dinner table, because the elders had difficulty with their English, but after dinner he would frequently gather the family together for lectures on American history and government. When he became ill, Bernard and David Greenglass considered it an honor to give him transfusions of their blood. Mrs. Tessie Greenglass, a shrewd evaluator of persons and events, always spoke of Harry Rosenberg with respect. "He was the most intelligent man in the world," she said on one occasion.

A frail, bookish lad, with weak eyes and a tendency toward hay fever, Julius was destined by his father to become a rabbi. He attended Hebrew school, the downtown Talmud Torah, at the same time that he studied at P.S. 96, and he went to the Hebrew High School on East Broadway after his regular classes at the Seward Park High School. Though his religious training kept pace with his secular studies, the combined schedule did not leave much room for sports or social affairs. Somewhere along the line he got restive. Refusing to become a rabbi, he entered the School of Technology at City College in June, 1934, one month after his sixteenth birthday, and thereby came close to breaking his father's heart.

Harry Rosenberg prided himself on his open-mindedness. Too fond a father to stand in his son's way, he tried honestly to be understanding. Then Julius became a convert to Communism, and in the first flush of conversion began to ridicule everything his father held dear. Julius seemed to have an answer to every question. His system of thought was closed. He itched to convert others; those who seemed slow, or unresponsive, he treated with condescension, as though sure of their eventual surrender; those who resisted with facts, like his father, he handled as enemies. In the face of such intolerant disrespect, Harry Rosenberg's studied air of tolerance crumbled; during arguments he vacillated between humiliation, despair, and rage. He ceased to brag about Julius among the neighbors and the men in the shop. To old friends, he remarked bitterly, "The barrel has overturned"—an expression in Yiddish suggesting that his son's whole character had changed.

Julius was a subway student. That is, he lived at home, and traveled underground daily to and from the City College campus. This meant renewal every evening of the struggle between him and his father. Even Julius felt the strain; frequently he would do his lessons at the nearby Greenglass apartment, where Ethel, a small, plump, dark-haired girl three years his senior, was sure to second his views. Ethel had literary and artistic pretensions. She liked to refer to herself as a poet. When she was very young, she had been a member of a Henry Street Settlement dramatic group. She had flirted with modern dancing. She studied piano with a private teacher for several years and took voice one year at Carnegie Hall Studios. Any new acquaintance learned in a surprisingly short time that Ethel had once been the youngest member of the Schola Cantorum under Hugh Ross at Carnegie Hall. If somebody admired her portable typewriter, she was quick to note that she had acquired this—as a bargain, almost a gift—from an actor associated with her in the Clark House Dramatic Group of which she had been a member, at the age of eighteen.

Despite all her posing, Ethel was a shallow girl with neither the talent, appearance, nor the personality to get anywhere as a singer, a dancer, or an actress. She had gone to work after graduating from high school in 1931, when she was sixteen, and she had been working more or less, for five years when she met Julius. She was a good girl, in the East Side fashion; she turned over to her family her whole salary, except for carfare and lunch money, right up to the day she married. During Ethel's first spell of employment, as a clerk with the National New York Shipping and Packing Co., she tried professional singing on the side, without success. Somewhere around 1934, when she was working as a stenographer at the Bell Textile Co., she joined the Communist party and became an active member in the Communist-controlled Local 65 of the United Retail and Wholesale Employees. She met Julius at a Party affair, and it was a joint interest in Communism, plus Ethel's determination to annex a man, rather than any mutual affinity for music, which drew them together. During his evening visits, Ethel would frequently type out his engineering reports, while Julius tested his ideology on David, who was several years younger and somewhat slower of mind, though by no means stupid. Out of all Julius' presents, the first was probably decisive: a chemistry set at a time when David was chemistry crazy. Between presents and propaganda, Ethel and Julius sandbagged David into the Party. The boy never had a chance to escape.

At City College, Julius Rosenberg scorned the Hillel Society, to his father's distress, but he engaged in all the feverish political maneuvering and agitation of the American Student Union and the Young Communist League. These activities slowed him up in class, or else he was not as smart as he assumed, for he ranked only seventy-ninth in a class of eighty-five graduating in February, 1939, with a degree of B.S. in electrical engineering. Four months after graduation, Julius Rosenberg, a professional man of sorts, married Ethel Greenglass, the frustrated singer. As a wedding present, David Greenglass joined the Young Communist League. During the first year of their marriage, they lived in a small Williamsburg flat with one of Julius' former classmates, Marcus Pogarsky, later called Page, and Pogarsky's wife. Julius tried a series of minor jobs during this period, including one as a tool designer for E. W. Bliss & Co., in Brooklyn. He and Mike Sidorovitch worked for a few months with an inventor named Paul Williams, who had an idea he was trying to translate into a device.

The Atom Spies

Julius Rosenberg was already taking his first steps toward becoming a Stalinist functionary. Out of an old New York splinter from an A.F. of L. union, the Communist party had fashioned the Federation of Architects, Engineers, Chemists and Technicians (CIO) as a spearhead in the scientific field. The various members of the Leftist technological clique from CCNY, and their women —the Rosenbergs, the Sidoroviches, the Pages, Joel Barr, and his sweetheart, Vivian Glassman, and many others—pooled their efforts to make the FAECT a going concern.

Ethel Rosenberg was particularly aware, as a result of her job experiences, of the employment-and-power possibilities in political trade unionism. She contributed free typing, and office work, to the ladies' auxiliary of the FAECT as soon as Julius, on September 3, 1940, assumed his duties as a civilian junior engineer at the Brooklyn supply office of the Signal Corps. Rosenberg pre-empted a little niche in the union, as its federal civil service chief. He handled appeals in disciplinary cases, grievances and the job placement of members. He reached out for national influence by the ancient bureaucratic route: he did the dirty day-to-day work. He might not have stuck to it so thoroughly except for Ethel, always the more aggressive of the two.

It was amazing how much Party activity the Rosenbergs managed to squeeze out of their lives, considering the fact that they were not particularly robust. Ethel had suffered since the age of thirteen from a spinal curvature which forced her to take to bed periodically with a backache. She also had a tendency toward low-blood pressure, which resulted in dizzy spells. On his part, Julius was likely to develop strep throat under tension. Nevertheless, the pair did their share of clamoring for peace during the Hitler pact, and they clamored for a second front after the pact. They attended meetings endlessly, and they signed the inevitable petitions for Communist causes and candidates. They collected funds for various Communist fronts, such as the Joint Anti-Fascist Refugee Committee. They urged others to join them in taking out $5,000 insurance with the Communist-controlled International Workers Order. They bought their copies of the *Daily Worker* (they were a two-newspaper family) at the regular newsstand, Madison and Rutgers streets, as well as other organs of the Party press, and they read them all from cover to cover.

Any empty corners in the existence of Ethel and Julius Rosenberg were plugged automatically by the FAECT. The first night club experience the Rosenbergs had was at an FAECT party at Café Society Downtown. When they signed a lease on an apartment at Knickerbocker Village, one of the East Side developments substituting vertical for horizontal overcrowding, they secured their furniture through the FAECT. Harry and Sylvia Steingart, active FAECT members, were leaving for jobs in California, so they turned over their furniture to the Rosenbergs, as a gesture of friendship and a way to save on storage charges. Later the Rosenbergs picked up a battered old piano, so Ethel could continue with her music. The FAECT crowd tended to live together; Michael and Ann Sidorovich secured an apartment above the Rosenberg apartment at Knickerbocker Village in 1942; others lived nearby.

The first Rosenberg child, Michael, was born at Knickerbocker Village on March 10, 1943, a month after Julius won promotion to associate engineering inspector for the Signal Corps. This was the second promotion for Julius. He had started as a junior engineer at $2,000 a year, moved up after a year and a half to the rank of assistant engineer, at $2,600. His new title carried a salary of $3,200, which in-grade raises later boosted to $3,600. Julius and Ethel Rosenberg were leading full and outwardly satisfying lives. Ethel kept particularly busy, since she did her own housework, including laundry, on top of her ideological chores. Yet Michael was a sickly, nervous child. Week in and week out, he had colds, sore throat, and fever. As he grew older, he became disturbed emotionally. Ethel took courses to help him, courses in child psychology and music for children; when these failed, she had to seek psychiatric counseling.

Contributing to the tension in the Rosenberg household may

have been a subconscious recognition by Michael's parents that things were too good to last. Because Russia decided in the middle of the war to use its Comintern register of all Communist and fellow-traveling scientists and technological experts in an emergency effort to keep pace with the solution of atomic mysteries, Julius was abruptly shoved into the work he had been angling for, and liked to say he was "fated for." He began spying as early as 1944, without abandoning almost open Communist work in the FAECT. From an espionage point of view, such a combination was preposterous, even though the Rosenbergs gave up buying the *Daily Worker* and attending Party meetings.

In the fall of 1944, when the storm clouds of investigation gathered around Julius' head, Ethel suffered her first prolonged illness, and she did not get out of bed until the following spring. Julius was suspended in February, 1945, and discharged the following month. He promptly went to work for Emerson Radio Co., one of the concerns whose war work he had been inspecting. His salary was $70 a week, which with overtime occasionally ran to $100. Julius Rosenberg remained dissatisfied; he had flatly denied ever having any Communist affiliations, which was the specified Stalinist course in those days, regardless of the evidence, and with a persistence that was almost compulsive, he kept starting one hopeless campaign after another for reinstatement to his former government job. Then in December, Emerson laid him off. The next step was the ill-fated East Side partnership with the Greenglass family, which seems to have had very little chance from the beginning of working out successfully.

One great shock to Julius Rosenberg was the death of his father. After five years of apparently honorable government service and gradually increased union prominence, Harry Rosenberg had been lulled almost to forgetting, if not forgiving, his son's radical departure in life. Then there was a flurry of controversy over Julius, and a spreading sense of disgrace on the East Side. The Secretary of War had personally ordered the discharge of Julius, it was whispered, and the whisper carried more than a hint of possible wartime betrayal of his country, so it seemed to Harry Rosenberg, and to others. Rosenberg, senior, still wanted to believe in the innocence of his son. He listened to Julius' story, but the young engineer's bluster had the effect of conceding the charge. Alone with his wife Sophie, a woman like himself in her sixties, suffering from high-blood pressure and failing eyesight, Harry Rosenberg rolled his head in despair. He would prefer not to see Julius any more unless it were absolutely necessary, he said. In 1946, Harry Rosenberg went to a hospital with kidney trouble. He was on the critical list for weeks, and was pulled back from the edge of death only by the transfusions of blood by devoted relatives. Then he improved, and he wanted to see his son Julius. One evening Julius came around alone to the hospital, and shaved his father in bed. During the night, after Julius left, Harry Rosenberg died of a blood clot. So far as anybody in the family knew, father and son, after so many bitter arguments, had arranged a sort of truce and had talked together peacefully, on that final evening.

Julius Rosenberg's internal insecurity may have inspired some of his pointless boasting in the presence of the Greenglass brothers, David and Bernie, when they were trying to make money out of their East Side machine shop after the war.

By espionage standards or any standards Julius was reckless. During the 1945 furlough of David Greenglass, he told his brother-in-law casually that he "stole the proximity fuse" from Emerson Radio while ostensibly inspecting the plant for the United States Army. He took out the data in a brief case he used to bring his lunch to work, he boasted, and no security officer laid a finger on him.

David Greenglass was keen on *Popular Science* magazine articles, and particularly keen on the possibility of interstellar space traveling. During one postwar discussion of this subject at the machine shop on East Houston Street, Julius Rosenberg contributed the information that the United States was working on a secret sky platform project, a large vessel which would be suspended at a point of no gravity between the moon and the earth and would revolve around the earth as a satellite.

In the presence of another workman at the shop, Julius Rosenberg confided to David Greenglass that American scientists had solved the problem of atomic energy for airplanes. When David asked about this later, Julius said the mathematics was already solved, he had gotten the figures from one of his contacts. When he wanted to pass information on to his friends, Rosenberg said, he went to a certain moving picture theater, and left microfilm in a certain alcove. If he wanted a personal interview, he left a code message at the alcove, which would set the stage for a rendezvous at a lonely spot out on Long Island.

In urging David periodically to return to school, with the financial assistance of his friends, Julius Rosenberg mentioned that he had several students attending upstate New York institutions. Something he said on another occasion convinced David that one of these institutions was Cornell.

Julius told David that he had been getting information of great value about General Electric in Schenectady. He spoke less specifically about receiving material from Cleveland. David connected this with a later description of the Warner-Swasey turret lathe plant which Julius Rosenberg said he inspected during a visit to one of his contacts in Ohio.

All this boasting impressed the Greenglass brothers, but it arose in their minds, with a nagging insistence, when affairs at the machine shop went haywire. Julius Rosenberg was probably incompetent as a machine-shop operator in the first place, because he did not have a sufficiently thorough understanding of what he was trying to sell, or what his machines could produce. With extracurricular activities draining his energies, the prospect was virtually hopeless. Lack of revenue at the shop left the Greenglass brothers poverty stricken, but Julius and Ethel Rosenberg managed to eat frequently at expensive restaurants and to take comparatively expensive vacations from time to time at Plattekill and other resorts. Nobody could say that the Rosenbergs lived on a lavish scale, so far as buying clothes or furniture was concerned, but they did live better than the Greenglasses, on the basis of a mysterious outside income.

When David got flat broke, as happened frequently, he could usually borrow from Julius Rosenberg. Julius made quite a show out of dividing in half whatever he happened to find in his pocketbook—$2, $10, or $20. The accumulating loan exceeded $300 in 1948, without arousing any feeling of gratitude in the minds of Ruth and David Greenglass. By this time, the couple had concluded they were being used, and that any money squeezed out of the Rosenbergs was just the return of some of their own.

The attitude of Ethel and Julius Rosenberg toward trouble at the shop was rather unrealistic. Ethel, around whose nose a pinched look had now settled, suggesting prissiness, fanaticism, or both, decided it was Ruth's fault, and Julius backed her up. David was all right, they said, but Ruth nagged him for money. While they buttered up David, they went as far as they dared— which was not too far—in criticizing Ruth's unfriendliness and lack of understanding. At Mrs. Tessie Greenglass' semi-compulsory Friday evening gatherings for the family, they whittled away at Ruth until they found the old lady herself rushing to Ruth's rescue.

In the psychological war over David, Ruth Greenglass could not afford to lose. She had as allies her husband's deep affection and the basic facts of the shop situation. As a result of her coaching, the arguments between David and Julius at the shop got hotter. Julius would add edge to his remarks until David almost automatically promised a punch in the nose, whereupon they would both cool off.

One day as they were sitting in a candy store at Avenue D and Houston Street, an argument between them reached such an unexpected peak of fury, before witnesses, that David did get up and take a swing at Julius, who ran out of the store in panic. Except for the intervention of his brother Bernie, David would have chased after his brother-in-law. Subsequently David felt ashamed. He apologized, but somehow the blow had touched Rosenberg's latent sense of persecution. Abandoning his old theory that David was a harmless, friendly man goaded to desperation by his wife, Julius Rosenberg informed relatives somberly that he realized now that David Greenglass had always had it in for him. David, on the other hand, insisted there was no real trouble between them. He and Julius had quarrels occasionally, he conceded, quarrels over personalities and over money, over the way the shop was run and contracts secured for the shop, but they remained good friends despite the quarrels, he said. Probably the best indication that David meant what he said was provided in 1949 when he got out of the machine-shop partnership and turned over his stock without payment or written promise of payment, so Julius would have a chance to make a go of the business on his own.

After that, Julius and Ethel Rosenberg had little to do with David and Ruth Greenglass until the emergency arose in 1950 over the arrest of Dr. Klaus Fuchs. Then the old tug of war over the soul, and the allegiance, of David Greenglass, was resumed with fresh intensity. Ethel and Julius had to keep David in line, not for economic advantage this time, but for their very lives. Ruth had to keep David faithful, for a variety of reasons including the future of their own children.

Around 8 A.M. on June 16, 1950, the day after David Greenglass was interrupted by FBI visitors as he was preparing the formula for his baby, three polite agents called at the Knickerbocker Village apartment of Julius Rosenberg. "We are from the FBI," one of them said. "We would like to talk to you." One was named Harrington and one Norton. Julius didn't catch the name of the third. He was thinking furiously as he said, "Come in, gentlemen."

Excusing himself, Julius drew his wife into the bathroom. "Shall I talk to them?" he said, desperately. She shrugged. "David did. It might look funny if you didn't."

Julius came out, and said, "I will talk to you, gentlemen, in a little while." He finished dressing Robert, who was four years younger than Michael, and tried to keep Michael quiet. Ethel made breakfast, and Julius shaved. One of the agents looked around the flat, and said, "We can't talk here. Would you like to come down to the office? We can have some coffee brought in."

The four men drove to Foley Square and rode up in the elevator to the FBI offices in the tower of the Federal Building. After prolonged questioning about David, one of the agents said conversationally, "Do you know that your brother-in-law said you told him to supply information for Russia?"

Julius Rosenberg almost shook out of his skin. "Will you bring him here and let him tell me that to my face?" he demanded.

"What will you do?"

"I will call him a liar to his face because that is not so. Look, gentlemen, you asked me to come down here to give some information concerning David Greenglass, and now you are trying to implicate me in something. I want to see a lawyer."

"Oh, we are not accusing you of anything," said the agent named Norton. "We are trying to help you."

The agent named Harrington suggested that Mr. Rosenberg might like a smoke, or a piece of gum. The third agent volunteered the thought that they could have some lunch sent in, but Julius Rosenberg had made up his mind.

"I want you to get in touch with the lawyer at my union, the Federation of Architects and Engineers," he said. "His name is Victor Rabinowitz."

After a couple of hours of fencing, the FBI did call the FAECT lawyer. Rabinowitz' partner got on the phone, and Rosenberg said he was down at the FBI. "Are you under arrest?" asked the lawyer. Rosenberg said he didn't know. "Ask the FBI if you are under arrest," instructed the lawyer. Rosenberg turned to Agent Norton, "Am I under arrest?" Norton shook his head. "He says no," Rosenberg said into the phone. "Then pick yourself up, and come down to our office," instructed the lawyer. Rosenberg made a little bow in the direction of the three agents. "Good-by, gentlemen," he said, and walked out of the office. In Foley Square he bought a copy of the *Post* with a picture of David Greenglass on the front page. It was the first inkling he had that David had been actually arrested.

Had David actually led the FBI to Julius, or was the FBI question just bluff? The fact that Julius had not been arrested, whereas David had been arrested, suggested a bluff, but Ethel and Julius had to know, and know quickly.

On June 17, Ruth Greenglass came home from the hospital on a stretcher. Despite the infections in her burns, which were still painful, she had insisted on going home. As members of the family had been doing for thirty-six years, Ethel Rosenberg took her two boys and went around to the old flat of her mother, Mrs. Tessie Greenglass, on Sheriff Street. She said the purpose of her visit was to see Bernie's wife Gladys, who was expected to return that day from a hospital. Gladys was not there, however. After a while Ruth came in, and rushed to her mother-in-law. She eyed Ethel warily. Quite formally, Ethel asked how Ruth was feeling. "I'm having trouble getting around with the burns, but I'll be all right," said Ruth. "How is Davy?" asked Ethel next. "All right," said Ruth, turning abruptly to Mrs. Tessie Greenglass. "Ma," she said quickly, "I have to pick up the baby. She is outside in the carriage near my mother's store. Good-by." Ethel stayed to pump Mrs. Tessie Greenglass for information, but to no avail.

On Saturday, Ruth and Mrs. Tessie Greenglass visited David at the Federal House of Detention. When they got back to Sheriff Street, they found Ethel waiting. Ethel had a flood of questions: how was David's health, how was he standing up under jail, and when could she go to see him?

Mrs. Tessie Greenglass scowled. "Well, look," she said, "Ruth is very tired and hungry. Suppose we sit down and eat, and talk later." Ethel had to accept. She tried to ease the atmosphere by describing a course in guitar that she was taking, but nobody listened. After the meal, Ruth announced she was going to pick up her baby, since it was time for its bath. This time Ethel re-

fused to be shaken off. She and Ruth went together to the up-
holstery shop which the Printz family ran on Rivington Street.

When she reached the carriage containing her baby, Ruth said,
"You know it is such a nice day, I think I will stay down with her
another ten minutes. Then I will take her upstairs for her bath."
The two women walked around the block. Finally Ethel could
contain herself no longer.

"You know how I feel toward Davy," she burst out. "You
know how I have always felt toward you, although I must say
you people have not always reciprocated, especially in the last
year. However that is beside the point. I'm going to stand by you
and help all I can, but I am Davy's sister and I have a right to
know what he is going to do? Is he going to plead guilty?"

Ruth flared up. "What are you asking silly questions for?" she
said. "David is not guilty, and I am not guilty! We have hired a
lawyer and we are going to fight the case in our own way."

Ethel Rosenberg said, "Look, I didn't know really what to
think. I had to hear it from your own lips."

With a grimace of distaste, Ruth said something about going
to a doctor. She hurried back to the store, where her mother
agreed that an immediate visit to the doctor was desirable.

Mrs. Printz took over the responsibility of the baby carriage
again, and Ruth set off toward the doctor's, followed by Ethel
Rosenberg. "I have to say good-by now," said Ruth when they
reached East Houston Street. Ethel came up and put her arms
around her sister-in-law and kissed her. Ruth Greenglass stood
rigidly under the kiss. "Good-by," she repeated, coldly, and the
two women parted.

Later that same afternoon, the entire Rosenberg family, Julius,
Ethel, and the boys, came to the photographic shop of Ben
Schneider at 99 Park Row. They ordered thirty-six passport
photos of themselves in a variety of poses, an almost unprece-
dented number, costing $9, which they paid in cash. Schneider
remembered the Rosenbergs well because the two boys acted
wild, and he had to ask their parents to leave the shop and come

back later for the prints, lest the boys destroy valuable equipment. Obviously, the Rosenbergs were finally girding themselves for an escape attempt to Mexico, Switzerland, Czechoslovakia, and Russia. But on Monday, Julius Rosenberg glanced out of the machine shop on East Houston Street and noticed FBI agent Harrington peering in. The agent waved his hand and walked on, making no effort at concealment. Thereafter the Rosenbergs were always uneasily conscious of surveillance. On the evening of July 17, more than a month after David's arrest, two agents came to the Knickerbocker Village apartment and took Julius away, under arrest.

Ethel Rosenberg gave an immediate indignant statement to the press, implying that the real culprit was her brother David.

Her husband had been "very much distressed," said Ethel, when David was arrested. "He felt very badly for Dave and his family," she said. "He told me, 'It's fantastic, it's just a lot of lies. It can't be true.' We were as sure then as we are sure now that my brother is innocent of all these charges."

One of the reporters asked mildly if her brother or her husband had ever been a Communist. Neither of them ever had, she said indignantly. Neither of them knew any Communists or Communist sympathizers, she added. Yet both had been arrested. Could either of them have been involved in espionage? "I've lived with my husband for eleven years," said Ethel Rosenberg, "and I just can't see it. It's impossible!"

3

After three balky and truculent appearances in which she refused on constitutional grounds to answer questions before a Federal Grand Jury investigating atomic espionage, Ethel Rosenberg was arrested August 12, 1950, on a charge of conspiracy to commit treason, and was held in jail, like her husband, for failure to produce $100,000 bail.

Temporarily, Mrs. Tessie Greenglass agreed to take Ethel's

sons, Michael, seven, and Robert, three. The old lady was less than happy about the arrangements. From the first she said it was impossible. Her blood pressure was over 200, she pointed out, and her $20 a month cold-water flat on the ground floor at 62 Sheriff Street, behind the boarded-up shop which her late husband had used for his Singer Sewing Machine repair shop, was not suitable for youngsters from Knickerbocker Village. Days after the arrival of the two boys, she was still growling at them, "I can't take care of you, I can't do it." If she continued taking care of them, despite her growling, it was simply because nobody else in the family seemed able to do it.

The two boys were very restless. They slept with Mrs. Tessie Greenglass in her bed in a tiny room whose window had to be kept closed because it faced one of the rat-ridden empty lots characteristic of modern East Side decay. They had trouble getting to sleep because the older kids in the neighborhood ran and yelled and kicked cans and smashed glass against brick in the empty lot on one side and in the empty lot to the rear, almost up to midnight. Even after they dozed off, little Robert was grinding his teeth in his sleep.

Because the flat lacked a toilet, the boys had to use a community one upstairs in the hall, and their noisiness annoyed other tenants. After arrangements were made for Michael to attend a play school, there was a comparative lull in the middle of the day during which Robert spent most of his time on the front sidewalk, playing listlessly with his red fire engine and "watching," as he said a dozen times a day, "for Mommy to come home." Then Michael returned and drove the younger boy to extremes of excitement and tears with his wild moods. The pair of them were too lively for the old lady.

Bernard Greenglass, who had secured a job as an examiner of prints in a silk house after leaving the Pitt Machine Products Co., phoned one day to say that his wife Gladys, long ill with Hodgkins disease, seemed to be dying, and that somebody would have to care for his twenty-three-months-old daughter Sharon.

Mrs. Tessie Greenglass keened over the news. She couldn't help, she wailed, she couldn't even do what she was trying to do. Bernie asked her to take it easy.

"Take it easy!" she shrilled. "How can I take it easy? I can't do nothing. I'm killed! I ought to be in a home."

At the age of sixty-eight, there was only a little gray in the black hair which Mrs. Tessie Greenglass wore combed back from her face. She looked sturdy enough, but she was "broken down in a variety of ways," besides her blood pressure, she told neighbors.

What bothered the old lady most was money trouble. Samuel, the oldest child and the only one to escape from the East Side, sent $5 a week out of his salary as a jewelry salesman. David had been giving $5 a week until he landed in jail. Bernard would help except that he had his own troubles. Ethel was in jail. Upstairs in the five-story tenement, in a $12-a-month flat, lived Miss Regina Feit, a sister of Mrs. Tessie Greenglass. A veteran member of the International Ladies Garment Workers Union (A. F. of L.), Miss Feit worked long hours as a dress operator, and appreciated a home-cooked dinner at the end of the day. For this she paid her sister $10 a week. "I get whatever falls from my sister's chin," Mrs. Tessie Greenglass would explain, not resentfully, but as one illuminating all the facets of a complex situation.

There may have been an element of pride in the fact that she was still needed in emergency, since Mrs. Tessie Greenglass never failed to mention to visitors that the other grandmother, Mrs. Sophie Rosenberg, was in less vigorous health than herself. She also made it clear that by caring for the children of Ethel and Julius she was not taking their side in the quarrel with David and Ruth. "I'm not like her [Grandma Rosenberg]," Mrs. Greenglass said. "I don't think something that belongs to me has to be perfect and that something that doesn't belong to me is no good. I'm not discriminating that way. If it's mine, but it's wrong, I say so. I saw Ethel in jail and I told her a few things. I had too many annoyances. David is doing a good thing."

David Greenglass was telling his full story. He made up his

mind at 2 A.M. on June 16, the day after his arrest. After talking for five hours at his apartment to the FBI agents who interrupted him when he was making the baby's formula, David went with the agents to FBI headquarters, where questioning was resumed. He maintained some reticences during this period.

During a lull in questioning early the next morning, David decided to seek legal advice before he rounded out his account. He was not worried about himself. He would take whatever penalty the courts provided, he said, but he wanted to work out some agreement, if possible, to help his wife Ruth. He gave his instructions over the phone to Louis Abel, a Navy veteran who had married Ruth's kid sister Dorothy, and who lived in an apartment at 87 Columbia Street, near the Greenglass apartment. Louis extracted the money from the hassock in his living room and took it over to the law office of O. John Rogge, a liberal lawyer whose split with the Communist party over events in Yugoslavia and other matters had been widely publicized. There had been $4,000 in the manila package handed David by Julius Rosenberg as escape money to Russia. Except for $100 which Ruth kept for herself at the last minute, it all went in the original package as a retainer to Rogge. This meant that the Soviet Union indirectly provided the cash which mapped out the legal procedure whereby David Greenglass became a devastating government witness in the first United States atomic-espionage trial resulting in a death penalty. When Ruth Greenglass was called before the Grand Jury, she talked without restraint. She was named subsequently as a coconspirator, but she was not arrested. Though her burns still bothered her, she was able to remain at home, taking care of her two children and even giving Mrs. Tessie Greenglass a hand from time to time.

Mrs. Tessie Greenglass remained as unpredictable as ever. One day toward the end of August, she announced that taking care of Ethel's children was becoming too expensive. She would have to break the independence of a lifetime, she said, and apply for relief the following morning.

The Atom Spies

Instead of going through with this plan, Mrs. Tessie Greenglass appeared after breakfast at the Pitt Machine Products Co., which had ground up thousands of dollars of her savings. The workmen there were still edgy from the impact of that visit a half hour later. "That tough-minded old lady gave me hell for not working," one of them explained. "Whew! You'd think she owned the place. I wasn't doing anything. Ethel gave instructions not to take any new work until the place was sold." There was a lawyer in the office at the Pitt Machine Products Co., talking with a prospective purchaser of the place, when Mrs. Greenglass materialized. She left a bee in his ear: unless the Greenglass family got its share of the money invested in the company, there would be a suit which would tie up any sale indefinitely, she threatened.

The widening rift between the families led to a solution of the desperate situation at the apartment of Mrs. Tessie Greenglass. Michael and Robert were removed to a children's shelter up in the Bronx, and Mrs. Tessie Greenglass was left with time to ponder over what had gone wrong with her life since she arrived on the East Side in 1904 as a girl of twenty-two from Poland. Obviously, the neighborhood had changed. "When I moved in," she recalled, "every house was Jewish people. If sorrow, the whole house in sorrow; if nice thing, the whole house has party. Now not so many houses, and different people." The newcomers ranged from some Irish to more Puerto Ricans to many European displaced persons. None of these had been hostile to her because of her children's troubles, Mrs. Greenglass conceded.

"Everybody showed me friendliness," she said, wonderingly, "more than I thought of. I wouldn't say it if not true. Certain people who hardly speak to me thought we were a very nice family."

Louis Solomon, an amiable pink-cheeked elderly real-estate man collecting rents in the house for the owner, his wife, offered the idea that people might have been better off in the old days when twelve cents would buy a pound of steak and a dime would purchase thirteen rolls. Painting three rooms used to cost $14, he said, and now painting one room was $15, and "the pipes so old it is every minute a plumber." Mrs. Greenglass noted tactfully that Mr. Solomon made no charge for the electricity she (and the boys) had been using in the upstairs hall toilet. She showed proudly how Mr. Solomon had fixed up a bathtub for her under a sort of table top next to the sink in the kitchen. She had a good stove in her apartment, she pointed out, though the draft through the ill-fitting doors from the unheated hallways in the building made warmth hard to achieve on cold days. Solomon said he kept the rents down as low as he could and anyway the tenants wouldn't pay any more. To a comment that at least 50,000 houses on the lower East Side must be more than half a century old, Solomon roared with laughter. "This one is older than me, and I'm 79," he said.

"When Mrs. Roosevelt was in the White House," remarked Mrs. Tessie Greenglass, with a curious clarity, "she said if you want nice people, supply them with nice things. Which is so, which is so. . , ."

As if the question of her own responsibility for the turn of events in the family was still stirring in her mind, Mrs. Tessie Greenglass recalled how she used to take part in the activities of settlement house mothers' clubs to help the children.

"I wouldn't say my children didn't grow up nicely until very lately and I can't understand what happened," she said. "In older times parents were so much stronger, but children of parents from foreign lands . . . we don't know how to read or write. We don't go where they go. There are so many different people. This I can tell you. You have a child under your arms until a certain age and then you can't butt in." Her expression changed and she said venomously, "I blame the Russian Embassy for poisoning my children."

Dismissing Ethel as a girl who "always fought hard for what she got," Mrs. Tessie Greenglass mourned at length over her "baby," her youngest child, David. She hardly heard from him during the war, she said, when she thought he was "pushing a wheelbarrow" at Los Alamos. "He got lots of medals and certificates from top men," she noted. "If he was not color blind, he would not be in this trouble. He would have been in the Navy."

"My husband was a Singer Sewing Machine man," she went on. "He died in 1948. The boys didn't go in with him, too bad, we would have it much better, each and every one of us, if they had. I never inquired too much into the children's lives. I thought what I don't know don't hurt me. David made more than his father, that's what I imagine so, but what came in the end? I can live on a glass of water, bread, and coffee, if only no heartache. This I know: if my children are well, and making a living for their children, I'm more than pleased. That's enough for me."

10. Trial and Punishment

SOON after Harry Gold began talking freely about his career in espionage, the FBI picked up Alfred Dean Slack, a chemical engineer and plant manager who had worked in Tennessee, Georgia, Rhode Island, and New York. Arrested on June 15, 1950, as he drove his car into the parking lot of the Sundure Paint Co., in Syracuse, New York, where he had been employed since the fall of 1948, Slack claimed that he was "violently opposed to the Communist ideology." Expressing confidence that "this mistake will be eventually explained," he declared he did not know anybody named Harry Gold.

Like every other exposed spy, Slack failed to fit the role. Here was an outdoor-looking man wearing rimless eyeglasses, a stocky, medium-sized taciturn fellow with a lined leathery face. On a farm near Clay, New York, he was building a Cope Cod bungalow with his own hands for his second wife and their two young sons. He subscribed to scientific magazines, played an organ in his living room, and carved wood as an outdoor hobby. None of the neighbors could recall anything political, or even controversial, about him.

Nevertheless, Slack came out of the same stream of Communism which produced the other Soviet spies. A native of Syracuse, born August 6, 1905, he had finished high school at the age of eighteen. Taking a job at the Eastman Kodak Laboratories in Rochester, he had placed himself on the same sort of day and night treadmill as Harry Gold by struggling for a college degree after working hours. He carried the additional burden of an unhappy early marriage.

One of Slack's fellow workers in the camera laboratories during this period of quiet desperation was a middle-aged Communist named Richard Briggs. Week in and week out, Briggs deplored the economic flaws of capitalism and praised the perfection of proletarian dictatorship. It was a day when even many American liberals had no notion of the police terror in the Soviet Union, the class rigidity there, the perversion of trade unions, the low living standard, the steady diet of propaganda, and the clamping of ideological yokes on science and literature. Particularly after a United States depression developed in 1929, Slack saw no reason to disagree with his Marxist tutor. Starting in 1936, when he had improved his status considerably at Eastman Kodak, Slack began turning over chemical formulas to Briggs for transmission to Russia. He accepted $100 or $200 for each report. Briggs died in 1939, but Slack continued to provide information through Harry Gold. He seems to have been Gold's first regular contact after the Philadelphian began courier work in 1940.

During the war, Eastman Kodak undertook to operate the Holston Ordnance Depot at Kingston, Tennessee, and Slack went down in 1943 as a department supervisor. Gold visited him periodically there.

While at the Tennessee Ordnance Depot, Slack turned over the formula for RDX, a mixture of TNT and cyclonite far stronger than TNT, which the Navy used in torpedoes and the Army used in bazooka rockets. RDX proved devastating in Western Europe against tanks and pillboxes, and it may have turned the tide against Axis submarines in the Caribbean. The Russians must have been overjoyed to get it, though they received a similar formula from Dr. Raymond Boyer in Canada.

Slack had operated on the fringe of the atomic net, without turning over, so far as it was known, any data on nuclear fission.

He was treated with noticeable severity so long as he pretended innocence. Held in $100,000 bail on a charge of wartime espionage, punishable by death, Slack went by car down to Tennessee on June 20, with handcuffs attached to a chain around his waist. Three armed deputy sheriffs went with him. Sympathetic villagers of Clay, led by the Rev. Owen E. Rutledge, a Methodist minister, and Charles H. Rickard, the local grover, meanwhile raised a fund to enable Mrs. Slack to finish her new house, so it could be sold or rented if necessary. Neighbors also helped her meet immediate living expenses. They thought of the Slacks as people in trouble, not as the family of a man who had intrigued against their own lives. They recalled the case of John M. Corson, a young New York physicist who became acquainted with Klaus Fuchs as a coworker at the Manhattan District Project during the war. When Fuchs was arrested in 1950, Corson immediately wired him: NATURALLY, DO NOT BELIEVE THE ACCUSATIONS. IF I CAN BE OF ANY SERVICE, CALL ON ME. Fuchs replied: THANK YOU. THERE IS NOTHING YOU CAN DO. THE EVIDENCE WILL CHANGE YOUR MIND. Though there was no evidence of any political involvement on Corson's part, his United States passport was lifted subsequently as a precaution.

Slack similarly disappointed those who had confidence in him without regard for the evidence. When he reached Tennessee, he decided to confess. Following a procedure worked out by the Department of Justice to recommend leniency for those who confessed, Assistant United States Attorney Meek did not ask the death penalty when Slack came before Federal Judge Taylor for sentencing on September 18, 1950. "In view of the fact that Slack resisted giving information to the Russian agents when he realized it was for Russia, the government is willing to accept a ten-year sentence," declared Meek. The Judge imposed fifteen years.

The Justice Department based its gentleness toward Slack on the ground that he had thrice refused to furnish the RDX formula before giving in. Gold overcame Slack's resistance, it was said, by picturing Russia as bearing the full land weight of Hitler's fury, while its allies delayed a second front. This was routine Communist propaganda in those days, avoiding any reference to the half-million United States trucks, the tremendous amount of railway and other equipment which according to John R. Deane in *The Strange Alliance,* provided the margin of superiority enabling the Russians to push back the Nazis from Leningrad and Moscow and Stalingrad. The Soviet propaganda omitted any hint of the millions of tons of gasoline and foodstuffs which went to Russia, along with far more United States military secrets than were ever furnished the United States by Russia, took no account at all of the tremendous British-American military effort in other theaters, or of the tying down of German troops to meet the invasion of Western Europe already being planned. Why should Slack receive any consideration for yielding to such obvious Communist propaganda? The Department of Justice said Harry Gold, who was Slack's courier, had threatened to expose Slack if he continued to be balky. This threat was always implicit in dealings by the apparatus with agents. As a spy of long experience, Slack must have felt its unseen weight before then. However restive Slack became momentarily in Tennessee, it is scarcely logical to assume that he was ever in doubt as to the ultimate destination of his stolen secrets.

Paraphrased fragments of a confession by Slack, made public by the Justice Department, confirmed Gold's story and set the stage for further prosecutions. The outcome of this particular prosecution really carried a private message to others exposed by Gold: if you tell what you know, and thereby help to unroll the net further, you may receive as much leniency as can be arranged through the courts; otherwise, you will get the legal limit. Taking shape behind the scenes was a tough but flexible new United States policy for dealing with an apparatus which had proved too successful for domestic comfort, or safety. As part of this policy, the FBI kept secret any leads in a confession opening up possible counterespionage trails, until those trails had been thoroughly explored.

Abe Brothman and Miriam Moskowitz ran afoul of the new policy when they were picked up by the FBI on July 29, 1950. Ostensibly they were charged with conspiracy to obstruct justice, but the actual charge amounted to espionage. The treatment they received matched the concealed crime, which had been outlawed by the statute of limitations. The indictment against them contained two counts. The first concerned the phony story they hatched with Gold to mislead the 1947 Federal Grand Jury investigating subversion. The second involved actual delivery of the story before the Grand Jury. Only the first count mentioned Miss Moskowitz, but Brothman got both barrels. Bail was set at $25,000 each after they pleaded not guilty early in August. Miss Moskowitz argued desperately for a reduction in bail to $1,000. "The spying activities of persons other than the two defendants have distorted this case out of all proportion," her lawyer declared. The prosecution replied that they both were involved in espionage, as a matter of fact, and that the real offense outlined by the indictment was perjury to conceal espionage.

"The government contends that the furtive meetings of these defendants were not in the nature of a Sunday-school picnic," United States Attorney Irving H. Saypol remarked dryly.

Brothman's wife Naomi started a separate proceeding for lower bail, only to abandon it when one of Saypol's assistants asked if she had a Communist record. Though the bail remained high, Brothman and Miss Moskowitz managed to raise the cash in a few weeks. They were tossed back into jail when the trial began in November. Their lawyers noted that Alger Hiss was not committed to prison during his trials, and that the eleven leaders of the United States Politburo were not committed during their treason trial until they became obstreperous in court. "We are in a different period now," said Saypol, curtly, and he was upheld by Federal Judge Irving Kaufman.

The prosecution built its case around Elizabeth T. Bentley and Harry Gold. Miss Bentley, who had been a school teacher before she entered on her lost decade (1935-45) as a Stalinist, wore a plum-colored woolen suit and an air of rock-ribbed New England respectability. She conceded without hesitation that she had been the mistress, as well as the espionage assistant, of Jacob Golos, but she quibbled a bit about her age, before listing it as forty-two. From time to time she stole documents for Golos, in accordance with "Communist ethics," she said. "I never thought of the problem of stealing, I simply carried out Party orders." Nor did she annoy Golos with questions. "You don't ask questions in the Communist party," she pointed out.

Having more or less set the stage, Miss Bentley told how Golos turned over Abe (The Penguin) Brothman to her as an informant in 1940. Arrangements were worked out during a dinner discussion at a Chinese restaurant on 33rd Street, between Sixth and Seventh Avenues, in New York. "Mr. Golos said in Mr. Brothman's presence that I was to be the representative of the Communist party from whom he was to take directives," she testified. Her duties included collecting Party dues, explaining new Party policies, and taking down technical explanations in shorthand. Most of the blueprints and data provided by Brothman were industrial in nature, but occasionally he reached into the military field. Once she recalled talk about a chemical "kettle" for Edgewater Arsenal. Her memory was unsupported by documentary evidence since she had always burned her original notes after typing a report for Golos.

Miss Bentley let the jury know that she and Brothman did not get along. Trying to be impersonal, she found him impertinent and inquisitive. He never paid his dues on time. Frequently he would keep her waiting hours in a restaurant for a rendezvous, or fail to appear at all. For his part, Brothman complained of Miss Bentley's lack of technical understanding as well as her lack of appreciation for past favors on the part of the apparatus. Nevertheless, when arrangements were made for a new contact, he got panicky. He was quite satisfied with Bentley, he asserted. He objected particularly to meeting a new contact without any direct introduction from her or Golos. From the fuss he made, Brothman may have suspected some threat or danger to himself. Reassured, he agreed to go along with the arrangement.

Harry Gold, as the next witness, was able to carry on the story by telling how he slid in alongside Brothman in the front seat of a parked car in New York one evening in September, 1941, and said, "Hello, Abe. I bring regards from Helen," Helen Sherman being Miss Bentley's Party name.

The difference between the testimony of Harry Gold and Miss Bentley was that he produced documentary evidence. From the depths of his capacious cellar closet in Philadelphia had come a folder marked "A. B.'s Stuff," and from the folder a card bearing a typewritten memo about the rendezvous based on instructions from his Soviet superior, Semen (Sam) Semenov. This read:

> Mon 10 p.m.
> N. 27 bet. 6 and 7 av.
> 2N9088
> Abe
> Helen

To nail Brothman to the rendezvous, the prosecution needed only to connect the auto license plate number, 2N9088, with the defendant. Unfortunately, Bureau of Motor Vehicle records for that year had been destroyed. Harry Gold remembered that Brothman tried to explain away his nervousness that evening by mentioning a ticket received for illegal parking in New York only a few weeks earlier. A citywide check of police station records ordered by Saypol showed that Brothman's car, bearing license plate 2N9088, did get in trouble for illegal parking on Cortland Street the previous August 15.

Miss Bentley had testified as though emotion might rip through her rather thin-skinned calm any moment, but Harry Gold proved to be stolidity itself in describing his general procedure as a courier. "I would be introduced by my Soviet superior to an American who would furnish me with information," he said, with such detachment as to create a passing wonder as to whether he considered himself an American or not.

"These introductions were of two kinds," he continued. "Either I was given a precise set of instructions as to how to get in contact with the American who would give the information, or it was a personal introduction. After that I was the sole contact for the greater part of the time with the Americans who were feeding me data for transmission to the Soviet Union. I would meet him, would give him very exact instructions as to what sort of information was desired. If there had been a previous courier in contact with him, I would first endeavor to clean up everything that had gone before. . . . I would discuss with the man what he had available. He would make definite commitments on certain dates to transfer information to me. I would come on those dates. . . ."

At the second meeting, which Brothman reached an hour and a half late, after three telephone calls made hash out of all their meticulous arrangements for secrecy, Gold listed what his superiors wanted: any processes involving the manufacture of aviation gasoline, any of the techniques used for the manufacture of articles from natural rubber; and secondly, processes used for the manufacture of synthetic rubber, manufacture of petroleum lubricants, processes for manufacture of colloidal graphite, processes for the manufacture of strategic organic chemicals, and processes for the manufacture of synthetic butyl alcohol (used as a solvent for smokeless powder).

"Plus," he testified, "any and all information which Abe might find available to him regarding matters of military interest."

Operating according to instructions, Harry Gold tried to crack down on Brothman after a while. "I told Abe he would have to mend his ways regarding two matters," he testified. "The first was the submission of fragmentary bits of information. Secondly, I said that he would have to start keeping appointments on time."

Vastly annoyed, Brothman replied that "apparently the Soviet

Union didn't appreciate the value of the material" he had submitted in the past. He said he had given the complete plans for the manufacture of high-octane gasoline. And he also said that he had given John (Golos) the plans for a turbine-type aircraft engine and that at a later date he had given Helen the plans for one of the first Jeep models.

Gold testified, "Abe told me that if it was matters of military importance that were desired, and if it were complete plans and complete descriptions of processes, that at that very minute there was on his desk at Hendricks the complete plans plus all of the descriptive material for the operation of a military explosive plant in Tennessee."

Brothman failed to appear, however, for the next rendezvous, at which he was to turn over the description of the Tennessee plant. He was completely unreliable, though sooner or later and in one form or another, he usually managed to deliver what he promised. Gold learned to retain fragmentary or unsatisfactory material without protest. As a result, blueprints and other documents from companies where Brothman worked or was employed as a consultant piled up in Gold's cellar, for eventual use at the trial.

With or without the help of memos from that capacious cellar, Gold was able to describe rendezvous after rendezvous with photographic clarity. He would say, "I set the date for Fifty-first Street and Lexington Avenue, northwest corner, a Bickford's followed by a cafeteria called either the Lane or the Park Lane and then a Translux Theatre. On the southwest corner there is a bank with a clock on the face of the building. . . ." Or, "It was in the doorway of a Horn & Hardart restaurant, which is on Twenty-third Street, on either Sixth or most likely Seventh-Avenue. It is not right on the corner. This Horn & Hardart has a very large window or windows and a very small doorway. . . ."

According to Gold, Brothman's Soviet standing varied according to his espionage performance, which was distinctly spotty. When Brothman left the large engineering company whose far-flung resources he had been tapping regularly, in order to go into business for himself, Gold stage-managed a magnificent hoax which more than anything else revealed the gullibility behind Brothman's surface cynicism.

A very important Soviet dignitary, an official from Moscow, was soon coming to the United States, Gold whispered to Brothman. This official had reasons of state for his trip, but his actual, concealed purpose was to meet Abraham Brothman, and to discuss the unusual work Brothman had been doing for the Soviet Union, and might do in the future. Gulping down the bait, Brothman said he would be glad indeed to meet the Soviet dignitary.

Gold reserved two rooms at the Lincoln Hotel for the historic meeting, which occurred in December, 1942. He put Semen Semenov, his Soviet superior, in one of the rooms, and he and Brothman went to the other around 8 P.M.

By prearrangement, Semenov knocked at the door about twenty minutes after Gold and Brothman arrived in their room. Gold introduced his boss as "George." The deception almost collapsed when "George" referred to Gold as "Harry" instead of as Frank Kessler, the name Gold was then using with Brothman. Fortunately, Brothman was too dazzled by the imaginary honor being paid him to catch the slip.

Semenov, who was a mathematician, kept Brothman off balance with an obviously rehearsed abstruse discussion. Then Brothman made his bid for a place in the Soviet sunshine by exhibiting a piece of equipment of special design used in connection with a nickel-catalyst process, an intricate and valuable gadget which Semenov properly praised. For hour after hour this verbal minuet continued. After Semenov left, Brothman walked as if on air through the hotel lobby into the night.

"Abe told me," Gold testified without expression at the trial, "that I had provided one of the most wonderful experiences of his life . . . had given him a thrill he could never forget. He told me he was so elated that he was going back at that hour,

272

2 A.M., to the Chemurgy offices to work the rest of the night. . . . He said he couldn't sleep. . . . He took a taxi and left. . . ."

Two concrete matters came up during the Semenov-Brothman conference. One was a demand by Semenov that Brothman give up his own business to work for one of a specified group of United States concerns. The other was an offer of stenographic help whenever he and Gold found it necessary during preparation of an espionage report.

When he emerged from his trance, Brothman summarily rejected the first idea, but accepted the second. Taking stenographic help, curiously enough, proved calamitous for him, since the government was able to locate Jennie Zawyrucha, the young stenographer who was hired, and put her on the stand to confirm weekly meetings with Gold and Brothman over a period of months, and even to cite the subject matter of some of their espionage reports.

Exposure of Brothman as a spy had legal relevancy only in so far as it provided a motive for his fake explanation before the 1947 Grand Jury about his acquaintance with Jacob Golos. When Gold reached the conspiracy between Miss Moskowitz, Brothman, and himself, he seemed less calm as a witness, but almost equally precise. Neither Miss Moskowitz nor Brothman dared to take the stand, so the defense tried the traditional tactic of desperation, that of discrediting the chief prosecution witness. Defense Counsel William Kleinman, a former assistant district attorney from Brooklyn with a hammer-and-tongs courtroom manner, concentrated on the lies Gold told about himself to Brothman and Miss Moskowitz. Every detail in Gold's compensatory imaginary life with a wife and children was turned over and over and over. Kleinman stripped the veil from Gold's death wish for his own brother, and all the other Freudian shenanigans which went on in that complex mind. In opening remarks, cross-examination, and summation, he hammered away at the theme that Gold was mentally irresponsible. Starting with the theory that Gold's "only purpose is to save his own rotten neck because his life is at stake," Kleinman worked up to the idea that Gold was driven by "insane hate" to try to "destroy" Brothman and Miss Moskowitz.

"Gold has a disordered mind, a devious mind, nothing that you or I can understand," roared Kleinman, ". . . this phony, this schizophrenic, this single-tracked switch mind, this fellow who dealt in cloak-and-dagger fashion with Soviet superiors, who had built up a completely false background for himself. . . ."

The jury decided that Gold might have been lying like a courier to Brothman and Miss Moskowitz but that he had told the truth in court. After three hours of deliberation, they found both defendants guilty. Judge Kaufman praised them for having reached a verdict that was intelligent and proper and a complete vindication of the jury system.

"What I do not understand and simply cannot fathom," he continued, "is why people seek to undermine the country which gave them every opportunity—opportunity for education, opportunity for livelihood, yes, and an opportunity for a fair trial such as they have received here."

On November 28, 1950, Brothman was sentenced by Judge Kaufman to seven years in prison and a $15,000 fine. Miss Moskowitz received two years and a $10,000 fine. These were the maximum penalties under the law for the offenses on which they had stood trial.

2

From the beginning, the trial of Ethel and Julius Rosenberg had the quality of high drama. Here two closely knit families engaged in a struggle to the death as two wives tried contradictory solutions for politically devious lives. Here national security seemed to tremble in the balance. For the first time, the theft of United States nuclear secrets was put to the test in an open court, and the shape of the subversive menace in American laboratories was brought into sharp focus. Nevertheless, like earlier proceedings growing out of the confession of Harry Gold, this case fell within the framework of the tough but flexible new United States policy toward Soviet espionage. Like Alfred Dean Slack, Ruth and David Greenglass encountered consideration and leniency from the moment they decided to come clean. Like Abe Brothman, Ethel and Julius Rosenberg felt the weight of maximum court severity after they ignored the evidence against them, and lied—lied so lamely and unconvincingly as to arouse wonder as to whether they were making a real bid for personal freedom or a mere defense of their ideology.

The sharp propoganda tone on both sides before the trial suggested the magnitude of the stakes. FBI Director Hoover, summarizing the facts, said Rosenberg had made himself available to Soviet espionage agents "so he could do the work for which he thought he was fated." Emanuel H. Bloch, who had previously represented such Communists as Marcel Scherer, Marion Bachrach and Steve Nelson, took over the defense of Julius Rosenberg. His father, Alexander Bloch, agreed to represent Ethel. The Blochs declared there was "not one iota of truth" to the charges.

Emanuel Bloch roared with laughter, for publication, over the government story of a treasonable rendezvous kept in Albuquerque by matching several halves of a box of Jello. "This is fantastic, something kids hear on a Lone Ranger TV program," said Bloch. Yet Hede Massing, ex-wife of Gerhart Eisler, in her autobiography, *This Deception,* published after the Rosenberg trial, declared that cutting of a box or package in two jagged halves was such a stereotyped recognition device in the Soviet underground that she objected to it as "rather primitive" when it was used on her first espionage journey to the United States.

After some reshuffling of indictments, the two Rosenbergs and Morton Sobell emerged as major defendants on a charge of conspiracy to transmit military secrets to Russia during the war. The Greenglasses were named as conspirators, but not as defendants. David had already pleaded guilty to another indictment and was awaiting sentence, whereas Ruth was neither arrested, nor prosecuted, under an arrangement with the government worked out by David's lawyer, O. John Rogge, in consideration of the services of the Greenglasses to the prosecution, and to the welfare of their country. Morton Sobell fitted into the case through his role in Rosenberg's marshaling of Leftist technicians for espionage, though he had nothing to do with Los Alamos or the atom bomb. Anatoli A. Yakovlev, the one-time Soviet superior of Harry Gold and Julius Rosenberg, got a listing as a defendant *in absentia*, since he was out of reach of prosecution. Legally speaking, it was a nice inclusive package, permitting the marshaling of evidence from various quarters.

The first skirmish came over bail. To discourage any new thought of flight, since Sobell had been returned forcibly from Mexico, and the Rosenbergs had flirted with the idea of trying the Mexican escape route to Russia, the defendants were being held in prohibitively high bail of $100,000 each. The defense tried to get the bail whittled down to $10,000, and the prosecution countered with a demand that bail be cancelled entirely. The prosecution talked sensationally of the atom bomb, and the defense lawyers shouted that their clients were being "framed." Emanuel Bloch added, "This case will be fought bitterly down the line. This is not a Gold or Greenglass with whom they are dealing." When everybody finished orating, Federal Judge Davis let the bail stay where it was.

David Greenglass and Julius Rosenberg stayed at the Federal House of Detention in New York, but they had no contact, particularly after David, in annoyance over reported efforts to exert pressure on his wife Ruth, threatened to punch his brother-in-law's nose at the first opportunity. For three days, David was kept in solitary confinement, without laces in his shoes or a belt to hold up his pants because the warden read, and believed, a possibly planted newspaper story that he was threatening suicide. Eventually David convinced the warden that nothing was farther from his mind than killing himself since he was fighting for the future of his wife and children. He was a quiet prisoner, absorbed most of the time in popular-science fiction. Meanwhile Julius Rosenberg averted his eyes from the future and took what queer comfort he could from the present. Meeting Eugene Dennis, national secretary of the Communist party, during an exercise period at the jail, he sneered that Dennis had chosen comparatively safe open-Party work instead of running real risks underground.

In a Federal prison for women, Ethel Rosenberg sang steadily. Hour after hour, she warbled "Good Night, Irene," "John Brown's Body," (which was also "Solidarity Forever"), Communist songs, patriotic songs, popular songs, everything and anything vocal, to the amazement of her fellow prisoners and the guards, who conceded that her voice was better than fair. She liked to sing, she said, and it kept up her courage.

The trial started March 6, 1951, and lasted slightly more than three weeks. It centered around two themes: the relation of Communism to espionage, and the relation of a brother to a sister. Emanuel Bloch set the defense pattern during selection of the jury. When a member of the panel under examination remarked that he felt prejudiced against Communists, Bloch arose impressively. "For the record," he said. "I want it understood by all jurors that there is no evidence that membership in the Communist party is involved. I don't want any impression that Communism is on trial." Federal Judge Irving R. Kaufman, who had presided at the Brothman trial, said quietly, "There is no evidence at all in this trial up to now," and excused the talesman who did not like Communists.

United States Attorney Saypol, another Brothman trial alumnus, met the challenge in his opening statement. "The evidence will show that the loyalty and the allegiance of the Rosenbergs and Sobell were not to our country, but to Communism, Communism in this country and Communism throughout the world," he said. "By their rank disloyalty these defendants joined with their coconspirators in a deliberate, carefully planned conspiracy

277

to deliver to the Soviet Union the information and the weapons the Soviet Union could use to destroy us."

Saypol said all three defendants were involved in a "ceaseless campaign to recruit promising members [of the Communist party] for their Soviet espionage ring." Bloch demanded a mistrial on the ground that harping on Communism was "inflammatory in character." Denying the motion, the court said it would rule on any evidence that Communism motivated acts of the defendants, if and when such evidence was produced. As the trial proceeded, Bloch soft-pedaled his claim that the open and conspiratorial sides of the Communist coin had no connection, and concentrated on a grinding effort to destroy the character of Ruth and David Greenglass. Eventually Judge Kaufman admitted the Communist background of the defendants as he would have admitted, he said, testimony involving the Elks or the Masons, or the Republican party, "if there were something about membership in that Party which would prove one of the elements of the offense." The casual connection between Communism and espionage in the present case was clear, he said. When Bloch continued to protest, the Judge said the defense argument was really a claim "that because a person might be a member of the Communist party he was entitled to certain immunities he wouldn't have if he were a member of some other party that didn't quite carry with it the same alleged stigma."

The first government witness, Max Elitcher, talking freely on the advice of his attorney, O. John Rogge, described the defendants' social and trade union careerism inside the Communist movement as well as their efforts to entice him into espionage. Defense lawyers hammered away at Elitcher for hours. Emanuel Bloch wrested an admission from the witness that he had sworn falsely, during his government service, that he was not a Communist, and therefore faced a possible perjury charge. Edward Kuntz, lawyer for Sobell, got Elitcher to concede that he had not told the FBI right away about his 1946 visit to Sobell's home.

"I was inclined to conceal it," said Elitcher.

"You lied to the FBI?" pursued the defense lawyer.

"I omitted to tell about it," said Elitcher, confirming the normal process of confession, which is by installments.

Anonymous mailed threats against Elitcher's life confirmed the public impression that the first of 118 announced government witnesses had riddled the defense. Subsequently Elizabeth T. Bentley and Harry Gold described indirect espionage contacts with Julius Rosenberg which proved almost equally devastating.

A middle-aged ex-schoolteacher, testifying carefully, Miss Bentley said she had worked for Jacob Golos, and for Anatol (Al) Gromov, first secretary of the Russian Embassy, among others. "The bulk of the work was collecting information from Communists employed in the United States government and passing it on to Communist superiors for transmission to Moscow," she declared. "The Communist party being part of the Communist International served only the interests of Moscow, whether it be in propaganda or espionage or sabotage." At various times, she said, she handled thirty-odd informants, including a man named Julius, who lived at Knickerbocker Village in New York.

On several occasions between the fall of 1942 and the fall of 1943, she said, the phone in her Greenwich Village apartment would ring late at night, and a voice would say, "This is Julius." Julius would leave a message for Golos. As a result of that message, she and Golos would usually drive to Knickerbocker Village a day or so later. Golos would leave her in the parked car and pace up and down the sidewalk, waiting for his contact, whom he described as an engineer. Then Julius would appear, he and Golos would go into a candy store, and after a while Golos would return alone with an envelope full of technical information, Miss Bentley said.

Emanuel Bloch did what he could to destroy the effect of Miss Bentley's evidence. However, neither he nor the prosecution seems to have tested her memory of Julius by sight, or sound. She did not know Harry Gold at all, Miss Bentley agreed. She had never been indicted for espionage despite her ex-spy queen status in the newspapers, she conceded. She was not quite as clear about her relationship with Golos as she had been in the Brothman trial, but neither did she claim that her liaison with him was a purely business one. One of the satisfactions of her espionage work was that as an espionage associate of Golos she had been able on occasion to give orders to Earl Browder, who served briefly during the war as the titular leader of the Communist party, U. S. A.

Between the Brothman and the Rosenberg trials, Harry Gold had been sentenced to twenty-nine years and 223 days in prison (thirty years, minus time in jail since his arrest), which was subject to considerable reduction for good behavior. Though he had never seen, or talked to, any of the three defendants in the Rosenberg case, he proved an important witness. By providing the first public account of his various meetings with Klaus Fuchs, in New York, Cambridge, and New Mexico, and using his own busy espionage life as a frame of reference, Gold created an atmosphere useful to the prosecution. He then focused on his brief, double-barreled encounter with the Greenglasses in Albuquerque on June 3, 1945, when the Jello-box fragment given him by Yakovlev was joined to the Jello-box fragment given Ruth Greenglass by Julius Rosenberg. In addition to the password—"I bring greetings from Julius"—Harry Gold nailed Julius Rosenberg to the rendezvous with a series of precise recollections.

Harry Gold's whole account meshed nicely with the Rosenberg-Greenglass history as presented by the prosecution. He told of Yakovlev's assignment of an extra stop at Albuquerque, on the way back from seeing Fuchs at Santa Fe, because the woman assigned to go to Albuquerque was unable to go. He described how he objected to the double load, only to be silenced by a glare from Yakovlev and the hissed comment, "That is an order!" Having met the Greenglasses, Gold testified, since he usually stayed with a contact once made, he had suggested picking up the threads on two occasions, but was coldly rebuffed by Yakov-lev. The hidden reason for the rebuffs, of course, was that Rosenberg had taken over contact work with Greenglass.

Tangling with Harry Gold on the witness stand was like questioning an encyclopedia: it could only provoke a spate of coldly accurate facts. Having read the Brothman trial record, and reached the obvious conclusion, Emanuel Bloch merely waved his hand when Gold finished testifying. "The defense has no cross-examination on this witness," he said.

While Gold held the limelight in the courtroom, an outside flurry hinted at the slowly burning secret fire of counterespionage which was being fed by various confessions. William Perl, a brilliant young aerodynamics expert (said to be second in his field in the United States only to Dr. Theodore Van Karmen) was arrested on a four-count indictment for perjury. Perl had been listed as a prospective government witness in the Rosenberg trial until his memory proved faulty. During a Grand Jury appearance, he had failed to remember knowing Julius Rosenberg and Morton Sobell, his City College classmates, Mr. and Mrs. Max Elitcher of Flushing, and Mr. and Mrs. Mike Sidorovich of Cleveland.

After Perl pleaded not guilty to the charge, his attorney, Raymond L. Wise, objected vehemently to a government suggestion that bail be fixed in the sum of $20,000. "Mr. Perl wants to help the government," declared Wise. "I have his promise to aid the government. Somehow the government has an idea he is lying, but he is not." Federal Judge Goddard suggested amiably that professors were supposed to have poor memories, and Wise agreed they were often absent-minded. Fixing of bail at $10,000 seemed to be in the making, when Assistant United States Attorney Foley charged that Miss Vivian Glassman, that old friend of Ethel and Julius Rosenberg, had offered Perl "a considerable sum of money" in Cleveland to flee from the United States. Perl had applied for a passport in February, Foley added. That was just a renewal of an old passport, said Wise soothingly, in hope of arranging a summer vacation in Europe. Several espionage

281

suspects had already fled, beyond possibility of recapture, two of them being associates of Perl, declared Foley, inexorably.

Noting that it was a little early to get a passport renewed in February for a summer vacation, Judge Goddard said he thought he would leave the bail figure at $20,000, after all.

William Perl, who had changed his name legally from Mutterperl in 1945, was born in New York, October 1, 1918, the son of a Russian father and a Polish mother, who became naturalized citizens. He attended high school in the Bronx before going to City College, where he obtained a degree of Bachelor of Science in electrical engineering, in 1938, and a master's degree in 1940. On the basis of a high mark in a civil-service examination, Perl was assigned in April, 1939, as an advisor to the National Aeronautics Committee, the research group of the United States Air Force. From time to time the Committee allowed him to take courses to improve his research quality. In 1944, Perl went to the Lewis Flight Propulsion Laboratory in Cleveland, where he directed fifteen researchers studying jet propulsion and supersonic flight. The National Aeronautics Committee returned him to Columbia University for further study; after he secured his doctorate in the fall of 1950 at Columbia, however, he resigned from government service in favor of teaching.

A handsome six-footer with dark wavy hair, Perl did not by his appearance suggest anything as lonely and equivocal as a spy. His wife Henrietta, a tall woman with ash-blond hair, said immediately after his arrest that she was sure of his innocence. "Neither of us is related to any of these people in the spy case," she declared. "Why, I don't even know any of them."

Study of the cast of characters in the Rosenberg trial did, however, suggest something of a coincidence. One tentative government witness, who was never called to the stand, was Mrs. Ann Sidorovich, the woman who according to the Greenglasses had been scheduled originally as their contact at Albuquerque, but had been unable to make the trip. When Perl was placed under arrest, a government statement claimed that the Sidoroviches had served as couriers between Cleveland and New York, until replaced by Gold. Asked flatly if Perl, who had balked so unexpectedly at acknowledging any acquaintance with the Sidoroviches, was believed by the government to have turned over secrets, United States Attorney Saypol said, "All I can say is that he was indicted in connection with the probe of a Soviet atomic spy ring."

The fact that Mrs. Sidorovich, like Mrs. Max Elitcher, was on the government list of witnesses, but did not testify, proved nothing. The government actually called only twenty-two out of its original list of 118 witnesses, on the ground that its basic case against the Rosenbergs was already overwhelming, and that duplication would not improve it. (Back of this policy of restraint might also have been a desire to conceal the extent of government information in various directions, until the time came to pounce on new defendants.)

Of the twenty-two witnesses who did appear for the government, eight described various phases of Morton Sobell's guilt-ridden flight to Mexico, two described security measures at Los Alamos during the war, and another two were relatives of Ruth Greenglass called to affirm minor details of her story.

Instead of Dr. J. Robert Oppenheimer, Dr. Harold C. Urey, and Lt. Gen. Leslie R. Groves, wartime leaders of the Manhattan District Project, who were listed as prospective government witnesses, several lesser experts eventually took the stand. One was Dr. Walter Koski, a nuclear physicist intimately connected with explosive lens-mold experiments at Los Alamos. He said recent Greenglass sketches, duplicating sketches turned over to Harry Gold and Julius Rosenberg during the war, revealed detonation details of the atom bomb so secret that they remained so classified at the time of the trial six years later. John Derry, an electrical engineer who had worked with General Groves, said the Greenglass material showed a "substantially perfected bomb" of the type used at Nagasaki.

The Atom Spies

Once the solid framework of testimony about the Soviet espionage of Sobell and the Rosenbergs had been erected by the prosecution, the trial focused more and more on the complex of relationships in the Greenglass and Rosenberg families. Quite clearly, the chances of the Rosenbergs had dwindled to a slender hope of discrediting their primary accuser, David Greenglass. A determined defense effort in this direction became more imperative than ever after Greenglass himself described details of Los Alamos experiments which he had passed on in 1945 to Soviet Russia, and yet which were still so confidential in 1951 in America that the Judge cleared the courtroom of spectators during his recital and instructed the stenographer to take no notes.

Emanuel Bloch whittled away relentlessly at David's hard choice of loyalties between his wife and his sister. David met questions head-on, no matter how intimate. He said he wasn't sure when he first fell in love with Ruth, since their relationship went back so far in childhood.

Q. At any rate, when you began to see your wife on a fiancé and fiancée basis, did you love her? A. I did.

Q. Did you love her when you married her? A. I did.

Q. And do you love her today? A. I do.

Q. You love her dearly, don't you? A. I do.

Q. Do you love her more than you love yourself? The Court. Oh, I think . . . A. (Loudly) I do.

Moving down to the original visit by Ruth Greenglass to Albuquerque, during which David agreed to act as a spy in exchange for his wife's company, because at that time he was at least partially persuaded that Russia as an ally had a right to wartime developments, Bloch made no effort to underline the government's ultra-delicate treatment of the Communist associations and attitudes of Ruth and David. That would only have bounced back at his own client. Instead, Bloch gambled for emotional sympathy with the jury.

"From the time you told your wife you were not interested and you wouldn't do this work, to the following morning when

284

you told her you would, did you consult with anybody?" Bloch pressed.

"I consulted with memories and voices in my mind," said David. "I felt it was the right thing to do at that time, according to my philosophy at that time. I had doubts almost as soon as I started to do it, though I did not tell Julius. I had a kind of hero-worship there and I did not want my hero to fail. That is why I did not stop the thing after I had the doubts."

"Did it occur to you at the time that you finally said to your wife, 'I will do this,' and then transmitted to her certain information, that there was a possible penalty of death for espionage?"

David Greenglass said, "Yes."

"When you said to your wife, 'Yes, I will do it'—is that correct?" pressed Bloch. "That is correct," said David Greenglass.

"Are you aware that you are smiling?" demanded Bloch. David Greenglass blinked and said, "Not very." It had looked, for a moment, as though he were smiling.

Coming down finally to his confession, David testified that he told his story "as it happened, that was all I was interested in getting out." Bloch nodded. "You were interested in getting out?" he said. Greenglass looked outraged. "I said I was interested in getting out the story, don't misconstrue my words!"

Q. Did you at any time think of your wife while you were down there telling your story to the FBI? A. Of course I thought of her.

Q. Did you think of your wife with respect to the fact that she may be a defendant in a criminal proceeding? A. I did.

Q. And was that one of the factors which motivated you in getting a lawyer? A. At that time I didn't even think about it. I got a lawyer to represent me in court, that is all.

Bloch angled repeatedly for some expression of hate toward Ethel or Julius Rosenberg, but David insisted his basic feeling of friendship for Julius remained, and that his affection for his sister was the same "today, yesterday, and as far back as I ever met her and knew her."

The Atom Spies

Neither Julius nor Ethel made any pretense of reciprocating such sentiments. Julius said he had "done everything to help Davy," only to discover that his brother-in-law "always had it in for me." Asked if "everything" included helping David to join the Communist party, Julius said, "I refuse to answer on the grounds of self-incrimination." Ethel said, "I once loved my brother, but I'd be pretty unnatural if I hadn't changed."

Julius and Ethel Rosenberg admitted almost everything alleged by government witnesses, up to the point of personal danger. Then they inserted denials, or refused to answer on constitutional grounds. Asked about classmates at City College, to take one out of score of examples, Julius mentioned Benjamin Yelsey, Marcus Pogarsky or Page, Joel Barr, Max Elitcher. "Was there a boy by the name of Perl or Mutterperl?" asked United States Attorney Saypol, with head cocked on one side, and a slight grin on his face. "I read in the newspapers about a man called Mutterperl," began Rosenberg, adding quickly, "I refuse to answer any question on the grounds that it might incriminate me."

"That's all I wanted to know," said Saypol. "If you had said you hadn't known him, I wouldn't have pressed you further."

Julius Rosenberg remembered Alfred Saurent. He had met Saurent originally as a roommate of Joel Barr in Greenwich Village, he testified. "I saw him last in early 1950," he continued. "I went to his home to borrow some money—$300. Got it, cash. Still owe it, and more. Saurent is now in Ithaca."

"Don't you know he is in Mexico?" purred Saypol. Immediately the defense lawyers were shouting objections. Emanuel Bloch and Edward Kuntz demanded a mistrial, on the grounds that the question was "highly inflammatory" as well as outrageous in various ways. Judge Kaufman remained calm. "I don't know what the excitement is," he said, "over asking whether a witness is in Mexico."

Rosenberg did not lie convincingly. When he had finished denying the entire espionage conversation which David Greenglass said took place during his first furlough from Los Alamos, Rosenberg was asked what actually was said.

"Well, I am working hard, and we [Ethel and himself] told them how we were, and we asked him how he was," he stammered. "He [David] told us he was fine; he said he was a machinist at that time, and he just repeated that he was a machinist."

The Court: Didn't you know he was a machinist in 1944?

"Yes," said Rosenberg, "but he said he was a machinist at that time. He just repeated that he was working on a secret project and I didn't press him on anything like that."

Sobell never did take the stand, or call any witnesses in his own behalf. Lawyers for the Rosenbergs put on only two minor witnesses besides their clients. A department-store employee testified that a console table at the Rosenberg home (which David Greenglass had said was a gift to Julius from his "friends," the Russians) resembled certain tables on sale at the store at various times. In rebuttal, the government produced Mrs. Evelyn Cox, a domestic who had worked for the Rosenbergs. She declared Mrs. Rosenberg had explained proudly to her that the handsome table was a present from a "friend" of her husband. Ethel Rosenberg had pictured herself as struggling valiantly with only occasional maid service, two or three weeks after the birth of a baby or during an illness, but Mrs. Cox said flatly she was employed by Ethel from September, 1944, throughout the year 1945, except for a summer vacation in 1945.

Julius and his lawyer scoffed at the idea that the Rosenbergs ever had any notion of leaving the country. While Julius was still on the stand, an FBI agent brought into the courtroom a photographer from a shop hardly a block away who recalled somebody resembling the description of Rosenberg, with two wild kids, coming in for passport photos. He wanted a look at Rosenberg to be sure, and when he took the look, he nodded. He was the next witness, a devastating one. He described the wild behavior of the Rosenberg boys, then recalled that Rosenberg had boasted that his wife had just inherited a large sum from a relative in France, and that the family was planning a trip to Europe to collect the inheritance.

In his summation, Emanuel Bloch declared David and Ruth Greenglass had "concocted a false story, and sold a bill of goods to the government." David, he said, was a man who had "disgraced the uniform of every soldier in the United States—a tricky, crafty man—not a man, but an animal."

Greenglass had "smirked" on the witness stand, said Bloch. "Any man willing to testify against his own sister is repulsive and revolting. Maybe some people enjoy lynching, but I wonder if you have ever come across a man who comes into court to bury his own sister, and smiles. Greenglass was arrogant. He had a right to be arrogant because he put it over the FBI and United States Attorney Saypol. He was smarter than the whole bunch. Ruth Greenglass got a hostage, an exchange hostage. She walked out, and put Ethel in. That was the deal. The Greenglasses would do anything for money, they are trying to murder people for money."

Greenglass testified he loved his wife more than his own life, shouted Bloch. "This explains why David Greenglass will bury his sister and brother-in-law to save his wife," he went on. "Greenglass figured that if he put the finger on someone it would lessen his own punishment. He had to find a clay pigeon." Bloch turned to point at the intensely listening Julius Rosenberg. "That man is the clay pigeon!"

United States Attorney Saypol, in his turn, argued that "the breach of family loyalty is that of an older sister and brother-in-law dragging an American soldier into the sordid business of betraying his country."

"The difference between the Greenglasses and Rosenbergs is that the Greenglasses have told the truth, tried to make amends, whereas the Rosenbergs have magnified their sins by their lying," he added.

"We know that these conspirators stole the most important scientific secrets ever known to mankind from this country and delivered them to the Soviet Union. We know of other henchmen of Rosenberg's in this plot by him, by Sobell, by the Soviet Union and its representatives and by other traitorous Americans, to deliver the safeguards to our security into the hands of a power that would wipe us off the face of the earth. We don't know all the details because the only living people who can supply the details are the defendants. . . ."

After a short period of deliberation on the evening of March 28, 1951, the jury found the Rosenbergs guilty. Several hours of further consideration the next morning led to the decision that Sobell was also guilty. When the jury reported, Judge Kaufman expressed his personal gratitude to the members. He praised the prosecution for a capable and fair presentation of the evidence, and said, "This is a sad day for America." Equally sober, United States Attorney Saypol said the conviction should be an occasion, not for exultation, but for reflection. "It is not possible for a great nation to be free from traitors," he said, "but this case shows it is possible ultimately to reach some of them and bring them to the bar of punishment."

Julius Rosenberg was rocking slightly in his chair when the verdict was delivered. He continued rocking. His wife shook her head slightly, shifted her chair against the leg of the marshal behind her, turned, and smiled apologetically. Sobell seemed more interested in the scurrying of reporters toward phones than anything else.

Before the imposition of sentence on April 5, 1951, Judge Kaufman was deluged with letters, 99 per cent of which urged the death penalty. The Judge visited the synagogue three times during the preceding week to seek divine guidance, it was said. He also visited Washington to confer with Attorney General McGrath. The night before the sentencing, he listened for an hour to a weeping appeal for clemency by Mrs. Tessie Greenglass, the sixty-nine-year-old mother of Ethel and David.

Defense attorney Emanuel Bloch in a last courtroom appeal cited an article in Vol. 56 of the *Yale Law Journal* declaring that the idea of a scientific monopoly on the principle of the atom bomb was illusionary. Judge Kaufman asked if the lawyer argued from this that turning over information to Russia was proper on the ground that Russia would eventually develop the same knowledge. Bloch said he did not make this argument but he did believe the American feeling that the country's entire security rested on the atom bomb was a huge exaggeration. Turning to the courtroom as a whole, the Judge said he had not requested the United States Attorney to make any recommendation because he felt the responsibility in the case was too great.

To Ethel and Julius Rosenberg, the Judge said, "I consider your crime worse than murder. In murder a criminal kills only his victim. Your conduct in putting into the hands of the Russians the A-bomb years before our best scientists predicted Russia would perfect the bomb has already caused, in my opinion, the Communist aggression in Korea, with the resultant casualties. . . . By your betrayal you undoubtedly have altered the course of history to the disadvantage of our country."

Though Julius Rosenberg was the "prime mover in the conspiracy," Judge Kaufman said, he was convinced Ethel was a "full-fledged partner."

"I am convinced beyond any doubt of your guilt," he told the Rosenbergs. "It is not in my power to forgive you. Only the Lord can find mercy for what you have done. The sentence of the court upon Julius and Ethel Rosenberg is for the crime for which you have been convicted. You are hereby sentenced to the punishment of death and it is ordered upon some day within the week beginning with Monday, May 21."

Turning to Sobell, the Judge said he had no doubt of his guilt, but he realized it was "a lesser degree because the evidence does not point to any act on your part in the atom-bomb project." He sentenced Sobell to thirty years in prison, noting that he would recommend against any parole, which might mean the full thirty years, or virtually a lifetime sentence.

Harold Phillips, one of Sobell's attorneys, said he thought the sentence "much too severe, even if all the statements made against him were in every way true." Emanuel Bloch promised an immediate appeal to the Circuit Court of Appeals on behalf of the Rosenbergs.

None of the defendants showed any emotion over the sentences. Returning to her cell in the basement at the Federal Building, Ethel Rosenberg burst into loud song. After rendering "One Fine Day," an aria from *Madame Butterfly,* she swung into a not particularly well-known song, called "America Is a Beautiful Country." From a nearby cell, Julius Rosenberg raised his voice to join his wife, and the pair sang together, mostly folk songs and popular melodies, for several hours.

David Greenglass appeared for sentencing on April 6, having received an extra day to spare him the sight of the punishment of his sister. His attorney, O. John Rogge, stressed the usefulness to the country of David's confession, and argued that if the government "wants people in his position to come forward and co-operate it must give him a pat on the back." Rogge suggested five years as a fair sentence, under the circumstances. United States Attorney Saypol thought fifteen years would be more reasonable, and Judge Kaufman accepted the United States Attorney's recommendation.

3

Never before in the history of the country, during war or peace, had a civilian court sentenced native-born Americans to death for espionage. Seldom, if ever, had a husband-and-wife team been sentenced by a Federal court to die for any crime. The only woman executed by Federal court order, so far as informal historians could recall at the time Ethel and Julius Rosenberg heard their sentences pronounced, was Mary Surratt, conspirator in the Lincoln assassination.

In dealing with the atomic conspirators, the Federal government experienced some embarrassment for lack of proper lethal facilities of its own in New York. The Department of Justice elected therefore to borrow the State machinery available at Sing Sing. Despite the specific date set by the court for an execution at the Ossining prison, no immediate contingency existed in the spring of 1951, since appeal would normally consume months, perhaps a year or more. No appeal court, not even the United States Supreme Court, it was pointed out, could alter the sentence, but it could upset the conviction. If the conviction were upheld, the sentencing jurist had a final sixty days, after exhaustion of the last resource of appeal, to reconsider his verdict in the light of any change in the situation. In other words, the door remained ajar for the prisoners to save their lives at the last minute by confessing.

Postponement of the climax of the case permitted development of debate over the severity of the sentences in circles which could not be called Communist or hysterically anti-Communist. Axis Sally and Tokyo Rose, it was pointed out, had received only ten-year terms for wartime treason, while four men who sold United States airplane secrets to the Nazis toward the start of the war received sentences ranging from five to fifteen years. Such cases, however, were not on even footing with the Rosenberg case if Judge Kaufman was right in weighing the nature of the weapons stolen, in addition to the fact of betrayal.

"The atom bomb was unknown when the espionage statute was drafted," the jurist had pointed out, in urging amendment of the law to permit death sentences for espionage in time of peace as well as in war. "I emphasize this because we must realize that we are dealing with missiles of destruction which can wipe out millions of Americans. The competitive advantage held by the United States in super-weapons has put a premium on the services of a new school of spies—the home-grown variety that places allegiance to a foreign power before loyalty to the United States. The punishment to be meted out in this case must therefore serve the maximum interest for the preservation of our society against those traitors in our midst."

In the major English atomic cases, Allan Nunn May received ten years in prison in 1946, and Klaus Fuchs got the maximum under the law, fourteen years, in 1950, when public opinion had stiffened. Both May and Fuchs made confessions of a sort.

In the United States, Dean (nonatomic) Slack and David (atomic) Greenglass received fifteen years each, while Harry (nonatomic and atomic) Gold got almost thirty years. All three confessed. Abe Brothman and Miriam Moskowitz, who covered up an atomic spy as well as participated in nonatomic espionage, received the maximum penalty under the statute chosen for their prosecution; they did not confess. It could be argued that the Rosenbergs deserved harsher treatment than others because they were closer to the Russians and had more influence in building and operating the net. Even so, there was overlapping. It didn't seem easy to differentiate between types of espionage, or between types of Communists, for that matter. Ruth Greenglass remained free to fight for her future, and that of her children, while her sister-in-law, Ethel Rosenberg, prepared for death in the chair at Sing Sing. Ruth seemed a more likable, less fanatic woman than Ethel, yet so far as overt conspiratorial acts were concerned, or even the relative damage done to the country, there was little to distinguish them. One had chosen by confession to unroll the net of which she had been a part, while the other had tried to conceal Soviet meddling in United States internal affairs; that was the basic difference.

Considerable public feeling, not confined to the more chauvinistic commentators in the newspapers, seemed to have developed for the sacrifice of blood on the altar of national security. Many sober observers felt on the other hand that inflicting the ultimate punishment on a confused couple like the Rosenbergs would prove less valuable, socially and politically, than a last-minute confession which would exhibit the legal machinery of democracy coping somewhat successfully with a highly elusive totalitarian conspiracy.

Meanwhile events began to move toward a decision. On April

11, 1951, Ethel Rosenberg was transferred to the death house at Sing Sing. A crowd of thirty persons saw her leave the Women's House of Detention at 10 Greenwich Street. Wearing a pink blouse, a gray plaid skirt, a gray coat with karakul collar and a black hat, she sat in the rear seat of a car with Mrs. Sarah Goldstein, a deputy marshal. According to United States Marshal Carroll, who had charge of the party, she chatted "gaily about spring and other matters" during the trip upstate. Upon arrival at Sing Sing, she was ticketed as Prisoner 110,510. She gave up $15 she was carrying and signed a waiver permitting receipt of inspected mail. Asked what led her to commit the crime, she replied, "I deny guilt." The women's sector of the death house, commodious but hardly cheerful, consisted of three cells, a corridor, and an exercise yard located inside a ten-foot high wall. It had been untenanted since the execution during the previous month of Mrs. Martha Beck, who with her lover had taken advantage of lonely-hearts correspondence to locate victims wealthy enough to be murdered. The four matrons who had been watching and waiting on Mrs. Beck, at $40 a day, were rehired to perform the same functions for Mrs. Rosenberg.

One week after the transfer, Emanuel Bloch came into court with a flamboyant order to show cause why the government should not be required to send Ethel Rosenberg back to New York City. A supporting affidavit by his client contended that the purpose of the shift to the death house was to "break" her and force a confession.

It has long been recognized [wrote Ethel Rosenberg with the literary fluency of which she was so proud] that the mental and physical pressures of the refined cruelties that man has devised equal the barbarity of the rack, the thumbscrew and the wheel. It is a living hell to be separated from the warmth, love, affection and strength of my husband, and for him to contemplate my incarceration in this terrible place. It is agony to sit in a cell located not even a stone's throw from the execution chamber. I am sealed in the gray walls of this prison as if in a tomb. I am alone in an entire building except for the matron who guards me. I see no other human being from morning to night, I have no occupation other than to sit immured in the aching soundlessness of my narrow cell. I have no recreation other than to walk a bare patch of ground surrounded by walls so high that my only view is a bare patch of sky. Sometimes I can see an airplane passing by; sometimes, a few birds; sometimes I hear the noise of a train in the distance. Otherwise, there is always dead silence. . . .

Though she was the sole occupant in the woman's wing of the death house, it was asserted that Ethel Rosenberg had a radio for entertainment. She could secure magazines on request from the matron on duty, who sat at a desk directly in front of her small, but well-lighted cell. If she wished a shower, she was escorted to the last cell, where such facilities were available. On clear days, she was allowed to play handball, and frequently did play handball with a matron for hours at a time, in the large exercise yard.

Having made no headway in his effort to bring his client back to New York, Emanuel Bloch tried a new tack in May. He demanded a mental examination of Ethel Rosenberg because of the "undue and unusual psychological pressures" being exerted against her, and he produced as a witness a prominent psychiatrist, who asserted that Ethel might go insane if kept in the death house.

The government said it was forced to send Ethel Rosenberg immediately to Sing Sing because no facilities existed in the Federal prison for women in New York for the segregation of a condemned prisoner, as required by law. Such facilities did exist in the Federal House of Detention, where Julius Rosenberg was kept. However, in mid-May, perhaps partly because of the hullabaloo, Julius was also transferred to the death house. Dressed neatly in a double-breasted new gray suit, a red tie with a palmleaf pattern, and a white handkerchief in his breast pocket, he rode up to Sing Sing in the company of Marshal Carroll and two deputies. He was enrolled as Prisoner No. 110,649. To the routine question: "To what do you attribute your criminal act?" he replied, "Neither I nor my wife is guilty." Warden Wilfred Denno explained that the Rosenbergs would be permitted to see each other, one hour a week, and to converse across a table in the presence of a keeper and a matron. Julius was not alone in his wing, since seven other doomed criminals were also awaiting their fate there.

In June, Federal Judge Goddard disposed of the lingering legal effort to free Ethel Rosenberg from the death house. No evidence had been presented to show any attempt to "break" the prisoner, he said, ruling that the transfer was "not unusual or cruel and inhuman within the meaning of the eighth amendment to the constitution." During this same month, relatives visited Ethel at Sing Sing to discuss the problem of handling her two sons, who had been kept for almost a year in a Bronx children's shelter, after Mrs. Tessie Greenglass, their maternal grandmother, proved unable to handle them. Now they could no longer remain at the children's shelter. Julius' mother, Mrs. Sophie Rosenberg, and a married sister, Mrs. Lena Cohen, with whom the old lady lived, offered to take care of the boys, and another sister of Julius, Mrs. Ethel Goldberg, promised to help as much as she could. Later in the summer, the boys visited the prison after every detail of the trip to Ossining had been planned in advance by Ethel Rosenberg in six letters. The boys were shy at first, but they ate candy from the prison canteen and they joined in singing folk songs with their parents before they left.

That summer the Circuit Court granted more time for filing amended briefs in the appeal. The Communist party thereupon decided on a campaign with the ostensible purpose of setting up Julius and Ethel Rosenberg as martyrs. The campaign was built around a series of articles in the *National Guardian,* a weekly newspaper established in 1948 as an organ of the American Labor party and gradually converted into a more blatant Stalinist propaganda sheet than the *Daily Worker* itself.

The campaign brought about a subtle shift of emphasis. Before and during the trial, the defense had argued that the government was trying to insinuate a false issue of Communism. Now the argument became that the Rosenbergs were being "crucified" because they were Communists. As Ethel Rosenberg wrote, in one of her literary effusions which were published in the *National Guardian* as letters: "It is because we were relentless, uncompromising, implacable in implementing our beliefs with action, that we sit today in the gray walls of Sing Sing awaiting we know not what further pain and sorrow and emptiness."

William A. Reuben, the reporter who wrote the series, stuck within a reasonably close framework of facts, but the *National Guardian,* in a series of precedes, boxes, and editorials carried the case into never-never land. "There was a special political objective in making a supreme example of the Rosenbergs, because of their left-wing politics," said the major precede to the opening piece in the series on August 22. "In police parlance, the 'atomic plot' involved was a 'closed case' before the Rosenbergs were brought into it. All the accused participants had confessed."

The *National Guardian* asserted that Julius Rosenberg's name came into the case only through an FBI search of David Greenglass' apartment which unearthed some paper with scribbled notes. Asked about these, David said they were old college math notes of his brother-in-law Julius. The silly implication left by the *National Guardian* statement was that the twelve-year-old math notes constituted the evidence against Rosenberg.

Reporter Reuben tried a number of side paths. Citing a dispatch from London to the effect that friends of Klaus Emil Julius Fuchs had called him "Julius" there, he raised the question as to whether references by Miss Elizabeth Bentley and Harry Gold to "Julius" might not have meant Fuchs, instead of Rosenberg. The *National Guardian* hailed this vagrant notion as "fresh evidence" justifying acquittal of the Rosenbergs. It was not fresh evidence, and it justified nothing. Miss Bentley's references to espionage meetings with an engineer named Julius living in Knickerbocker Village, New York City, dated back to 1942 when

Fuchs was working on the gaseous diffusion process in Birmingham, England. Similarly, references to "Julius" heard by Gold during his visit to the Greenglasses in Albuquerque were tied to a relative of the Greenglasses, living in New York. Fuchs was no relative of the Greenglasses and he was not living in New York at that time.

Harry Gold, holder of the Order of the Red Star, which among other things entitles recipients to free rides on the Moscow subways, was denounced by the *National Guardian* as an "anti-Soviet adventurer," because he had confessed, and the amazing oblique suggestion was offered that the Soviet Union could, if it wished, have developed an atom bomb during the war.

> In the Summer, 1945, issue of the Journal of Physics of the U.S.S.R., Soviet physicist Veksler published a paper describing two of the key devices underlying the principles of atomic explosion. This was at the time of, or prior to, the New Mexico atomic tests and the U.S. bombing of Hiroshima and Nagasaki. Why the Soviets did not themselves develop an atomic bomb for use in World War II may be a matter of humanist and scientific instead of military speculation. But at any rate at least two of the "secrets" that formed the basis for the charges against the Rosenbergs were familiar to Soviet scientists in 1945.

The 1945 Veksler paper, well known to American physicists, describes the principle of the synchrotron, an improved version of the cyclotron. It was a theoretical paper which did not indicate that such a machine was then built, and there has been no evidence since then that it was ever built. Neither the synchrotron, nor the cyclotron, was in any way related to "the principles of atomic explosion."

The *National Guardian* arguments—from the point of view of anybody who knew anything about physics or about the evidence in the case—seemed so preposterous as to arouse suspicion that the Communist party was not trying too hard to achieve the impossible—vindication of the Rosenbergs—and would be satisfied if a token campaign kept the spies silent until they reached the electric chair.

Perhaps the most mischievous phase of the Communist campaign in the Rosenberg case consisted in trying to squeeze out some racial and religious advantage for the Party. The most conspicuous box in the opening article of the *National Guardian* series was a quotation that the Reichstag fire in Germany set the stage for the "terror, the persecution and attempted political and economic annihilation of the Jews." The front-page picture of the Rosenbergs carried a reference to France's famous anti-Semitic military case: "Is this the Dreyfus case of cold-war America?"

Anybody familiar with the personal history of Julius Rosenberg knew he had broken his father's heart by refusing to complete rabbinical training, and that he had repudiated his religion entirely when he embraced Communism. Nevertheless, at his trial, he slipped in occasional references which could have been cultural vestiges or conscious efforts to portray himself in a false light. Bogging down during one attempt to explain why he preferred the Russian form of government, he said, "I felt that the Soviet government made a lot of progress . . . and at the same time I felt that they contributed a major share in destroying the Hitler beast who killed six million of my coreligionists, and I feel emotional about that thing."

Asked about the gift of a watch from the Russians, Rosenberg went into a long history of watches starting with a Waltham given him by his father "for *bar mizvah.*" Asked about an espionage rendezvous at Christmas time, Rosenberg dragged in Hanukkah. Careful reading of his testimony created an inescapable impression that he had tried unscrupulously to wrap himself in the Judaism which he repudiated as a young man in college.

When the *National Guardian* campaign culminated in the formation of a National Committee to Secure Justice in the Rosenberg Case, the racial and religious appeal deepened. "It is a relevant fact," said an appeal for members to serve on the Committee, dated November 10, 1951, which came to the author of this book, "that the alleged political opinions of Ethel and Julius Rosenberg were a major element in the case. Fear that the Rosenbergs were also victims of religious bigotry was expressed, immediately following the trial, by the leading Jewish press and by other newspapers in this country."

It was not a fact that the leading Jewish press and other newspapers had blamed the conviction of the Rosenbergs on their religion. With the exception of a few ultra-reactionaries like Representative Rankin (D-Miss.) there had been no public misuse of the case for rabble-rousing purposes, until the Communist party decided to see what propaganda advantages it could secure.

Americans pretty generally seemed to realize that if a man brought up as a Protestant, a Catholic, or a Jew joined the Communist party he thereby cut loose from his religious training, his community ties, his family, and his country. The fact that one or two convicted spies bore what were called "Jewish names" meant nothing, any more than any conclusion could be drawn about Brooklynites or Italian Americans because of the arrest of two Italian-Americans in Brooklyn for passing counterfeit $10 bills. The law in the United States treated offenders on an individual basis, without reference to color, religion, or national origin.

Whether the Communist willingness to arouse anti-Semitism in the guise of fighting it in the Rosenberg case would get anywhere was doubtful. The public generally was becoming more sophisticated in such matters. It had the assurance from FBI Director Hoover that Jews were not proportionately more prominent in the Communist party than other groups. Some Jewish intellectuals had been conspicuous in the influx of idealists into the Party during its anti-Fascist phase in the thirties, but the same intellectuals had led the exodus when the rigidity, cruelty, and immorality of Communism became apparent. By 1950 hardly any Jew of prominence remained in the Party. Jewish scientists remembered how their coreligionists had been turned over to the Gestapo by Stalin at the time of the Nazi-Soviet pact. Jewish writers stressed the increasing anti-Semitism of Communism, in the satellite countries, in Soviet policy toward Palestine, and in a dozen other ways. Jewish labor leaders were in the forefront of the effort to cleanse the unions of Communist influence.

Nobody could isolate any personal anti-Semitism in the Rosenberg case. The chief prosecution witnesses, as well as the three defendants, were Jews. The Judge was a Jew. The prosecutor was a son of Jewish immigrants who had settled in the same depressed East Side area which had produced the Rosenbergs and the Greenglasses. Despite all these facts, the National Committee to Secure Justice in the Rosenberg Case, consisting of Joseph Brainin, Dr. Katherine Dodd, B. Z. Goldberg, the Rev. Spencer Kennard, John T. McManus, William A. Reuben, and Dr. Gene Weltfish, sharpened the religious issue in a pamphlet issued in the winter of 1951-52. For some reason, their drive did not gain much headway, even after the Progressive party ran a series of Midwest meetings in January and February, 1952, to whip up sentiment.

An example of the Communist efforts in this direction appeared in the January 20, 1952, issue of the *Daily Worker*. A two-page spread, titled "Anti-Semitism and the Rosenbergs" carried the subtitle, "Was the death sentence imposed on Julius and Ethel Rosenberg caused in part by anti-Semitism? . . ." The article went on to say, ". . . did the government seize upon the Rosenbergs for conviction and death because they were not only Jews, but also radicals? Was the government here exploiting the case to advance anti-communist hysteria by strengthening the Jew-Communist-atom spy stereotype in the public mind? Some people may be shocked at this suggestion. But the Sacco-Vanzetti and Tom Mooney frameups, as well as Scottsboro and the routine frameups of countless Negroes are indisputable facts of history." The article continued in this vein, with the Communists showing no qualms in stimulating and exploiting anti-Semitism for their own ends while seeming to deplore it.

Early in January, 1952, the Rosenberg-Sobell appeal was heard by Circuit Court Judges Jerome Frank, Thomas Swan, and

Harrie Chase. Calling it the "most dramatic and celebrated case in the annals of American jurisprudence," Emanuel Bloch charged that the Rosenbergs had been convicted as a result of a "deal" between the Greenglasses and the government. Two assistant United States attorneys replied that the guilt of the Rosenbergs was "too plain to admit of dispute." Harold Phillips, arguing for Sobell, said his client had been deprived of a fair trial, among other reasons, because statements about his Communist party membership had been allowed as evidence.

The appellate court reserved decision. While the public waited for a ruling, a gruesome item in the Broadway column of Leonard Lyons called attention to the Rosenbergs' awful dilemma of confession or possible death. Julius, it seemed, had required some fairly extensive dentistry while in Sing Sing. With the shadow of possible execution moving closer day by day, the prison dentist decided on temporary bridgework, since otherwise the State would be put to unnecessary expense. Rosenberg appealed to the Warden in a fury, demanding permanent bridgework on the ground that his release was only a matter of time. According to the latest report, the Warden upheld the prison dentist, and refused the request for permanent bridgework.

On February 25, 1952, the Court of Appeals sharpened the dreadful alternative facing the Rosenbergs by confirming unanimously their conviction in the lower court.

Index

A

Abe Brothman Associates, **46, 54, 76, 185,** 271, 273
Abel, Mrs. Dorothy (sister of Ruth Greenglass), 200, 259
Abel, Louis, 206, 259
Aberdeen Ordnance School, 208
A. F. of L., 246, 258
Abingdon, England, 177
Abington, Philadelphia, 52, 54-55
Abraham Lincoln Brigade, 147
Abraham Lincoln School, 136
Absolute Ethyl Alcohol, 39
Acheson, Dean, 17-18
Adams, Arthur Alexandrovitch, 130-31, 137-46, 166-67
Adams, Eric, 127
Aerosol Bomb, 72
Aiken, S. C., 14
Aircraft Turbine Engine, 271
Akers, Sir Wallace, 111
Alamogordo, N. M., 3, 6, 9, 11, 79, 94, 145
Alaska, 131, 146
Albuquerque, N. M., 3, 5-7, 23, 201-03, 209-10, 213-17, 280, 283, 298
Alexander Suvorov, 107
Alichanian, Abram, 97, 197
Alichanian, Artyom, 97, 197
Alice in Wonderland, 178
Aliptekin, Issa Yusuf Bey, 196
Alsos, Goudsmit, Samuel A., 103
Alsos Mission, 101-3
Altavilla, Enrico, 195
Aluminum Nitrate, 134
American Association of Scientific Workers, 163
American Chemical Society, 66
American Labor Party, 296
American League Against War and Fascism, 159
American Newspaper Guild, 18
American Peace Mobilization, 232

American Review of the Soviet Union, 96
American Russian Institute, 151
American-Soviet Science Society, 159
American Student Union, 18, 158, 245
American Youth Congress, 18, 232
Amtorg Trading Corp., 38, 63, 70, 76, 138, 174
Angelov, Lieutenant ("Baxter"), 112, 114
Antiaircraft Shells, 119
Anti-Semitism, 35-36, 93, 103, 190, 299, 300-1
Appellate Court, 302
Argonne National Laboratory, 82, 113-14, 136, 177
Arlington, Va., 169
Army Air Force Research, 38, 41
Army Intelligence (U. S.), 20, 135-37
Arthur H. Thomas Co., 44
Ashenden: the Secret Agent, 131
Association of Scientific Workers of Great Britain, 121
Atomic Bombs, 3, 57, 196, 209, 210
Atomic Bomb Patent (1940), 188, 193
Atomic Detonator (flat lens mold), 4, 214-18, 224, 242, 283
Atomic Energy Commission, 13, 146, 162, 182
Atomic Information Exchange, 182
Atomic Piles, 102, 113, 115
Aviation Gasoline, 270
Axis Sally, 292

B

Bachrach, Marion, 275
"Back, Bacon, Badeau, Bagley," 124, 125
Baker, Rudy ("Ralph Bowman," "Al"), 156-57, 166-67
Bar Mizvah, 299
Barr, Joel, 202, 246, 286
Barry, Art, 163
Batory, 167
Beck, Mrs. Martha, 294
Bell Telephone Co., Montreal, 127

303

Index

Bell Telephone Laboratories, 239
Bellet, Dr., 186
Bell Textile Co., N.Y., 245
Benedict, Manson, 173-74
Bentley, Elizabeth T. ("Helen Sherman"), 48, 58-64, 66, 74, 76, 78, 82, 241, 267-69, 279-80, 297-98
Berkeley, California, 132, 147
Berle, A. A., 17
Berlin, 93
Bernay, Eric, 138, 166
Berne, Switzerland, 29
Bernstein's Fish Grotto, San Francisco, 160
Betatrons, 104
Beth Israel Hospital, N.Y., 203
Bethe, Hans, 176-77, 212
Birkby, Fred G. (FBI), 187
Birmingham University, 89
Black Light, 220
Black, Tom ("Troy Niles"), 35-39, 41, 47, 72-74
Bloch, Alexander, 275
Bloch, Emmanuel H., 275-81, 284-86, 288-91, 294-95, 302
Board of Economic Warfare, 20
Bohr, Niels ("Baker"), 11, 93, 98-99, 160, 212
Borisoglevsk, Voronezh, U.S.S.R., 44
Bow Street Court, London, 181
Boyer, Anita Cohen, 122
Boyer, Raymond ("The Professor"), 121-23, 264
Brahms' Violin Concerto, 62
Brainin, Joseph, 301
Brandt, Hilda ("Heiss," "Warm," "Kalt"), 87-88
Bransten, Louise, 151, 160
Brazil, 153
Briggs, Richard, 264
Bristol University, 88
British Army Intelligence, 91, 100
British Communist Party, 88, 91
British Intelligence (M.I. 5), 81-82, 110, 113, 117-18, 178, 182, 188
British Ministry of Supply, Atomic Energy Division, 192
British Museum, 117-18
Brixton Prison, London, 188
Brooklyn College, 223
Brooklyn Eagle, 147
Brooklyn Polytechnic Institute, 146-47, 222
Brothman, Abe ("The Penguin"), 47-56, 58-78, 185, 267-75, 277-78, 280-81, 293
Brothman Laboratory, 60
Brothman, Naomi, 49, 70-72, 75, 267
Browder, Earl, 66, 139, 158, 280
Burdenko, Soviet Surgeon General, 160
Bureau of Motor Vehicles, 269
Burgess, Forrest (FBI), 187
Burt, Colonel, 110, 117-18, 120
Bush, Vannevar, 15
Byelostrov, 195
Byrnes, Secretary of State, 12

C

California Institute of Technology, 173
Calutron, 149
Cambridge, England, 90, 95, 111
Cambridge, Mass., 82, 175-76
Camden, N. J., 30
Campbell, John, 11
Canada, 58, 66, 82, 89, 106, 190
Canadian Affairs, 123
Canadian Association for Scientific Workers, 122
Canadian Royal Commission, 128
Canadian Spy Rings, 12, 54, 66, 78, 82, 106-32
Cannery Workers Union, 158
Canol Project, 137
Carbon, 14, 159
Carr, Sam, 109, 117, 128-29
Carrington, John W., viii
Carroll, U. S. Marshal, 294-95
Cavendish Laboratory, 99, 111
Census Bureau, 232
Central Control Commission, 66
Chadwick, Sir James, 90
Chaglich, Yugoslavia, 148
Chain-Reacting Piles, 101
Chalk River Plant, 112, 191
Chambers, Whittaker, 17, 109, 146
Chapin, John Hitchcock, 140-46
Chappaqua, N. Y., 213
Chase, Judge Harrie, 302
Chemical-Metallurgical Engineering, 69
CHEKA, 107
Chevalier, Haakon, 150, 151, 155
China Union Press, 196
Churchill, Winston, 182
CIO, 15, 223, 236, 246
Circuit Court, 302
City College, N. Y., 158, 169, 221, 230-32, 235, 242-46, 282, 286
Civil Rights Congress, 163
Clark, Charles, 145
Clark House Dramatic Group, 244
Clay, N. Y., 263, 265
Clayton Continuous Soap Process, 39
Clearly, Gottlieb, Friendly & Cox, 75
Cleveland, 140-42
Clinton Engineer Works (Oak Ridge), 114
Cockcroft, Dr., 112
Cohen, Elliot E., vii
Cohen, Karl, 173-74
Cohen, Mrs. Lena, 296
Cohn, Victor, 96
Collins, Richard J., 14
Colloidal Graphite, 270
Colorado Committee for the First Amendment, 163
Columbia University, 40, 47, 63, 98, 135-36, 140, 148-49, 173, 282
Comintern Register, 248
Commandos, 100
Commercial Solvents, 39
Communist, 231

Communist Espionage Machine, 22-26, 32, 39, 42, 47, 54, 59, 82, 90, 128, 130-32, 136, 150-62, 165-69, 172-80, 184-85, 196, 201, 204, 207, 209-10, 212-19, 224-27, 230, 232-42, 246, 248-50, 264, 266, 268-73, 275, 278-80, 284

Communist Party, 36, 39-40, 66, 78, 83, 86-88, 90, 133-34, 136, 139, 147-48, 150-60, 162-64, 194, 202, 209, 220, 222-24, 230-37, 242, 245-48, 267-68, 277-80, 286, 296, 298-302

Communist Propaganda, 14-15, 36-37, 83, 86, 91, 97, 103, 108, 123, 132-33, 136, 150-52, 158, 162-64, 210, 220-26, 230-35, 239, 243-47, 264-68, 296-301

Communist "Third Period," 35, 133, 220

Conant, James B., 15, 173

Condon, Edward U., 127, 159

Confessions, 170-71, 179-81, 183-84, 186-88

"Controlled Schizophrenia," 83, 182

Copenhagen, 165, 194

Coplon, Judith, 192

Cornell University, 140, 250

Corson, John M., 265

Cosmic Rays, 97, 165, 191, 193, 196

Counter-Intelligence Corps (CIC), 145, 158-59, 161

Court of Appeals, 302

Cox, Ethel, 287

Creutz, E. C., 144

Crimea, 102

Critical Mass, 90, 176, 218

Crouch, Paul, 152-53

Cultural and Scientific Conference for World Peace, 163

Curie, Irène, 98

Curie, Marie, 98

Curtis-Bennet, Derek, 91

Cyclotron, 96, 149, 159, 298

Czechoslovakia, 165, 168

D

Daily Worker, 39, 209, 231, 247-48, 296, 301

Danish Underground, 100

Danziger, William, 168-69

Davidman, Joy, vii

Davis, Charlotte, 158-59

Davis, Federal Judge, 276

Davis, Robert R., 158-59

Dayton, Ohio, 38, 41

De Courcy, Kenneth, 196

De Witt Clinton High School, N. Y., 158

Denmark, 99

Dennis, Eugene, 277

Denno, Warden Wilfred, 296

Department of Agriculture, 20

Department of Justice, 18, 265-66, 291-92

Derry, John A., 9, 283

Dickstein, Representative, 236-37

Dodd, Katherine, 301

Doyle, Bernadette, 158, 161

Dnepropetrovsk, 97

Drexel Institute, 40, 66

Dreyfus Case, 299

Duluth, Minn., 29

E

Earl Theatre, Bronx, N. Y., 43, 45

Eastman Kodak Laboratories, Rochester, N. Y., 263-64

Edinburgh University, 88, 194

Edison, 54

Edgewater Arensal, 268

Einsohn, Herman & Diane, 206

Einstein, Albert, 14, 92-94, 103-04

Eisler, Gerhart, 275

El Paso, Tex., 5

Electronics Corp. of America, 138

Elitcher, Helene, 233-38, 240-41, 281, 283

Elitcher, Max, 230-41, 278-79, 281, 286

Elmhurst, Queens, N. Y., 60

Eltenton, Dolly, 151

Eltenton, George C., 151, 155

Emerson Radio Co., 248-49

Engineering Society Library, 64

Eniwetok, 13, 224

Escape Routes, 165-68, 184-85, 195-96, 200-04, 256, 276

E. W. Bliss & Co., N. Y., 245

Ewert, Arthur, 153

F

Farago, Ladislas, vii

"Farmer," Fermi, Enrico, 11, 93-94, 98, 176, 189

FBI, 11, 18-20, 22, 27, 34, 37, 55-72, 74-77, 91, 110-11, 126-28, 130-31, 140, 142, 145, 159-62, 166, 169, 171-72, 178, 183-84, 186-87, 189, 200-01, 207, 226, 229, 241-42, 252-54, 256, 258-59, 263, 266-67, 278-79, 285, 287, 297

Federal House of Detention, N.Y.C., 254, 276, 291, 295

Federation of American Scientists, 16

Federation of Architects, Engineers, Chemists and Technicians, 24, 35, 40, 136, 147, 152, 158, 242, 246-48, 253

Federation of Artists, Engineers, Chemists and Technicians, 213

Federation of Atomic Scientists, 14, 16

Feit, Regina, 258

Fermi, Enrico ("Farmer"), 11, 93-94, 98, 176, 189

Fernald, Ohio, 13

Field, Frederick Vanderbilt, 122

Finland, 165, 197

Fire Control, 234, 237

Foley, Assistant U. S. Attorney, 281-82

Foote, Alexander, 115, 130

Foster, William Z., 159

Fox, Irving D., 158-59, 161

Index

France, 88-89, 190
Franco, 129
Franco-American Chemical Co., 39
Frank, Judge Jerome, 302
Franklin Institute, 66
Franks, Sir Oliver, 182
"Fred," 41
French Atomic Energy Commission, 99
Frisch, O. R., 93
Fuchs, Rev. Emil, 81-82, 84-88, 94, 179
Fuchs, Klaus ("Golia"?), 5-6, 19-20, 23, 46, 60, 79-92, 94-96, 104, 108, 110-11, 120, 126-28, 132-33, 135-36, 165, 172-84, 186-89, 192-94, 200-01, 203, 242, 252, 265, 280, 293, 297-98

G

G & R Engineering Co., 225
"Galya, Gini, Golya, Green," 109-11, 124, 189
Gamow, George, 176
Gardiner, Gerald, 120-21
Gaseous Diffusion Plant, 13, 135, 173
General Electric, Schenectady, N. Y., 192, 233, 237-38, 250
German Atomic Research, 92
Gestapo, 81, 95, 301
Giner de Los Rios, Manuel, 169
Glasgow University, 89
Glassman, Vivian, 246, 281
"Gloria," 50
Goddard, Federal Judge, 281-82, 296
Gold, Harry ("Dave," "Raymond," "Frank Kessler"), 3-9, 17, 19, 23, 26-83, 90, 95-96, 118, 132, 172-76, 181, 183-86, 202-03, 218, 239, 263-67, 269-76, 279-81, 293, 297-98
Gold, Joseph, 29-30, 34, 52-54, 69, 185, 187
Goldberg, B. Z., 301
Goldberg, Mrs. Ethel, 296
Golden Bear Honor Society, 147
Goldstein, Deputy Marshal Sarah, 294
Golodnitsky, Celia (Gold), 29-31, 33-34, 42-43, 50-56, 69, 185
Golodnitsky, Heinrich (Harry Gold), 29-30
Golodnitsky, Samuel (Gold), 29-30, 33-34, 51-54, 69, 185, 187
Golos, Jacob N. ("Raisin," "John," "Mr. Chester," "Timmy," "Yasha"), 48, 58-59, 61, 63-68, 76-77, 109, 184, 268-69, 271, 273, 279-80
Goudsmit, Samuel A., 101
Gouverneur Hospital, N. Y., 203
Gouzenko, Igor, 54, 106-10, 112, 114, 117, 119, 121-23, 126, 128, 130, 167, 188
Green Bay, Wis., 132
Greenglass, Barbara, 203-05
Greenglass, Barnet, 220
Greenglass, Bernard, 220, 225-26, 228-29, 243, 249-51, 257-58

Greenglass, David ("I. Jackson"), 3-9, 19, 23, 165, 167-68, 172, 199-216, 218-29, 242-43, 245, 259, 261-62, 275-78, 280, 282-89, 291, 293, 297-98, 302
Greenglass, Gladys, 257
Greenglass, Ruth (Printz), 3-7, 23, 199-216, 218-19, 222-29, 251-52, 254-56, 258-59, 275-76, 278, 280, 282, 284-86, 288, 293, 298, 302
Greenglass, Samuel, 220, 258
Greenglass, Stephen, 200, 205, 227
Greenglass, Tessie, 220-21, 225, 243, 251, 254, 257-61, 289, 296
Gromov, Anatol ("Al"), 59, 82, 279
Groves, Maj. Gen. Leslie R., 10-11, 107, 113-14, 145, 155-57, 283
Guided Missiles, 234

H

Haaren Aviation High School, 221
Hahn, Otto, 93, 102
Halban, H. H., 98-99, 112, 190
Halperin, Israel ("Bacon"), 124-27
Halsall, Thompson, 181
Hamilton, John D. M., 27
Handbook for Spies, Alexander Foote, 115, 130
Hanford, Wash., 11, 80, 107, 176
Hanukkah, 299
Harrington (FBI), 252-53, 256
Harrison, Katherine Puening (Mrs. J. Robert Oppenheimer), 154-55, 157
Harvard University, 121, 127, 173, 208
Harwell, England, 165, 177-78, 180-82, 187, 189, 192-96
Hawaii, 146
Hawkins, David, 162-64
Hawkins, Frances Pockman, 163
Heart Research, 186
Heavy Water, 97-100, 115, 135
Hebrew High School, N.Y.C., 243
Heiman, Julius, 139
Heineman, Mrs. Robert B., 175-76, 183
Heisenberg, Werner, 102-04
Helsinki, 166, 195
Henry Street Settlement, 244
Herald Tribune, 203
Hewlitt, Johnson (Red Dean of Canterbury), 134
Hickenlooper, Senator, 113
Hotel Hilton, Albuquerque, 4
Himmler, Heinrich, 93
Hiroshima, 10, 79, 102, 114, 219, 298
Hiskey, Clarence F. (Szczechowski), 132-37, 139-41, 143, 145-46, 148, 152, 157, 242
Hiskey, Marcia Sand, 133-34, 136, 141, 143, 146
Hiss, Alger, 17, 91, 146, 267
Hiss, Donald, 17
Hitler, 17, 84, 86, 101, 190, 264, 299
Hitler-Stalin Pact, 18, 89, 95, 108, 133-34, 246, 301

306

Hohenzollerns, 84
Hollandia, 52
Hollister Co., 34
Hollywood Writers Mobilization, 14
Holmesburg Prison, 187
Holston Ordnance Depot, Tenn., 264
Holtzoff, Federal Judge, 162
Holy Cross Parochial School, 133
Hoodless, Carter, 66, 77
Hoover, John E., 19, 34-35, 110, 275, 300
House of Lords, 127
House Un-American Activities Committee, 132, 162
Houtermans, 104
Hydro, Lake Tinnsjo Ferryboat, 100
Hydrogen Bomb, 14-16, 57, 168, 177, 191, 196-97

I

Il Tempo, 195, 197
Impulse Dynamo, 96
Industrial Espionage, 20-21, 38-42, 62, 74, 264, 268, 270-72
In Fact, 134
Infrared Rays, 104
Institute for Advanced Study, 93
Institute of Pacific Relations, 151
Institute of World Affairs, 148
Intelligence Digest, 196
International Brigade, 129, 154
International Ladies Garment Workers Union, 258
International Publishers, N. Y., 134
International Telephone & Telegraph Co., 222
International Workers Order, 247
Isle of Man, 88
Isotope Separations, 97
Italy, 58, 165, 188
Ivanov, Peter, 155, 157, 159

J

Jackson, Gardner, viii
James, Henry, 27
Jeeps, 271
Jekyll-and-Hyde, 83
Jello Box, Recognition Device, 5, 214, 216, 275, 280
Jersey City, N. J., 34, 36
Johns Hopkins University, 189
Johnson, Secretary of Defense Louis, 182
Joint Anti-Fascist Refugee Committee, 159, 246
Joint Congressional Committee on Atomic Energy, 13, 173, 183
Joliot, Dr. Frédéric (Joliot-Curie), 98-99, 190
Joshua Handy Hemp Works, Cal., 208
Journal of Physics of the U.S.S.R., 298

Jowitt, Viscount, 127-28
Judaism, 299
Jung, C. G., 32

K

K-25 Plant, Oak Ridge, 135, 137, **173-74**
Kaiser Wilhelm Institute, 93
Kamen, Martin, 159-61
Kapitza, Peter, 96, 151
Kasperov, Gregory, 159-61
Kaufman, Federal Judge, 267, 274, 277-78, 286, 289-92
Kellex Corp., 173
Kennard, Rev. Spencer, 301
"Kessler, Arabella," 50-52, 54-55, 69
"Kessler, David," 49-52, 54-55, 69, 72, 176
"Kessler, Essie," 49-52, 54-55, 69, 72, 176
"Kessler, Frank" (Harry Gold), 48-49, 51, 53, 68-69, 73
Kharkov, 97
Kheifets, Gregory, 151, 159-61
Khevinov, Nikolai ("Martin"), 117
Kiel, Germany, 81-83, 85
Kiernan, Thomas, 75
Kiev, Russia, 29
Kindred Street, Philadelphia, 45
King's College, 117
Kirkpatrick, Dr., 68
Kistiakowsky, George, 208, 212
Kleinman, William, 273-74
Knickerbocker Village, N.Y.C., 213
Knoxville Peace Council, 134
Knoxville, Tenn., 133-34
Korea, 13, 22, 169, 290
Koski, Walter, 283
Kouznetskov, Colonel General, 128
Kowarski, L., 98-99
Kriegstagbuch, 19
Krypton, Barium Emissions, 93
Kualja, Sinkiang (China), 196
Kuntz, Edward, 278-79, 286

L

Labor-Progressive (Communist) Party, 109, 123
La Crosse State Teachers College, 133
La Crosse, Wisconsin, 133
Lake Como, Italy, 188-89, 194
Lambert, Rudy, 147, 152
Lange, 95
Lanolin, 39
Lansdale, Jr., Colonel John L., 137
Lawrence, Dr. Ernest O., 149, 160
Lawrence, Dr. John, 160
Lend-Lease, 19, 266
Leningrad, 91, 97, 150, 166, 266
Lenin Institute, Moscow, 149
Leningrad Institute, 150
Leopold, Inspector, 110

Index

Lenin, 35
Levitov, Edith, 168-69
Lewis Flight Propulsion Laboratory, Cleveland, 282
Lewis, John (FBI), 171
Life, 115
Lilienthal, David E., 146, 182
Lincoln Assassination, 291
Little Rock, Ark., 29
Lincoln Hotel, N. Y., 272
Liverpool, England, 90
Liverpool University, 193-94
Lomanitz, Giovanni Rossi, 158-59, 161
Loomis Institute, 140
Los Alamos, N. M., 4, 7, 19, 80, 83, 107, 114, 128, 149, 155-56, 159-60, 162, 176-77, 182, 200-01, 208-10, 212, 216-18, 224-25, 227, 262, 276, 283-84, 287
Los Angeles Junior College, 158
Low Countries, 89
Lowrey, Wilhelmina, 150
Lunan, David Gordon ("Back"), 123-26
Lutheranism, 84-85
Lyons, Leonard, 302

M

MacArthur, General, 18
Madison Square Garden, 45
Manhattan Engineering District Project, 10, 22, 94, 104, 107, 113, 131, 136, 140, 145, 157, 159, 160, 173, 189, 208, 283
Manhattan Trust Co., 205
Manning, Edward T., 143-46, 166
Martin, Francis, 134
Marxian Philosophy, 82, 91
Marxist Study Groups, 21, 132, 150, 163, 230-31
Massachusetts Institute of Technology, 41, 126, 227
Massing, Hede, 275
Matthews, Federal Judge, 146
May, Dr. Allan Nunn ("Alek"), 82, 107, 111-22, 124, 126, 128, 132, 150, 163, 183, 191-92, 293
May, Kenneth, 147-48, 150-56, 162, 164
May, Ruth McGovney, 148, 152-53
May, Samuel Chester, 147-48
Mazerall, Edward ("Bagley"), 124-26
Meek, Assistant U. S. Attorney, 265
Meitner, Lise, 93
Metallurgical Laboratory, University of Chicago, 113, 115, 131, 136-37, 140, 143-45, 191
Mexican Police, 170-71
Mexico, 58, 66, 130, 165
Mexico City, 165, 167-70
Mikhailov, Pavel, 139
Milch, Air Marshal, 104
Miller, Dr. Louis, 139
Minneapolis Tribune, 96
Modelski, General, 99
Momento Sera, 197
Montgomery, Morrell Quentin, 51

Montreal, 112, 114, 116, 121, 122
Montreal Laboratory, 112
Mooney, Tom, 301
Moscow "Center," 21, 114, 116, 125, 128, 169
Moscow Engineering Economic Institute, 43
Moskowitz, Miriam, 59-61, 64-66, 68-70, 72-75, 185, 267, 273-74, 293
Motinov, Lieutenant Colonel, 107-08
Murphy, Attorney General, 58
Murray, James Sterling, 145, 157, 162
Mussolini, 190
MVD, 107, 130, 150

Mc

McCarran Committee, 151
McGill University, 121-22, 124
McDonald, U. S. Commissioner, 169
McGranery, Federal Judge, 27, 187
McGrath, Attorney General, 289
McGuire, viii
McKenzie-Papineau Battalion, 129
McMahon, Senator, 173-74, 183
McManus, John T., 301
McMaster University, 125
McMillan, Edward M., 149
McMillan, Dr., 186

N

Nagasaki, 10, 79, 219, 242, 283, 298
National Academy of Science, 149
National Aeronautics Committee, 282
National Bureau of Standards, 127, 159, 233
National City Bank, 205
National Committee on Atomic Information, 15
National Committee to Secure Justice, 299-301
National Council of the Arts, Sciences and Professions, 163
National Guardian, 296-300
National New York Shipping & Packing Co., N. Y., 245
National Research Council (Canada), 112, 124
National Sugar Refinery Co., 53
Naval Aviation Supply Depot, 52
Navy Bureau of Ordnance, 231, 239
Navy Communist Party Cell, 233
Nazi Atomic Research, 100-04
Nazis, 79, 86-87, 91, 94, 266
Nazi "Purification Period," 103
Needleman, Gibby, 70-72, 75
Nelson, Steve (Mesarosh), 147-49, 152-59, 161-62, 164, 166-67, 275
Nevada, 13
New Deal, 17
New Denmark, Wisconsin, 132

New Leader, 107
New Masses, 134, 138
New York Federal Grand Jury, 74-78, 118, 185, 267, 281
New York Post, viii, 199, 254
New York Times, 197
New York University, 227
"Nigger Nate," 50
Nightingale, M. S., 127
Nickel-catalyst Process, 272
NKVD, 19-20, 38, 107-08, 130, 137, 147, 150, 154, 156
Nordblom, Mr. and Mrs. Hans, 195
Norsk Hydro Co., 98, 100
Northwestern University, 101
Norton (FBI), 252-53
Norway, 98, 100
Norwegian Underground, 100
Novick, Samuel, 138-39, 156
N.R.A., 37
Nuclear Fission, 90, 94
Nuclear Reactor Engines, 13

O

Oakland Workers School, 151
Oak Ridge, Tenn., 11, 107, 131, 135, 174, 208
O'Brien (FBI agent), 63, 65-68
OGPU, 107
Office of Naval Intelligence, 19-20
Official Secrets Act, 123
Oliver, Justice, 121
Oppenheimer, Frank, 154-56, 159, 162
Oppenheimer, J. Robert, 11, 82, 149, 154-57, 163, 212, 283
Oppenheimer, Jacquenette, 154-56
Order of the Red Star, 298
Organic Chemicals, 270
Oster, Dr. Gerald, 96
Ottawa, 112, 122, 123
Out of Bondage, 59
Out of My Later Years, Einstein, 93
Ovakimian, Gaik Badalovich, 58

P

Paducah, Ky., 13
Page, Marcus (Pogarsky), 245-46, 286
Passport Office, 129
Pasternak, Max, 169
Peden, Jack (FBI), 171
Peekskill, N. Y., 71
Peerless Laboratories, N.Y.C., 222
Peierls, Rudolph E., 89-90, 94, 173-74
Pennsylvania Station, N.Y.C., 38, 48, 72
Pennsylvania Sugar Co., 33-34, 37, 40-42, 53, 66
Pereira, 68
Perl, Henrietta, 282
Perl, William (Mutterperl), 281-83, 286
Perrin, Michael, 181

Perry's Chemical Engineer's Handbook, 62
Petawawa, Ontario, 115, 125, 191
Peter Cooper Hotel, N. Y., 138-39
Peters, J. ("Alexander Stevens"), 109
Petroleum Lubricants, 270
Philadelphia General Hospital, 186
Philadelphia Navy Yard, 41
Phillips, Harold, 290-91, 302
Phoenix, Ariz., 5
Phosphorus, Radioactive, 160
Physical Review, 98
Picture Post, 117
Pilat, Avice, viii
Pitt Machine Products Co., 225, 228, 257, 260
Plaza de Colón, 167-68, 204-05
Plutonium, 11, 57, 80, 102-03, 114-15, 149
Poland, 99
Pontecorvo, Antonio, 192, 195
Pontecorvo, Bruno, 99, 165-66, 188-98
Pontecorvo, Gil, 190
Pontecorvo, Guido, 189, 194
Pontecorvo, Mariana Nordblom, 190, 195, 198
Pontecorvo, Massimo, 189
Pontecorvo, Tito, 192
Popular Science, 249
Potsdam Conference, 11
Pratt Institute, N. Y., 222
Pravda, 107-08
Princeton University, 93, 127
Proceedings, Society of London, "Artificial Radioactivity Produced by Neutron Bombardment," 189, 193
Progressive Party, 301
Project Cyclone, 168
Proximity Fuse, 249

Q

Quakers, 85, 88
Queens University, Kingston, 124

R

Rabinowitch, Eugene, vii
Rabinowitz, Victor, 253
Radar, 125-26, 138, 165, 194
Radiation Laboratory, Berkeley, 147, 150, 152-56, 158-60, 162, 192
Radio-Foote Spy Ring, 105-06
Rankin, Representative, 300
Rascher, Dr., 104
Rathman, George (CIC), 161
RDX Formula, 123, 264-65
Reactor, 191
Reader's Digest, 19
Reeves Instrument Co., 168, 238, 240-41
Reichstag, 87, 299
Reid, Ed, 146
Religious Socialists, 84

Index

Report of the Royal Commission to Investigate the Facts Relating to and the Circumstances Surrounding the Communication by Public Officials and Other Persons in Trust of Secret and Confidential Information to Foreign Agents, 109-12, 114, 117, 128, 130
Resident Director, 167, 169
Resins, 67
Reuben, William A., 297, 301
Rhenium, 133
Rich, Gustav, 33-34, 40-42, 53, 68-69, 74
Richards, Matthias, 32
Rickard, Charles H., 265
Riesel, Victor, 196-97
Rockets, 168, 196
Rogge, O. John, 259, 276, 278, 291
Rogov, Lieutenant Colonel ("Jan"), 123-26
Roosevelt, Franklin D., 17, 94, 166
Roosevelt, Mrs. Franklin D., 18, 261
Rose, Fred, 109-10, 122-23, 127
Rosenberg, Ethel (Greenglass), 6, 201, 207, 209-10, 212-15, 217, 219-21, 224-26, 228, 232, 235, 244-48, 250-61, 274-75, 277-78, 283-97, 300-02
Rosenberg, Harry, 242-44, 248-49
Rosenberg, Julius, 3, 5, 23-24, 184, 201-07, 209-16, 218-21, 224-29, 232-59, 274-81, 283-97, 300-02
Rosenberg, Michael, 247, 256-60, 287, 296
Rosenberg, Robert, 253, 256-60, 287, 296
Rosenberg, Mrs. Sophie, 296
R.O.T.C., 133, 136
"Rover Boys" (FBI), 58, 68, 74
Royal Canadian Mounted Police, 108
Russelsheim, Germany, 84
Russian Émigrés, 28, 38, 220, 222, 282
Russian Purchasing Commission, 76
Russian War Relief, 159
Rutherford, Lord, 96
Rutland, Vt., 140
Rutledge, Rev. Owen E., 265

S

Sachs, Alexander, 94
Sacco-Vanzetti Case, 301
SAM (Substitute Alloy Material) Laboratory, 135, 140, 173-74
Sand, Marcia, 133
Santa Fe, N. M., 6, 19, 79, 81, 83, 160, 176, 209, 210, 212, 280
Saurent, Alfred, 202, 286
Saypol, U. S. Attorney Irving H., viii, 267, 269, 277-78, 286, 288-89, 291
Schein, David, 225, 229
Scherer, Lena Davis, 152
Scherer, Marcel, 147, 152, 275
Schneider, Ben, 255-56
Schneiderman, William, 150, 153
Schola Cantorum, 244
Schroeder, Rex (FBI), 171

Schumann, 103
Scotland Yard, 91, 110, 117, 128
Scottsboro Case, 301
Seaborg, Glenn T., 149
Segre, Emilio, 189
Selzinger, 192
Semenov, Semen M. ("Sam"), 44, 49, 174, 269, 272-73
Serini, Emilio, 194
Seward Park High School, N.Y.C., 243
Shannon (FBI), 63, 65-68
Sharswood Public School, 31
Shawcross, Sir Hartley, 121
Sheffield, Ala., 134
Shell Development Co., 151
Shell Oil Co., 148, 150
Sherwood, Miriam Rebecca, 136, 146
Sidorovich, Anne and Mike, 213-14, 245-47, 281-83
Sillitoe, Sir Percy, 178, 188
Silvermaster, Nathan G., 20
Singer, Kurt, 87, 91
Sing Sing, 292-97
Sinkiang Province, China, 196-97
Skardon, William J., 178-83, 187-88
Skinner, Deputy Director (Harwell), 193
Slack, Alfred Dean, 263-66, 275, 293
Smith, Durnford ("Badeau"), 124-26
Smith, Paul, 38-41, 44, 47
Smyth Report on Atomic Energy, 90, 108, 115, 120
Sobell Affidavit, 170
Sobell, Helen Gurewitz, 168, 170, 235, 237
Sobell, Louis, 168
Sobell, Mark, 168-69
Sobell, Morton ("Morty Sowell," "Morty Levitov," "M. Sand," "Marvin Salt," "N. Sand," "Morton Salt"), 165, 168-72, 231-35, 238-42, 275-78, 281, 283-84, 287, 289-91, 302
Sobell, Sydney, 168, 170
Social Democratic Party (Germany), 84-86
Society for the Protection of Science and Learning, 88
Sokolov, Major ("Davie"), 110
Solomon, Louis, 260-61
South Philadelphia High School for Boys, 32
Soviet Academy of Sciences, 96
Soviet Consulate, San Francisco, 155, 157, 159
Soviet Consulate, N. Y., 8, 43, 139
Soviet Embassy, Washington, 157
Soviet Embassy in Ottawa, 106, 110, 188, 191
Soviet Embassy, Stockholm, 195
Soviet Military Intelligence, 130
Soviet Naval Intelligence, 130
Soviet Russia Today, 140
Soviet Scientists, 96
Spain, 129, 147, 154
Spanish Loyalists, 129
Speaking Frankly, 12

Stalin, Joseph, 11-12, 16-17, 95, 190, 196-97, 301
Stalin Prize, 97, 197
Stalingrad, 91, 266
Stalinist Purges, 95
Stanford University, 154, 162
State Department, 110, 167
Statements Relating to the Atomic Bomb, 90-91
Steiger, Dr., 186
Steingart, Harry and Sylvia, 247
Stevens Hotel, Cleveland, 142
Stockholm, 139, 166, 195
Stone, Victoria, 139, 166
Strauss, Supply Minister, 193-94
Strong, General, 20
Sundure Paint Co., N. Y., 263
Sunny of Chinatown, Rego Park, N. Y., 68
Suratt, Mary, 291
Swan, Judge Thomas, 302
Sweden, 100, 165
Switzerland, 105, 165, 168, 185
Synchrotron, 298
Synthetic Butyl Alcohol, 270
Synthetic Rubber, 270
Szczechowski, 132
Szilard, Leo, 93-94, 98

T

Tampico, 169
Tass, 117
Taylor, Federal Judge, 265
Taylor, L. G. (FBI), 171
Teddington Station, England, 80
Teller, Edward, 176
"The Penguin" (Abe Brothman), 59
The Strange Alliance, 266
The [London] *Times*, 117
The World's 30 Greatest Spies, Kurt Singer, 87
Thermo-Nuclear Weapons, 58
This Deception, Hede Massing, 275
Thoreau, 29
Tito, 153
Togliatti, 153
Tokyo Rose, 292
Tolman, Richard C., 173
Topsy's Rest, Forest Hills, N. Y., 75
Towne Scientific School, University of Pennsylvania, 33-34
Tracer Bullets, 41
Transformer Corp. of America, 156
Trinity College, Cambridge, 111
Tritium, 191
Truman, Harry S., 11, 15, 57, 114, 166, 177, 197
Try and Stop Me, Bennett Cerf, 80
Tube Alloy Project, 94, 104, 111
TVA, 134

U

U 233, 144, 119
U 235, 97, 102, 114-15, 119, 125, 135, 149, 173
U 235 Enriched, 107, 119
U 238, 149
Union Carbide & Carbon Chemicals Corp., 173
Unions, 22, 222-23, 233, 246-47
United Electrical, Radio and Machine Workers, 222-23
United Office and Professional Workers, 223
United Nations, 99, 109
United Retail and Wholesale Workers, 223, 245
United States Internal Revenue Bureau, 190
United States Signal Corps, 24, 232-33, 235-36, 246-48
University of Brunswick, 124
University of California, 147-54, 156-62, 164
University of Chicago, 113, 137, 149, 227
University of Colorado, 163
University of Illinois, 140
University of Kiel, 81, 85, 87, 179
University of Leipzig, 85
University of Michigan, 232
University of Minnesota, 162
University of Rome, 189
University of Tennessee, 133-34, 143, 148
University of Wisconsin, 132-33, 135, 157
Urals, 102
Uranium, 11, 57, 82, 93-94, 97-98, 100, 115, 121, 126, 145, 149, 176, 201
Urey, Harold C., 98, 135, 173, 212, 283

V

V. . . ., Norman, 122
Van Karmen, Theodore, 281
Vansittart, Lord, 127
"Varitrons," 97, 197-98
Vassar College, 48, 58
Veksler (Soviet Physicist), 298
Vemork, Norway, 100
Vera Cruz, 169
Virulainen, Minister of the Interior and Mrs. Johannes, 195
Volk's Café, N.Y.C., 44-45

W

Wagner, Admiral, 19
Wakefield Prison, Yorkshire, 121
Warner-Swasey, Cleveland, 250
War Office, British, 181
Washington Post, 58
Webb, Under-Secretary of State James E., 182
Wegman, Samuel J., 138-39
Weinberg, Joseph W. ("Joe"), 132, 157-59, 161-62, 164
Weinberg, Muriel, 157, 161

Index

Weimar Republic, 85
Wells Survey, Inc., Okla., 191
Weltfish, Gene, 301
Wen-Hao, Wang, 196-97
West Side High School, Newark, N. J.,
  73
Whitehead, Inspector, 110
White Horse, Yukon Territory, 141
Whitney, Anita, 151
Williams, Paul, 245
Wilmer, George, 105
Wilmer, Joanna, 105
Witczak, "Bunia," 129
Witczak, Ignace, 129
World Tourists, Inc., 58
WPA, 134
Wrong, Hume, 182

X

Xavier University, 41

Y

Yakovlev, Anatoli A. ("John"), 5, 8, 9,
  43-47, 60, 80-82, 174-76, 239, 276, 280-
  81
Yale Law Journal, 289
Yelsey, Benjamin, 286
Young Communist League, 47, 63, 85,
  133, 158, 221, 231-32, 245
Young Progressives, 163

Z

Zabotin, Colonel ("Grant"), 107-09, 112,
  114-17, 122, 124-25, 128-29, 191
Zarubin, George N. ("Rudolf"), 108
Zawyrucha, Jean ("Jennie"), 72-73, 273
Zeyher Manufacturing Co., 52
Zindle, Harold (CIC), 161
Zlotowski, Ignace (Chief Soviet Atom
  Spy), 99
Zubilin, Vassili, 157, 159